"There is a Samurai saying, *He who is well prepared has won half the battle.* To prepare for the battle with the markets you have to win the information war. This means getting better, faster and more accurate information than your opponents can get. By using the tools, trading tactics and strategies revealed in my friend Toni Turner's second edition of *A Beginner's Guide to Day Trading Online*, you will be armed with the skills needed to help you win your battle with the markets."

Steve Nison, CMT
President—*www.candlecharts.com*
Author of *Japanese Candlestick Charting Techniques*

"This book is the essence of what trading is all about. Toni beautifully describes and fully explains in excellent terms, what influences the markets and what investors need to do in order to make effective trading decisions. I believe all traders will absolutely benefit from the knowledge packed in these pages. Two things I strong recommend people who are investing do: one, read this book, and two: re-read this book. It will surely help you achieve your trading goals, which is to make money in the markets. Every trader, from a beginner to the advanced professional should have this book!"

John Person, CTA
President—Nationalfutures.com

"Toni Turner has the uncanny ability to take the very complicated subject of trading and break it down so that everyone can understand it. To master a given subject is to have a very firm grasp of the basics. That is what Toni gives you. There are only a handful of trading educators that I would recommend listening to and she is one of them."

Hubert Senters
*www.tradethemarkets.com*

"Toni Turner's information-packed guide leads you through techniques and tactics you'll need to become a winning trader, and does it in an upbeat, easy-to-understand format. Read the book if you want to know how the market works and how to make it work for you."

Greg Capra
President of Pristine.com

2ND EDITION

# a beginner's
## guide to
# day trading
# online

## TONI TURNER

Adams Media
Avon, Massachusetts

Published by Adams Media, an F+W Publications Company
57 Littlefield Street
Avon, MA 02322
*www.adamsmedia.com*

ISBN 10: 1-59337-686-3
ISBN 13: 978-1-59337-686-4

Printed in Canada.

J I H G F E

**Library of Congress Cataloging-in-Publication Data**
is available from publisher.

This publication is designed to provide accurate and authoritative information with regard to the subject matter covered. It is sold with the understanding that the publisher is not engaged in rendering legal, accounting, or other professional advice. If legal advice or other expert assistance is required, the services of a competent professional person should be sought.

—From a *Declaration of Principles* jointly adopted by a Committee of the American Bar Association and a Committee of Publishers and Associations

Many of the designations used by manufacturers and sellers to distinguish their product are claimed as trademarks. Where those designations appear in this book and Adams Media was aware of a trademark claim, the designations have been printed with initial capital letters.

RealTick® graphics used with permission of Townsend Analytics, Ltd. © 1986–2007 Townsend Analytics, Ltd. All rights reserved. RealTick is a registered trademark of Townsend Analytics, Ltd. Any unauthorized reproduction, alteration, or use of RealTick is strictly prohibited. Authorized use of RealTick does not constitute an endorsement by Townsend Analytics of this book. Townsend Analytics does not guarantee the accuracy or warrant any representations made in this book.

*This book is available at quantity discounts for bulk purchases.*
*For information, please call 1-800-289-0963.*

# Dedication

*I dedicate this book to my daughter, Adrienne.*
*Your intelligence, wit, beauty, and sense of inner balance*
*remain constant sources of joy and inspiration to me.*

# Contents

Benefits of Day Trading: The Good News | The Flip Side: Wall Street Takes No Prisoners | What Does a Day Trader Look Like? | To Trade or Not to Trade? | Author's Note | Center Point: The Power of Commitment

The First Traders | The Birth of Wall Street | Who Are Wall Street's Biggest Party Animals? The Bulls and the Bears | The Land of Greed and Fear | Supply and Demand or How Much Will You Pay for That Cookie? | Price: The Bottom Line | The New York Stock Exchange | The NASDAQ Stock Market | The American Stock Exchange, or Amex | Where You Come In | The Bid and Ask, or Offer: What They Mean | NASDAQ Level II System | The Ringmaster, CNBC | Center Point: Empower Your Personal Beliefs

Your Day Trading Stash: A Reality Check | Choose Your Weapon | What Type of Trader Are You: Part-time or Full-time? | Trading with an Online Broker: Which One Is Right for You? | Advantages of Using a Direct-access Trading Platform | Should You Open Two Trading Accounts? | Slippage and Commissions: How They Affect Your Wallet | Trading On Margin: How to Do It and Still Sleep at Night | Develop a Simple Business Plan | Create a Success-oriented Environment | Paper Trading: Should You Do It? | Center Point: Your Vision: Life's Invitation to Greatness

# Foreword

In late 1999, everyone and their grandmother's nursing home attendant was a stock market genius. People bought stock based on sound fundamentals such as "page views." If it didn't work out for them that very first day, well, shoot, they just gripped that bucking bronco tight and hoped for the best—stop-loss orders were for wimps. And it worked! This strategy shined supreme for a while, but started gathering rust in the second quarter of 2000. Soon after, this technique that had made so many people so much money became the one sure way to get a good flogging. Did people adapt? No. Most people got flogged.

By the time the year 2000 rolled around, I had been trading for more than a decade, had experienced the crash of 1987, and had already accumulated a nice series of trading mistakes under my belt. Therefore, when the market imploded, I wasn't a neophyte and readily switched to the short side to make my profits. Many people I knew were not able to make this smooth transition and adjust their trading styles to the current market environment. Instead, they continued to focus on what had been working. After all, the Internet was changing the world one click at a time. It really was different this time. Sigh. They were getting hurt . . . bad.

This was frustrating to watch, and I started looking for trading books that I could hand to my friends and family that were active in the market, but didn't "get it." Most of these books were too technical, too dry, or too positive that the Dow was going to 36,000. Just as I was about to throw in the towel, I came across Toni Turner's book, *A Beginner's Guide to Day Trading Online*. The text was truly a breath of fresh air.

When I started trading, I attended seminars, visited Web sites, talked to brokers, and generally looked for information anywhere I could get it. The information was often times dry and contradictory. What I secretly wanted, however, was to be able to take an experienced trader down to the local Starbucks, fill them up with coffee, and let them talk about trading. This is the feeling I got while reading Toni's book. It was a pleasure to recommend the book to friends who were just starting out in the markets. They could read it quickly, grasp how the markets worked, and learn different ways to trade—instead of just buying stock and hoping for the best.

The book begins discussing the lifestyle of a short-term trader, including the very first traders, Uggh and Oog. There is also a quick description of how the markets work, and where the individual trader fits in under the whole scheme of things. From there, Toni lucidly and entertainingly discusses how to set up and treat your trading as a business, and then how to get in the right mindset to start doing this as a profession. I wholeheartedly agree with her idea of "Trading to trade well, not to make money." That idea in and of itself will save traders a lot of frustration and heartache.

From there, Toni reviews basic technical analysis and trading setups, and this is why I eagerly hand over this book to the new and intermediate trader. I get e-mails all the time asking about moving averages, basic chart patterns, and various oscillators. My response to these questions is very simple—get Toni's book! She explains them in that same "talking over a cup of coffee" style that I love, doing a much better job describing these tools than I could ever do.

As in any profession, it is critical that an individual understand their working environment if they hope to succeed. The Internet and online trading have truly been a revolution in the financial industry. It is very easy to open up an account online and start clicking the buy and sell buttons. The fact that this process is "easy," however, is misleading. It just means that the uneducated investor can get skewered much more quickly today than he could ten years ago. There isn't anyone I know who would presume he could go to an airport without a pilot's license, sneak into a 747, and take off down the runway to experiment whether his first flight would be successful. Yet, nearly everyone I know will try his or her hand at online trading with minimum knowledge to see how it works out. In the end, it doesn't work this way.

Toni's book, in my opinion, is the quickest way for newer traders to get up to speed with how to trade the markets for a living. This updated edition discusses key changes that have occurred in the markets since the book was first written, including changes that have revolutionized the world of trading. If a trader is longing to find someone they can meet at Starbucks and learn the ropes of this never-dull business, then they need look no further than these pages.

John F. Carter
Author, *Mastering the Trade*
President, *www.tradethemarkets.com*

# Acknowledgments

I just exhaled, seemingly for the first time in months. It's a wonderful feeling! A moment ago, I completed the revision and second edition of my first book, *A Beginner's Guide to Day Trading Online.* (My other two books to date are *A Beginner's Guide to Short-Term Trading* and *Short-Term Trading in the New Stock Market.*)

Writing-wise, this book was my firstborn. It has its own special personality—its own special place in the fabric of my life.

Like children, books involve many more people than the originator to bring its pages to life.

Many people contributed to the final product, and to them, I give heartfelt thanks. I can only write these books because each of you offers so much help in the process.

To my husband Mike, thank you for enduring yet one more book in-process. Once again, you've endured vague answers, dead houseplants, late dinners, and solitary weekends. Thank you for your constant council, support, and hugs.

To my daughter, Adrienne, thank you for your encouragement, humor, and wisdom. You are a delight, a bright light, and a true blessing.

To my family Chuck, Tammy, and Gail, Missy, Jenny, and John, thank you so much for your support and understanding when I "go underground."

To my assistant, Tina Hoesli, thank you so much for your fast and efficient contributions, and for the many times you cheered me on.

To my editor, Jill Alexander, thank you for putting a "strong hand in the middle of my back" and pushing me forward. You are one patient and talented editor, and I wish to thank you for bringing this book to a wonderful completion.

To my agent, Deidre Knight, as always, mega-agent, a huge "thank you." I couldn't do these books without you. You are the best!

To the great people at Townsend Analytics, Ltd., creators and developers of RealTick software, especially Mike Felix and Sarah Neis, thank you so much for your support.

To John Carter, thank you for taking time out of your busy schedule to write a timely and informative foreword.

To my incredible friends who offer the greatest network of support a writer could have, especially Joyce Smith, Jacqueline Middleton, Pam Hastings, and Penny Lavoie. Yes, Penny, as you advised, throughout this book, "I used happy crayons."

And, finally, thank you to Beverly Pickens, Mary Ellen, and Courtney, office coordinators extraordinaire, who offered chocolate and encouragement several times a day . . .

Thank you again to each one of you! God bless.

# Introduction

Welcome to the wild, wild world of day trading. Hang on tight, because if you jump aboard, it will be the most exhilarating, most terrifying ride you'll ever take!

The stock market is the monster of all roller coasters, lifting traders to hair-raising highs, then dropping them to the lowest lows, with no regard for their screams. Adrenaline junkies become addicted to the excitement. The timid among us endure or quit.

Day trading, or *active trading*, as it is sometimes called, is the not-so-gentle art of buying and selling stocks during the course of a trading day. It has exploded in popularity in the last decade, and savvy traders are raking in substantial returns. Since 1995, when the Dow Jones Industrial Average opened the year at 3,834, the most-watched index in the world has now rocketed to highs over 11,000. Not to be outdone, the benchmark Standard & Poor's Index (S&P), and its rowdy cohort, the NASDAQ Composite, have also etched dramatic cycles.

Stock prices have gone ballistic, soaring skyward though the glorious bull market of the late 1990s, skidding south through the down-and-dirty bear market of the early 2000s, and then shooting higher, once again.

The resultant volatility has encouraged a growing number of people to forsake the "buy and hold" rule of investing. We've learned that what goes up . . . can come down hard and fast. We've learned that global events now impact the markets so rapidly, we'd best know how to "get when the gettin' is good." And, we've discovered, sometimes painfully, that complacency is the root of shrinking profits.

The earliest day traders popped onto the scene in the early 1990s. Many of the original players were known as "SOES bandits," (SOES stands for "small order entry system") who learned how to navigate the newly accessible Internet. The bandits traded stocks on NASDAQ Level II screens and shot their orders—many times hundreds, even thousands, per day—to the "floor" of that electronic exchange.

As the Internet grew in popularity, we learned to research the stock market. Once regarded as a world of dark, esoteric secrets understood only by card-carrying members of the Puckered-Brow-in-a-Suit group, the financial arena now opened its doors and beckoned to those of us passionate enough to do our own research. We quickly discovered that we could not only conduct our own due diligence, we could also understand the market's motivation. For example, if inflation threatens to rear its annoying head, the Federal Reserve Board raises interest rates. That forces corporations to pay more for bank loans, thus affecting their earnings. Result? Falling stock prices.

Charles Schwab opened the first discount brokerage house in 1995. Other discount brokers burst on the scene, and offered their services online. No longer chained to a telephone and our broker's availability, we hopped onto our online trading accounts to buy, sell, set automatic stops, and review market action.

By 1997, America had fallen in love with the stock market. Mother Market swooned with the lavish attention, and stock market prices cavorted to higher highs. (They fell to lower lows, too, but no one seemed to notice.) Quickly, the word got out that you could buy and sell stocks in your online account all day long, and grab big bucks in minutes to hours. Viola! The new breed of market players, known as "day traders," were born.

Of course, focused traders needed serious tools. Direct-access brokers quickly came to the rescue. They developed highly sophisticated trading platforms that used NASDAQ Level II SOES screens for order entry, as well as ultra-fast access to market internals and intricate price charts and indicators.

If you were active in the markets during the mid-nineties to the early twenty-first century, you know the rest of the story. As mentioned earlier, the markets soared to nosebleed tops in January, 2000. Euphoria reigned. The stock market reigned as the conversational topic of all cocktail parties and television talk shows. Traders made—and lost—fortunes in a heartbeat.

But what goes up comes down, and by spring of 2000, the stock market—lead by the overly-inflated NASDAQ and its rambunctious dot.coms—started losing air. By October of 2002, the powerful technology index had fallen from its highs of 5,132 to a low of 1,108.

Day traders who could not, or would not, sell short—and worse, those who held stubbornly to their thoughts of previous glory—lost their accounts. Some, known as scalpers, lost their profits to the April 2001 decimalization change that dramatically narrowed the price between the inside bid and offer (the best price at that moment, in which stocks are purchased and sold).

Still, bear markets don't last forever, either, and by 2003, optimism returned to the financial arena. Prices bubbled higher.

At present, with a new bull market steaming away, new trading products have exploded onto the scene. Besides equities and options, traders now have a choice of Exchange Traded Funds (ETFs), E-mini and mini-sized Dow stock index futures, and single-stock futures. Previously the domain of banks and institutions, now Forex markets (trading global currencies and their futures contracts), are available to individual traders.

Online brokers and direct-access brokers have streamlined their platforms to maximum levels of speed and efficiency.

"Okay, I get it," you reply. "As traders, we jump onto the Internet and pull up the news and charts we need on a stock. Quickly, we switch over to our online trading execution system, and click the stock we want to buy, at the perfect entry point, of course. Then we sit back with a cup of coffee and rake in the big profits. Right?"

Right.

Well . . . sometimes.

I've had that exact scenario happen to me. But not always.

Once, early in my trading career, you would have found me slumped over my keyboard, wondering, "What in the heck am I doing wrong?" I watched my trading account lose money by the bucket loads. And it wasn't money I could afford to lose. I lived off that account. I pulled the mortgage payment, the electric bill, my daughter's college tuition, and mounting credit card payments out of it. You've never seen an account balance drop so fast!

One day, I sold all of my stocks (it didn't take long, I'd lost a lot of equity) and spent a couple of weeks wandering around in a state of misery. When I finally finished feeling sorry for myself, I got mad. Who did this market think it was, taking all of my money? One word kept nagging me: knowledge. I didn't know enough.

Some jobs you can fake with a little moxie and a lot of charm, but you can't fake day trading. You can't wander into this rough-and-tumble arena without knowledge. The market eats ignorant players for breakfast.

I know. I was one of them. I made a million mistakes. I suffered losses so grim that my friends and family begged me to quit. But I come from a "long line of stubborn."

I persisted. I read books on technical analysis that I didn't understand. I watched CNBC until my eyes glazed over. Then one day, a friend introduced me to a terrific couple who were real day traders. They invited me to their home, showed me their computer setup, and explained how they traded. A new world opened to me. I realized day trading was far more difficult and involved than I had previously thought.

I knuckled under, enrolled in trading techniques and strategy classes, and studied like crazy. Six months later, when my nontrading friends asked me how my trading was going, I'd grit my teeth and answer defiantly, "I'm losing less."

They rolled their eyes.

After a while, I broke even. Then came the day, nearly a year after I'd started, when I began to make money—consistently. Not gobs of money, but a decent living.

As success became routine, it occurred to me that I could help others do what I do. I imagined there must be many people who would like to work out of their homes, be their own bosses, set their own schedules, and make a tidy profit each week.

Why, though, should these beginning traders make the same mistakes I did—there's standing-room only in the Dumb Mistakes Trading Room—if I can help them skip some of the nastier, account-breaking rungs on the ladder to mastery?

When I started trading, I wished for a book that spoke to me in clear and direct terms that I could grasp quickly and easily. I wished for a book that would tell me, "when the market's doing this, don't trade," or "when a stock's doing this, go for it." When my losses finally turned into consistent wins, I decided to write that book.

In the following pages, I'm going to talk to you as one good friend talks to another. If you decide trading is for you, I'll explain how to do it without losing your shirt or blouse. I'll tell you the absolute, nitty-gritty of what you're wading into *before* you make your first trade, not *after*. I'll show you how to preserve your principal and make money.

I wish someone had explained these things to me, early on, in a way I could understand. It would have saved me big bucks. So here it is, fellow traders, from me to you.

And, here's to your good wealth!

# CHAPTER 1

# This Ain't No Dress Rehearsal!

## BENEFITS OF DAY TRADING: THE GOOD NEWS

Day trading is a made-to-order profession. By and large, you can work when and where you want to. You can structure your days as you chose, working from your office or home, or even when traveling, when need be.

If you think of it as a small business, the initial investment in equipment—a good computer, one to three monitors, fast Internet hookup, and software—is relatively inexpensive.

You can live anywhere. If you decide to move to Bangor, Maine, from Yee-haw Junction, Florida, just dismantle your electronic monsters, pack them up, and go. If you long to go skiing for a week and can afford it, take your account *flat* (trader's jargon for taking your account to cash), and go.

As an active trader, you're independent and answer to no one but yourself. Forget reporting to a nasty boss. You can stay in bed when you have the flu. You don't have to wear a tie that chokes you or high heels that dislocate your back. You can trade in a torn T-shirt, flannel shorts, and duck slippers.

You'll develop your own style, fast-paced or easy-going. Days when the market is highly volatile, you can, and should, take the day off. Run errands, play with your kids, or go shopping with the money you saved by staying out of the market on a whippy, choppy day.

## THE FLIP SIDE: WALL STREET TAKES NO PRISONERS

All of the above is the good news. Now, let's look at the less-than-charming realities you need to know before you place that first trade.

When I first started trading, I crawled into bed one night with a bowl of praline ice cream and *Trading for a Living*.

In the opening pages, author Dr. Alexander Elder writes, "Markets operate without normal human helpfulness. Every trader tries to hit others. Every trade

1

gets hit by others. The trading highway is lettered with wrecks. Trading is the most dangerous human endeavor, short of war."

"Humph," I thought. "Dr. Elder certainly has a negative attitude."

A few weeks and one bloodied trading account later, I knew Dr. Elder was right on the money. In the hands of the wrong person, trading can be hazardous to one's wealth.

Here's another reality statement: This business crushes most who enter its doors. Nearly 80% of those who try, quit. They lose their trading accounts by ignorance, trading too much, or taking foolish risks. Some can't handle the stress.

You can earn substantial profits day trading. If the rewards are high, however, so are the tradeoffs. The stock market is a ruthless arena. *Newsweek* once called Wall Street "the avenue of avarice." It's inhabited by the sharpest minds in the world, all intent on grabbing your money as fast as possible. It's a greed-against-greed, fear-versus-fear, trader-battling-trader, if-you-die-I-win world. Every day. No mercy. The more you lose, the harder I laugh.

"But buying a stock can be a complacent click on my computer screen," you say, puzzled. "I don't see the greed and fear connection."

Take my word for it. When I began trading, I didn't see the connection either, but I learned in short order, and the lesson was expensive—*very* expensive.

The best way to start trading is slowly, calmly, and armed with knowledge you've already accumulated. Watch CNBC or another financial network every day for several weeks, so you can internalize market rhythms. Soak up the gist of the "if, then," logic. *If* this happens on Wall Street, *then* that usually follows. Stare at market indicators and absorb how they act in relation to one another. Listen to market gurus and keep track as to whether their predictions come true.

Place paper trades for a few weeks. I'll explain how in Chapter 3. Keep in mind, though, that while paper trading is good practice, it doesn't accurately portray how real trades play out. Reason? The absence of emotion.

If you listen and heed my advice, it will save you money and headaches. Every caveat I give you in the pages that follow comes from a lesson I learned the hard way. If you learn from the lessons, you'll keep your losses small and your gains high.

I jumped into trading head first, assuming I knew what I was doing. I didn't.

As a successful investor, I imagined trading was the same thing, but at a faster pace. Not true. Comparing trading and investing is like comparing hamsters with kangaroos. Yes, the time frames are different, but mindsets are different, too. So are entry points, exit points, and risk-reward ratios. Traders concern themselves with market and stock trends, whereas investors want stocks that outperform the overall market.

Please go slowly when you enter this profession. A cautious turtle will keep his or her money, then make more. An impetuous hare will end up in the briar patch.

## WHAT DOES A DAY TRADER LOOK LIKE?

Traders in the trenches insist we need three things to trade successfully, namely, the "Three Bs," or *Bucks, Brains,* and, uh, . . . *Boldness* (polite substitute for actual word). They're right.

First, of course, is *bucks.* Anyone who says you can start trading with $2,000 or less is blowing smoke. Why? Because, at some point in time, you are going to lose money. You may make it back, but you will lose it first. Show me a successful trader who says he or she didn't lose money learning how to trade, and I'll show you someone growing a Pinocchio nose! If losing money stops your heart, trading is not your game.

Next comes *brains.* I'm going to assume you own mental horsepower if you're reading this book.

If you don't know what I mean by *boldness*, you will, if you stick around the financial markets long enough. This profession gives you confidence and mental toughness not only when you're trading, but in every area of your life. After all, if you're a day trader, you survive in one of the toughest arenas in the world.

My nontrading friends ask me repeatedly, "How do you do that all day? Isn't it risky?"

You bet. If you don't love jumping blindfolded into the dark unknown, with no guarantee whether you'll land on a pile of feather pillows or into a crater of hot lava, please don't trade.

Successful traders know how to act swiftly. Many times you'll have one second to make a decision that may affect your account by thousands of dollars. If your middle name is Waffle, you'll be happier investing.

The best traders also multitask easily. They scan charts, while listening to CNBC, while watching a list of major market indicators and mentally computing their relationship to one another, while keeping an eye on one or more stock positions, while remembering the strategy and stops for each trade, while executing a momentum play or two, while . . .

Successful traders also pay attention to their intuition. By intuition, I don't mean you should buy a stock because you have a "gut feeling" it's going to fly. That's never a good idea. I mean you can use the gut feeling developed by all good traders through experience—the hunch that tells you something in the market is good, or amiss, before the actual event takes place.

The traders holding the fattest wallets have the ability to change their minds in a nanosecond. Being right or wrong has nothing to do with it. They know that sticking to a decision they made hours, or even minutes, ago just to prove they are "right" is the worst thing a trader can do.

Emotional discipline is a must. The best traders monitor their emotions constantly. In *Trading for a Living*, Dr. Elder writes, "Your feelings have an immediate impact on your account equity. You may have a brilliant trading system, but if you feel frightened, arrogant, or upset, your account is sure to suffer."

I've traded while feeling scared, smug, and sad. During those times, I've always lost money. One emotion I still allow myself, however, is pure, self congratulation. After I close a great trade, I say, "You go, girl," and I grab a piece of chocolate.

This is the perfect moment for you to pause for introspection and conduct a reality check as to whether or not you'd be happy and prosperous as an active trader. Forget your ego. Be completely honest and ask yourself these questions: "Can I chance losing part of my account?" "Do I think fast and stay cool under stress?" "Can I control my emotions?"

## TO TRADE OR NOT TO TRADE?

As one of my best friends says about life, "This ain't no dress rehearsal."

Neither is trading. You can't "sort of" ride a roller coaster. Either you're hurtling through space at mach two with your hair on fire or you're standing on the ground below. You can't do both. To dangle one foot outside the speeding car is mighty dangerous.

Before you start to trade:

➤ Study this book and others on the Recommended Reading List located in the back of the book.
➤ Explore high-quality trading chat rooms on the Internet; analyze what their members say. Most offer free trial memberships.
➤ Consider taking a trading course from a reputable school.
➤ Attend a "money" show or traders' conference.
➤ Join a local trading group and talk to other traders. You learn from every kind of trader, whether they trade stocks, commodities, or jelly beans.

## AUTHOR'S NOTE

Learning to trade successfully was the most vitalizing, yet the most difficult, undertaking of my life.

As with all professions, the good times, when everything fell into place, delivered a sense of self-satisfaction and composure. The not-so-good times, when everything I touched knocked me down, gave way to discouragement and frustration.

To cope with the challenging times, I studied principles gleaned from motivational teachings. I hoped that if I stepped back from the trading world and observed larger truths of life from a different vantage point, it would empower me to persevere. It did.

Each "Center Point" in this text summarizes various concepts and observations that kept me centered on my goal of becoming an accomplished trader. They also benefited other areas of my life.

I trust you will find these messages to be valuable handrails as you make your way over the stepping stones to success.

## CENTER POINT: THE POWER OF COMMITMENT

*"Until one is committed, there is hesitance, the chance to draw back, always ineffectiveness. Concerning all acts of initiative (and creation), there is one elementary truth, the ignorance of which kills countless ideas and splendid plans: that the moment one definitely commits oneself, then providence moves, too. A whole stream of events issues from the decision, raising in one's favor all manner of unforeseen incidents and meetings and material assistance, which no man could have dreamt would come his way."*

—William Hutchinson Murray

When you fully commit to a goal, the focus of positive energy onto a desired result is like programming a missile to "lock on" to a moving target; the missile automatically pursues the target no matter how elusive it becomes.

The act of commitment also attracts exciting, new opportunities to your doorstep, leading to dramatic changes in your life.

Perhaps you've noticed that successful people are not always the best or the brightest, the quickest or strongest. Yet they're always the ones who do whatever it takes to succeed.

A goal without commitment results in a nonentity, and usually falls by the wayside from a lack of interest by its beholder. Only when we fully commit to a dream are we able to access the highest possibilities of our being.

Commitment requires you to identify a clear, realistic, and positive goal. Next, declare your intention to achieve that goal, while maintaining the belief that it's already a reality in your life. If your inner commitment to your goal remains strong and unwavering, it will remove obstacles that fall onto your path and deliver you to your objective.

Personal greatness comes from fully engaging and fully participating in a process that generates life by drawing on your inner, transformative resources. When you truly commit to a goal or vision, the universe responds with positive results "with which no man could have dreamt would come his way."

# CHAPTER 2

# Wall Street: A View from the Top of the Skyscraper

## THE FIRST TRADERS

The act of trading dates back to the original cave neighbors, Uggh and Oog. One day, Uggh reflected that he, himself, was darn good at hunting animals for meat, while his neighbor, Oog, was a heck of a fisherman. So, Uggh motioned Oog over and grunted his observations to him. The two men agreed to swap meat for fish, and day trading was born.

## THE BIRTH OF WALL STREET

Fast-forward a million years or so to a more civilized world. In 1644, the Dutch West India Company in New Amsterdam (later named New York City) decided too many cows wandered around the island of Manhattan. The company decreed, "Resolved, that a fence shall be made, beginning at the Great Bouewery, and extending to Emanuel's plantation, and all area to repair thither on Monday, 4th April, with tools to build a fence." The resulting barricade was an earthen embankment, studded with uprooted tree trunks, at the southern tip of Manhattan.

A few years later, in 1653, Governor Peter Stuyvesant knew that the British were about to attack and guessed they would arrive by land. He ordered local residents, mostly soldiers and Dutch colonists, to raise the fence and dig a moat the length of it.

But Stuyvesant missed the boat. The British didn't attack by land. They came by sea in 1664, anchored off Coney Island, and captured the settlement without firing a shot. Later, they burned the wall. The street that ran alongside survived, though, and retained its name—Wall Street.

The New York Stock Exchange was born in New York City, when the first Congress met in Federal Hall in 1789 to assume the debts of the new colonies and government. The Congress issued about $80 million in government notes, creating an exciting new market in securities. These securities, along with additional stocks, bonds, orders for commodities, and warehouse receipts, were put up for sale to the public. Traders gathered each day under the sycamore tree at 68–70 Wall Street to buy and sell.

To participate in this market, many investors helped fund American companies by buying shares of ownership. The investors had equity and could prove so by the certificates of stock issued by the company, in exchange for the equity capital given by the investor. That stock proved the investor's participation, and so secured the debt. That's why shares of stock are alternately called *stocks*, *equities*, and *securities.*

The stock market began trading formally in 1792, and public auctions of securities were halted to regulate business. Two dozen brokers formed a club and continued to meet under the buttonwood tree, or in the Tontine Coffee House at the corner of Water and Wall streets. Fierce competition ran rampant among them, and instead of focusing on their customers, they fought to protect themselves and their commissions. Public outrage rang loud, and over time, the brokers established brokerage houses that offered stocks to the public at fair prices.

In 1827, a new Merchants Exchange building, erected at Wall and Hanover streets, housed the New York Stock and Exchange Board. By 1842, the American Stock Exchange opened its doors. Both exchanges enforced strict rules governing the sale of stocks, and Wall Street began its evolution as one of the world's most important financial centers.


## WHO ARE WALL STREET'S BIGGEST PARTY ANIMALS?
## THE BULLS AND THE BEARS

New York City gradually swallowed Manhattan's farmland, but references to animals carried through on Wall Street.

No matter which exchange we participate in, four animals describe the types of traders: bulls, bears, hogs, and sheep. An old Street saying goes: "Bulls make money, and bears make money, but hogs get slaughtered."

A bull fights by striking up with his horns. If you're a bull, you believe the stock market is going to rise in value. You're a buyer.

Bears fight by striking down with their paws. As a bear, you speculate that stock prices will fall and make your profits from a declining market. Therefore, you're a seller.

Have you already figured out who the hogs are? Hogs bet all of their money on big, risky positions, then get slaughtered when the market turns against them. The market always knows when hogs overeat—it skewers greedy gluttons every time.

Instead of relying on their own knowledge and experience, sheep follow tips, gurus, or anybody with a tambourine. Sometimes they act bullish, sometimes they roar like bears. But when the market turns suddenly volatile, dim-witted sheep get shorn in a hurry.

Each day in the market is a giant tug-of-war between the bulls and the bears. As a wise trader, you'll decide before you put on a trade who is in power. In a strong, rising market, bulls rule, profiting from the soaring prices. Unless you're a contrarian (a market participant who takes the opposite side of the current trend—not a good idea for a new trader), you'll strap on your horns and buy. When the market turns weak and prices fall, bears rule, profiting as prices trend lower. In a bear market, you either stand aside or learn the art of selling short.

When volatility indicators show that the bulls and bears are engaging in a no-win battle, smart traders observe from the sidelines. Knowing when to trade and when not to trade is the hallmark of a seasoned trader. Believe it or not, it takes immense discipline to watch the market whirl around you, and not jump in. Forcing trades when market conditions are whippy and unpredictable is labeled *greed*. And we know what happens to hogs.

## THE LAND OF GREED AND FEAR

Greed and fear rule the financial markets. These two emotions motivate nearly all market players—institutional managers, stockbrokers, investors, traders, the taxi driver that plays "hot tips"—and you.

"Me?" you gasp. "Not a chance. I'm a very nice person. Greed and fear will never rule any part of my life."

Sure they will. As a novice trader, greed and fear will be your constant companions.

Is that something to be ashamed of? Absolutely not. Are you the only trader experiencing these emotions? No. You have plenty of company. One of our goals in this book is to face these emotions and understand them. That way, you can get them behind you, where they belong.

What do these emotions look like?

Say you buy a stock at the perfect entry point. Within minutes, the price rises even higher than you expected. A little voice whispers in your ear, "This baby's gonna fly. Why don't you take all the money in your trading account and buy as many shares as you can? You'll make a killing." *Greed.*

Or you buy a stock, and it moves up two points. It's your predetermined profit exit, and you think, "This is the sensible place to take profits. But this stock might push higher. I'm staying in." *Greed.*

Typically, when strong stocks explode in a bull market, greed explodes in direct proportion. But there's a downside. These same stocks fizzle as fast as, and usually faster than, they mushroom. The falling price detonates panic (*fear*), and everyone runs for the door with less money than they came in with.

Let's take a look at another example: Convinced a particular stock would shoot up at the market's open the following morning, you took a hefty position home the night before (*greed*). The next morning, though, the market opens way down (*fear*). Your stock crashes like a boulder off a cliff, as selling runs rampant. Panic twists your heart and your stomach. The blood pounds in your ears as you watch a big portion of your trading account dissolve into the blinking red prices on your monitor.

"Is there a way around this?" you ask. "Can I trade without greed and fear?"

Absolutely. If you learn how to control these two destructive emotions by replacing them with positive ones, if you read this book and others, if you study and apply what you learn in a disciplined, cool-headed fashion, then you'll have the edge over 99% of all market players.

## SUPPLY AND DEMAND OR HOW MUCH WILL YOU PAY FOR THAT COOKIE?

Think back to your childhood. Remember the day you misbehaved, and your mother punished you by forbidding you access to the cookie jar?

For the past couple of days, you hadn't thought about cookies at all, hadn't even asked for one.

All of a sudden, though, cookies were off-limits, and you could think of nothing else. You stood and stared at the big earthenware jar, picturing the mouth-watering goodies inside. You wished more than anything in the world that you could nibble on the crunchy oatmeal and taste the soft, sweet morsels of chocolate melting on your tongue. At that moment, you'd give a week's allowance for a cookie.

Why did you ignore the cookies one day, and focus on them the next? Supply and demand. Suddenly, your supply was cut off. Human nature dictates that when supply gets low, that item becomes intensely desirable, meaning in high demand.

Let's say the following day, you mother decides you've been punished enough and returns your privileges to the cookie jar. You quickly push a chair up to the counter, scramble onto it, and stand on your tiptoes until you reach the jar. You can't wait to taste those cookies. Smacking your lips in anticipation, you lift the lid. One, lonely cookie stares back at you. Only one? Well, heck it's better than none.

Suddenly behind you, you hear the sound of scuffling feet. Your older brother runs into the kitchen. He shoulders you aside, nearly knocking you off the chair, and jams his hand into the cookie jar. "Only one cookie?" he yells. "It's mine." *Demand.*

"No, it's mine," you reply. *Demand.*

He's taller than you, and he holds the cookie (*limited supply*) over his head, taunting you. "What will ya' give me for it?"

Your mind races. You've already spent most of your allowance this week, but now you're willing to give up the rest of it for what seems to be the only cookie in the world (*demand*). "I'll give you seventy-five cents."

He sneers. "You gotta be kidding. It's worth more than that. Remember, this is the only cookie left in the entire universe, and I have it." He waves the cookie higher over his head. "How much?"

Your mind races to another quarter you'd seen earlier on your dresser. "Okay. A dollar. That's all I have!"

He agrees, and you run upstairs, promptly returning to exchange money for the cookie.

A minute later, you sit on the back stoop, taking tiny nibbles of the cookie, savoring every crumb of it. Why didn't you pop it in your mouth, chew absent-mindedly, and gulp it down, as you usually did? Because your supply was limited, this added value to the cookie.

The next afternoon, a bunch of the neighborhood kids come over. While you and your friends play, your mother dons her apron and starts to bake. Soon, she holds out a platter of freshly baked cookies. You and your friends grab handfuls of cookies and gobble some down, maybe shoving one or two in your pockets for later. After mumbling your thanks, you run outside to play.

Why didn't you savor each bite, as you did before? Because now there's an abundance of supply. Everyone can have cookies, with plenty left over. The demand has lessened.

Supply and demand manipulate human emotions, which turns full circle to manipulate supply and demand. Just as a cookie shortage causes children of all ages to desire them more, the shortage of an attractive stock at a given price causes market players to desire it more. Those who control the stock demand higher prices because buyers agree to pay those prices.

Limited supply equals high demand. How high a price will you pay? That depends on your level of risk and the perceived reward.

Here's a classic case of supply and demand in trading: An attractive stock breaks through its intraday high of $49—a good omen for it to rise even higher. You buy a few hundred shares just over the breakout price, at $49.10. Within an hour, the price climbs nearly a point, to $50. Coincidentally, $50 is yesterday's high, or the highest price it reached during yesterday's trading.

Let's backtrack. Yesterday, when it reached that high of $50, many traders bought shares at that price there, thinking it would go higher. Instead, it fell to $47. As it fell, the traders who bought at $50 held on, and said, "If this stupid stock ever goes back up to fifty, I'm getting rid of it. At least I'll get out even."

Okay, we're back to the present day, and the stock just hit $50, yesterday's high. *Smack.* All the traders who are waiting to get out even sell at $50. Supply. *Lots of supply* (big platter of cookies). To make matters worse, traders who bought the stock today—you included—notice the supply, predict a pullback, and offer theirs for sale.

That creates too much stock for sale at $50 (supply) and nobody's buying, meaning *limited demand.*

To get rid of it, sellers make it more attractive by lowering the price. They offer it out at $49.90, then $49.75 . . . then $49.70 . . . then $49.50, as well as increments in-between.

Finally, at $49.20, the sell off peters out. Supply dwindles (most of the cookies have been eaten). At $49, the stock's price looks attractive once again, and buyers start nibbling. Demand increases, sellers raise their prices, and the process repeats itself.

## PRICE: THE BOTTOM LINE

Just as the most important aspect of real estate is "location, location, location," the most important aspect of the stock market is "price, price, price." Price is the bottom line, the end result, the last word. All analyses, whether fundamental or technical; all guru proclamations; all market movements, whether ruled by greed or fear or even uncertainty; boil down to a single element: price. Simply put, price rules.

For every transaction in the stock market, there has to be a buyer and a seller. You, the buyer, and the seller agree on a certain value of a given equity at the same time. Equity and money exchange hands. Price represents a shared consensus at the moment of transaction.

Does this agreement on price mean you have the same emotions about that stock? No. Just the opposite. At the moment you buy the stock, you believe it's a bargain. You think it will increase in value so you can sell it at a higher price and pad your pockets from that increase. The trader who sold it to you, however, feels sure that stock will fall and is delighted to dispose of it.

Please keep this in mind whenever you place a trade. The trader who is buying the stock from you, or selling it to you, holds the opposite opinion of the stock's future direction. The minute you complete the trade, you're both at risk because the next "tick," or price movement in the stock, will prove which of you was right. And only one of you gets to win!

Why do prices up and down? They move because of supply and demand, generated by our old buddies, greed and fear. When you, the buyer, and the other guy, the seller, disagree about the value of the stock in question, the disagreement causes the stock price to change.

This change, or fluctuation, creates opportunity for you to make money. You assess the risks in the fluctuating prices and act according to your risk tolerance. The trick is to predict price movement accurately enough of the time that your profits are larger than your losses.

## THE NEW YORK STOCK EXCHANGE

Although several equities exchanges operate across the United States, our three largest are the New York, NASDAQ, and American Stock Exchange.

The present-day New York Stock Exchange (NYSE) was established on the principle that customer orders must be handled in a fair and efficient manner, and that the investor's interest comes first.

Located at 11 Wall Street, the NYSE (*www.nyse.com*) lists more than 2,700 stocks. You can observe the floor of the NYSE live, every weekday morning, on CNBC and other financial networks.

The stocks traded on the NYSE are referred to as "listed" securities. Many are icons of American industry, such as General Electric, Boeing, IBM, and Johnson & Johnson. In addition to other "blue chips" like these, the NYSE lists a wide variety of equities, from high-tech companies, to Exchange Traded Funds (ETFs), to non-U.S. companies listed on other global exchanges.

For the sake of efficiency, all financial instruments are assigned symbols. Listed securities consist of symbols consisting of one to three letters. For example, Sprint/Nextel's symbol is S, Alcoa Aluminum's symbol is AA, and Caterpillar's symbol is CAT. The NYSE, itself, is a publicly-held company, and trades on its own exchange under the symbol NYX.

Thirty equities, the majority of which are listed on the NYSE, make up the venerable Dow Jones Industrial Average. "The Dow," as it's often referred to, is the most closely watched market indicator in the world and is generally perceived to mirror the state of the American economy. You can buy and sell the Dow in a single stock, known as an exchange traded fund (we'll talk more about ETFs later) with the symbol DIA.

The Dow Jones 20 Transportation Average and the Dow Jones 15 Utilities Average serve as colleagues to the Industrial Average. The NYSE Composite Index reflects the price movements of all stocks listed on the New York Stock Exchange.

Listed stocks have earned a reputation of behaving in a dignified manner and at a more reasonable pace than their wilder, more volatile counterparts on the NASDAQ. That means NYSE stocks are many times easier for traders to "catch" at the proper entry point, so there's not as much tendency to chase them. Remember, though, when Mother Market feels really cantankerous, any stock—listed, or otherwise—can mirror her behavior.

### The NYSE: How It Operates

The financial world has changed in the last few years, with consolidation acting as a major catalyst. One of the most prominent examples took place in 2006, when the NYSE merged with the fully-electronic ArcaEx. To date, the merger (which also included the Pacific Stock Exchange) represents the largest integration ever accomplished among securities exchanges.

At present, the NYSE, or "Big Board," as it is sometimes called, trades as an integrated or hybrid market; it operates as a floor-based central auction system and an automatic, electronic market.

On the NYSE floor, different "posts," each representing a different stock, pepper the floor of the Exchange. At each post, a specialist (think "auctioneer") conducts a two-way auction between buyers and sellers and provides a market for that stock. Only one specialist represents each stock; for example, IBM has only one specialist. Specialists, however, can represent more than one stock.

Even though specialists still rule the NYSE trading floor, all buy/sell orders now arrive on the floor electronically. In addition, the NYSE's Direct+ automatic system fills a large percentage of trades.

## THE NASDAQ STOCK MARKET

The NASDAQ Stock Market (*www.NASDAQ.com*) opened in February 1971. Formerly, NASDAQ designated an acronym that stood for the National Association of Securities Dealers Automated Quotron. Now, the word NASDAQ stands on its own.

The NASDAQ is the largest fully-electronic stock market in the United States. Currently, it lists nearly 3,300 companies and trades more shares per day than any other major U.S. market. The exchange, itself, is a publicly held company, and trades under the symbol NDAQ.

Because it's electronic, you won't see the "floor of the NASDAQ." Still, you've probably seen the NASDAQ MarketSite Tower on television. This dazzling, cylindrical electronic billboard, located at 43rd and Broadway in New York City's Time Square, flashes constant market news and advertisements onto the seven-story high building. Inside, the MarketSite Broadcast Studio transmits market updates to financial networks, such as CNBC, Bloomberg TV, and Reuters.

Although the NASDAQ is also home to retail, communications, biotechnology, financial services, and transportation and media companies, when announcers and journalists refer to the NASDAQ, they often describe it as "tech-heavy." That's because technology stocks like Microsoft Corp. (MSFT), Oracle Corp., (ORCL) and Google Inc. (GOOG) take up a large share of the NASDAQ pie. When there's a "tech-wreck," technology stocks crash. Since these stocks tend to move in tandem, when a tech-wreck occurs, it usually pulls the entire NASDAQ market down with it.

As you've noticed by now, NASDAQ-listed stocks typically have symbols consisting of four letters.

The NASDAQ 100 Index lists 100 of the top nonfinancial stocks in the market. The NASDAQ Composite is an index comprising all issues traded on that exchange. Both the NASDAQ 100 and Composite act as important indicators that traders watch throughout the day. You can trade the NASDAQ 100 Index in a single stock, symbol QQQQ.

Active NASDAQ stocks are the day trader's playground. Trading many of these issues makes a roller coaster ride feel like a quiet walk in the park. The more attention a NASDAQ stock receives, the more volatile it can be, skyrocketing multiple points in minutes to hours, then falling even faster, taking a boatload of screaming traders with it.

Since I am adamant about keeping one's trading account on the plus side, I suggest new traders buy and sell the kinder, gentler NYSE stocks when they begin. There's less chance of losing one's shirt.

### The NASDAQ: How It Operates

As I stated before, the NASDAQ is a single electronic system. The NASDAQ's version of specialists are called "market makers," and many of them represent brokerage houses you'll recognize: Prudential, Merrill Lynch, Schwab, and Goldman Sachs. They execute orders for their firm's customers and trade their firm's account. They also maintain liquidity in the stock, which is their responsibility. Unlike listed stocks where a single specialist orchestrates most of the trades, the NASDAQ allows many market makers to "make a market" in a stock at any given time.

In the old days of the late 1990s, we day traders would stare at Level II screens that displayed buy and sell orders by each stock's market makers, and play head games with the MMs. In the office where I traded all day, we'd yell, "Check out Cranky Computers—Goldman's on the bid." That translated into "Goldman Sachs is buying Cranky Computers." And, if 800-pound gorilla Goldman was buying a stock, it meant the price would skyrocket. We'd plunge right in and buy, too.

We soon learned that Goldman was pretending to buy certain stocks, and was using us traders for bait. While the market maker made himself apparent on the bid (buy) side of our screens, he was actually using another broker to sell his shares on the ask (sell) side.

The onset of decimalization in 2001 took away the large spread between the bid and the ask prices, which reduced market maker profits. That, plus the upgrading of direct-access trading platforms available to individual traders created a more level playing field between them and us. Most of us are no longer glued to our Level II screens, and we no longer play the same games with market makers. Heck, they usually won, anyway.

## THE AMERICAN STOCK EXCHANGE, OR AMEX

The American Stock Exchange, or Amex (*www.amex.com*), is the third most active market in the United States, after the NYSE and NASDAQ. The exchange was founded in 1842, in New York City. It resides at 86 Trinity Place in lower Manhattan.

The Amex lists equities, options, and ETFs, and trades similarly to the NYSE, with specialists maintaining orderly markets through electronic systems. Amex stocks are also referred to as "listed" securities and contain three letters.

For a quick look at how the Amex is doing as a whole, check the Amex Composite Index, which includes all common stocks listed on the Amex.

## WHERE YOU COME IN

Although we'll talk a lot more in upcoming chapters about executing trades, let's talk briefly about the two paths you can take: directing your order to an online broker, or executing through your direct-access trading platform.

Say you want to buy 300 shares of Boeing Co. (BA), at the market, which means "at the current posted price." Basically, your order can be filled one of two ways:

1. You call your broker and give your broker the order, or you can bring up your online account and send the order to your broker via the Internet. When your broker receives it, he electronically directs it to a specialist or market maker at the target exchange. Once your order is filled, your broker is notified of the fill (the precise number of shares and price your order was filled at), and he sends you a confirmation. This can take seconds to minutes.
2. You execute the order yourself, through your direct-access broker, from a NASDAQ Level II screen order entry system (detailed in the next chapter). Your order goes directly to an exchange or market maker, and once filled, you see instantaneous confirmation.

## THE BID AND ASK, OR OFFER: WHAT THEY MEAN

When you jump onto your online account and request a quote for Oracle Corp. (ORCL), the quote display might show something like: *Bid: 13.78, Ask: 13.79.*

➤ That means $13.78 is the *inside bid*, or highest price you can demand if you want to sell ORCL as a *market order*.
➤ The other, $13.79 is the *inside ask*, or *inside offer*. ("Ask" and "offer" are interchangeable terms.) It represents the lowest price you can buy ORCL if you want to buy at the market price.
➤ The "spread" is the one-cent difference between the two prices.

When you get a quote from any exchange, whether verbal or written, the bid is always announced first, and then the ask or offer, second. These are also known as "Level I" quotes.

## NASDAQ LEVEL II SYSTEM

When you ask for a quote from your online broker, the inside bid and ask or offer prices are displayed. Again, these are called Level I quotes.

When you open an account with a direct-access broker, however, the broker will provide you with a trading platform that includes Level II order entry screens. These windows display all of the market participants for a selected stock. By the way, don't let the NASDAQ part confuse you. Although the NASDAQ originated Level II screens, their quote information covers all actively traded stocks, on all exchanges.

Serious active traders open accounts with direct-access brokers to gain access to Level II screens because the quote systems offer transparency. That means you can see bids and asks from nearly all of the current market participants posting buy/sell orders, not just the inside (best) bid and inside (best) ask. On a high-volume stock, a Level II screen boasts a long line of specialists (indicated by their exchanges) and market makers waiting at the bid, and another line waiting at the ask, showing different prices.

You'll see exchange names such as CIN (Cincinnati Stock Exchange), BSE (Boston Stock Exchange), and ARCAX (ArcaEx). You'll also see market makers representing brokers such as Goldman Sacks (GSCO), Merrill Lynch (MLCO), and Morgan Stanley (MSCO). Independent market makers also hop in and out of the lines.

Other primary participants you'll see listed are the electronic communications networks (ECNs). They by-pass the exchanges and link buyers and sellers automatically. You could say they are "trader co-ops." You will see their order books posted in Level II screens with designations such as BRUTBK (Brut ECN) and INET (Inet ATS, Inc.). If you use a direct-access broker, you'll be able to preference the ECN of your choice. That's appealing to some traders, because their commissions vary.

## THE RINGMASTER, CNBC

The CNBC (*www.cnbc.com*) television network covers the world's markets and keeps us informed on a minute-by-minute basis of important events pertaining to global finances. CNN also reports business news, Bloomberg television and radio networks provide excellent television and radio coverage, and you'll want to read the various financial papers.

As important as it is to stay informed on financial news, take care how you apply the news to your trades. News can work for you or against you.

Let's say that it's midmorning on a bullish day, and your positions are edging up nicely. Suddenly, Ben Bernanke appears on CNBC, and tells the world that U.S. stocks are overpriced and inflation is on the rise. A statement like that from someone as powerful as our Federal Reserve Chairman sends everyone running toward the doors.

If you started taking profits at the same time Mr. Bernanke came to the end of the sentence, you did the right thing.

Far more often, you'll hear network commentators interviewing financial gurus. You'll hear experts, including mutual fund managers, prominent technical advisors, CEOs of companies, and authors of how-to financial books—once in a while they flavor the soup with a market astrologer—forecast their opinions about the markets' future or a particular stock's future.

Want to see a stock move fast? Watch what happens to the price of Sensational Software the moment Marvin Mutual Fund Manager swears on CNBC that it's going to be the next Microsoft. Sensational rockets straight up, point after point. Finally, it quivers for a second, then—look out below! Enjoy watching it as amusing entertainment. But no stock chasing, please. When stocks run on news, wise traders keep their fingers off the keyboard. Why?

➤ First of all, word leaks out early in the morning on which stocks the experts will tout. That means the stock may have already absorbed a lot of buying and is ready to pull back.

➤ Second, news announced on CNBC, or any other financial network, was broadcasted over professional news systems earlier in the day. Institutional trading offices across the country become aware of the news long before CNBC announces it to us.

➤ Third, those who already own a touted stock use the run-up to take unexpected profits.

For these reasons, be assured if a stock runs because of broadcast news, it's usually the amateur traders who give it a quick upward throttle. The market makers sit in the corners drooling, waiting for these traders to run the stock up, so they, the market makers, can short it (sell it) and drive it back down. Neophyte traders end up buying at the highest price of the day, then watch it fall in horror, with no buyers to sell it back to.

In conclusion, a wise trader uses news as he or she uses a temperature gauge for the markets. Trust me, it's best to leave impulse news buying to those with disposable trading accounts.

And now, since this is an interactive book, it's your turn. From this point on, at the end of each chapter, you will find a quiz that relates to the chapter content. Please don't skip it. Completing the answers by writing them down will test your absorption and make you a better trader, faster.

# QUIZ
||||||||||||||||

## Questions

1. True or false? When volatility indicators show the bulls and bears are fighting a volatile battle, and neither is winning, wise traders stand aside.

2. What two emotions rule the financial markets?

3. Which two fundamental principles dictate stock prices? Give a brief explanation.

4. True or false? Since price equals a shared consensus of the value of a stock, the buyer and seller also share the same opinion of the future worth of the stock.

5. On what kind of system does the New York Stock Exchange operate?

6. True or false? NYSE specialists have only one responsibility—to pair orders between buyers and sellers.

7. Overall, which sector dominates the NASDAQ?

8. True or false? Unlike NYSE stocks, which have one specialist per stock, active NASDAQ stocks have many market makers fielding orders at one time.

9. Define the term spread.

10. True or false? The safest strategy for making big bucks is to wait for a CNBC expert to tout a stock, then buy lots of it—and fast.

## Answers

1. True. Successful, seasoned traders recognize whippy, trendless, market patterns and refrain from trading.

2. Greed and fear

3. Supply and demand. Limited supply of a desirable stock causes high demand. Oversupply of a stock at prices perceived to be inflated causes expanded supply, and therefore, low demand.

4. False. The buyer and seller have opposite opinions of the future worth of the stock. The buyer assumes it will rise in value; the seller assumes it will decrease in value.

5. The NYSE operates on a hybrid system that combines the traditional specialist central auction system with an electronic system.

6. False. Specialists not only pair, or match, orders, they also act as the customer's agent by recording and matching limit orders; they provide liquidity by filling orders from their own accounts when necessary; and they keep a fair and orderly market in their stock(s).

7. Technology

8. True

9. The spread is the monetary difference between a stock's posted inside bid and inside ask, or offer price.

10. Very, very false!

## CENTER POINT: EMPOWER YOUR PERSONAL BELIEFS

*"Your potential is unlimited. Aspire to a high place. Believe in your abilities, in your tastes, in your own judgment. Imagine and perceive that which you wish to be. Back your image with enthusiasm and courage. Feel the reality of your "new" self; live in the expectancy of greater things and your subconscious will actualize them."*

—Brian Adams

Our personal beliefs form the texture of our lives. When nourished with energy and action, our self-beliefs act as powerful forces for achieving our goals and dreams. They access resources deep within us and direct these resources to support and achieve desired outcomes.

Those who go about their day-to-day lives without positive personal belief systems resemble airplanes with no flight crews and no autopilots. They flounder with no goals or destinations and so end up with life's "leftovers."

Those who believe they are on the path to compelling futures, and feel confident in their abilities, find their paths consistently strewn with opportunities.

When you establish a belief about yourself, the process is an internal one; each belief, consciously or unconsciously, begins with a choice. After that choice is made, be it positive or negative, it filters communications with the outside world and colors your perceptions with certain attitudes. The more ingrained those beliefs become, the more difficult they are to change.

Beliefs are the most powerful force in the world. On a global scale, diverse belief systems cause cultures to draw boundaries, ideologies to clash, and wars to be fought. On a personal level, what we believe to be true about ourselves appears in our lives as our lives.

What do you believe about yourself? Do you see yourself as a strong and capable person who will succeed in attaining the vision you hold for yourself? Or do you see yourself as ineffective and overwhelmed? Either way, you'll be right. Your beliefs will dictate the circumstances in your life—your reality.

Much as an electrician rewires circuits in a faulty electrical system, if we want to succeed and achieve our highest potential, we must replace any negative beliefs we hold about ourselves with positive ones. Once attained, that foundation of powerful beliefs will help us on our path to success and fulfillment!

# CHAPTER 3

# Day Trading Is Your Business: Let's Set It Up That Way

Day trading is a business, just like any other, and in this chapter we'll talk about setting it up quickly and efficiently.

First, we'll identify your trading objectives. Are you a part-time or full-time trader? Next, we'll talk about your weapon of choice. Do you want to trade stocks, ETFs (exchange traded funds), or mini stock index futures? (Although I won't discuss forex, or currencies trading, in this text, forex traders will find the technical analysis explanations in this book apply nicely to that market.)

We'll talk about the nature of the money you plan to trade with, and make sure it's in your best interests to use it. You'll decide on your broker, whether online or direct-access. We'll streamline a custom brokerage account, define slippage, commissions, and margin. You'll develop a business plan, and make sure your environment is trading-friendly. Finally, we'll look at the pros and cons of paper trading.

## YOUR DAY TRADING STASH: A REALITY CHECK

By now, you've probably allocated a sum of money you intend to use for your trading account. Let's talk about the nature of that money, and take a hard, but necessary, look at reality. Here are two important rules to consider.

The first rule is that you never trade with "scared money." That means you never, ever, trade with money that, if lost, will diminish your lifestyle or that of your family. Why? When you trade with scared money, fear colors your decision-making abilities. You'll make the worst possible trading choice and lose the money—fast. Trust me. I've done it.

That leads us to the second rule, which is a variation on the preceding theme: Trade *only* with money you can afford to lose.

It's unfortunate, but true. Novice traders lose money. I know many traders who've lost their entire trading account, and worse—houses, furniture, cars, you name it—when they started. Please don't add your name to that casualty list. If you can't afford to lose the money you've buttonholed for trading, don't touch it. Postpone your trading career until you've pocketed a separate, expendable, stake.

Once you've targeted the money for your account, figure it's going to take from six months to a year before you consistently take money out of the market.

## CHOOSE YOUR WEAPON

In my second book, *A Beginner's Guide to Short-Term Trading*, I wrote that America is having a love affair with the stock market. That's still true, and the love affair intensifies with each year. Traders have learned how to profit from Mother Market's bad moods, as well as her good ones, and are opening their arms to the wide variety of trading and investing products that have flooded the marketplace.

You'll want to match your trading vehicles to your personality and lifestyle. One of the biggest mistakes novice traders make is to dive headfirst into a highly volatile stock, or futures contract, because their neighbor trades it. Comparing yourself to others in this occupation—whether it's what they trade, how they trade it, or how much money they make—is a time waster.

Assess your personality, and decide whether you can tolerate high-risk environments, or whether you operate better in low-risk settings. Then consider your trading choices. Although there are others, most new traders choose stocks, ETFs, or mini stock index futures.

➤ Stocks are the most popular choice, probably because they have been around the longest. You can find highly volatile stocks, or quiet, calmer versions. Price per share ranges from a few cents (penny stocks, or "pink sheet" stocks) to hundreds of dollars.

➤ ETFs (exchange traded funds) are the rising stars of the industry. Traded as a single stock that represents a basket of stocks, they invite market players to invest in industry groups such as semiconductors or banks, stock indexes like the Dow, NASDAQ, or S&P 500, and countries, such as Japan, Indonesia, or Brazil. Currently, nearly 200 ETFs (also called "tracking stocks") trade on the exchanges, but many don't have the average daily share volume to provide precision entries and exits. Those that do are well worth looking into. Volatility wise, most high-volume ETFs trade with a bit more stability than some of their wild and wooly stock cousins.

➤ Mini stock index futures, such as the mini-sized Dow, E-mini S&P 500, E-mini NASDAQ 100, and E-mini Russell 2000 contracts have also gained immense popularity. Leverage for the mini contracts is hefty, and you don't need the $25,000 minimum account balance that the Securities and Exchange Commission (SEC) requires active traders to maintain at all times in equities' trading accounts. Still, trading mini index futures is a fast and furious game that involves substantial risk. As with all trading vehicles, please go slowly and study the market from the sidelines before you ante up.

## WHAT TYPE OF TRADER ARE YOU: PART-TIME OR FULL-TIME?

Before you start trading, establish your goals. How much time do you plan to devote to this profession? Do you intend to be a part-time or full-time trader?

Most traders glue their backsides to their chair from market's open until it closes, taking advantage of every profit nuance offered during market hours. Others work at alternative jobs and trade two or three days a week. I know a few hot-shot traders who trade two hours a day, during the market's most volatile periods, from the opening bell at 9:30 A.M. (Eastern Standard Time) to 10:30, and then again from 3:00 to 4:00 P.M., when the market closes.

### The Part-time Trader

Now that you've defined the time you wish to devote to trading, let's take a closer look at your objectives:

➤ Do you plan to place three or fewer trades during the day?
➤ Are you content to be a "swing" trader or position trader, meaning you're happy to hold a position for two days to two weeks, or longer?
➤ Do you intend to study trading as much as possible in your spare time, but have no intention of giving up every waking minute to it?

If these objectives describe your trading plans, you're probably a part-time trader, and an online account with a discount broker should be sufficient for your needs. You'll choose to establish an office in your home or other office area, where you can set up a computer with one to two monitors, and a television.

### The Serious Trader

The following defines the serious trader:

➤ Do you plan to trade every day the market's open and place more than three trades a day?
➤ Is your goal to execute trades with precision entries and exits?

➤ Do you want to make fast profits, sometimes jumping in and out of a stock within seconds, to minutes?
➤ Are you dedicated to studying technical analysis and charts until your eyes cross?
➤ Is your objective to eventually trade for a living?

If these objectives describe your trading goals, you'll need to consider a trading platform with a fast connection to the Internet, such as DSL, cable, or T-1 line. You can work out of your home, or in an office with other traders.

## TRADING WITH AN ONLINE BROKER: WHICH ONE IS RIGHT FOR YOU?

Trading via the Internet with an online broker has revolutionized the stock market. In the old days, you drove downtown and entered a stately looking office building. Soon, a dignified stockbroker wearing a dark suit and a condescending manner ushered you into a mahogany-paneled office and opened an account for you. When that broker bought or sold stock, the commission cost you upward of $100 per trade. Of course, the broker researched the stock, and if you eventually made a nice profit, it covered the commission.

How things have changed! Nowadays, online brokers offer an array of inexpensive services and eagerly await your business. You'll probably never see their office or personally meet their staff.

### Opening Your Account

To open an account, most brokerage houses invite you to download the account application online, fill it out, and e-mail it back to them. Then you can mail your check, or make arrangements for wiring funds from your checking account directly into their designated account.

If you intend to open an online account with a discount broker, find one that offers:

➤ Reasonably low commission rates
➤ A Web site that is accessible and easy to navigate, with graphics that snap on the screen rapidly. Check to make sure the site doesn't slow to a crawl when you move from screen to screen.
➤ A well-organized trading screen with safety catches built in to guard against data entry errors
➤ A quick confirmation system, real-time portfolio updates, and account balances

➤ Comprehensive and easily accessible research data
➤ Alternative ways of reaching them. What happens when the market plunges hard, and causes panic selling? Are orders accepted and filled, or does their system jam? If their servers go down, can their brokers be reached by phone—fast?
➤ Low margin rates; you'll be surprised at how they differ.
➤ A reasonable minimum dollar amount required to open an account—if any. (If you qualify as a "pattern day trader," defined by the SEC as an account holder who makes four, or more, round-trip trades during five business days, the law requires that your account must maintain a $25,000 minimum balance all times.)

When it comes to brokers, I believe in word-of-mouth. Ask other traders which online brokers are reliable and cost-efficient, then call the most highly recommended ones and ask them to mail you information. Remember, mega-low commission rates sometimes translate into mega-low customer service.

Here is a selection of popular online brokers, with their Web addresses and telephone numbers:

➤ A.B. Watley Direct, Inc. *www.abwatley.com* 888-733-9000
➤ Charles Schwab & Co. Inc. *www.schwab.com* 866-855-9102
➤ E*Trade Financial *https://us.etrade.com* 800-387-2331
➤ Fidelity *www.fidelity.com* 800-544-6666
➤ Interactive Brokers *www.interactivebrokers.com* 877-442-2757
➤ Scottrade *www.discountbroker.com* 800-619-7283
➤ Terra Nova Trading, L.L.C. *www.terranovaonline.com* 866-866-6546
➤ TD Ameritrade *www.tdameritrade.com* 800-454-9272

Many new traders begin by trading with an online discount broker, and later move to a direct-access broker. Although online brokers have upgraded their trading systems substantially in the past few years, and many offer Level II systems to their high volume clients, the ultrasophisticated trading platforms with order routing choices are still mainly offered by direct-access brokers.

Also, if you choose to trade mini stock index futures or any other futures contracts, you will have to open a separate account with a futures broker. Although a few brokerage houses offer multi-asset accounts, most require a separate account for futures trading.

## ADVANTAGES OF USING A DIRECT-ACCESS TRADING PLATFORM

A major reason day trading has exploded as a profession is the rapid advancement of technology made available to the public. Now you can look inside the market and see the same financial information that used to be privy only to stockbrokers. Streaming price quotes on Level II screens, customizable charts, scans, ticker tapes, and up-to-the-minute news are as close as your computer.

If you plan to be a serious trader and play with the pros, you need access to all this information, plus an order entry system that gives you nanosecond access to the markets.

Direct-access brokers offer high-quality trading software in which you can open dozens of windows on one page—windows that include charts on customizable time frames, a long menu of customizable chart indicators, Total View Level II order entry screens with order routing choices and settings for discretionary order configurations, hot key accessibility, alarms, ticker tapes, market minders with sorting capabilities, market internals, and market-related news items.

Unlike traditional online discount brokers who fill your order using *their* choice of market makers or electronic communications networks (ECNs), direct-access brokers provide you with order entry screens that let *you* control your execution route.

If you plan to trade actively, speed will be an essential tool. Speed ensures you can enter and exit a trade at the best possible price. And, the speed with which you and your equipment act not only levels the playing field, it gives you the edge over other market players who want your money.

For optimum trading speed and accuracy, your orders need direct routing to the exchanges. Serious traders don't have time to wait for their Internet broker to fill an order. Instead, traders click on a buy or sell button on their system's order entry screen that routes their order directly to specialists/market makers or ECNs. In a split-second, they see their order displayed or filled.

Currently, three basic quote systems define the trading scene: Level I, Level II, and Level III. A Level I quote is what you see when you ask for a quote from an online broker, or the inside bid and ask. Level III quote screens are used by only specialists and market makers and allow them to change the prices of buy and sell orders.

A Level Level II quote system is actually a moving screen that is constantly being updated. It shows the various prices and lot sizes at which a stock is bid and offered and the exchanges, market makers, and ECNs. Most traders add a Time & Sales screen to their Level II screen. Time & Sales displays the actual

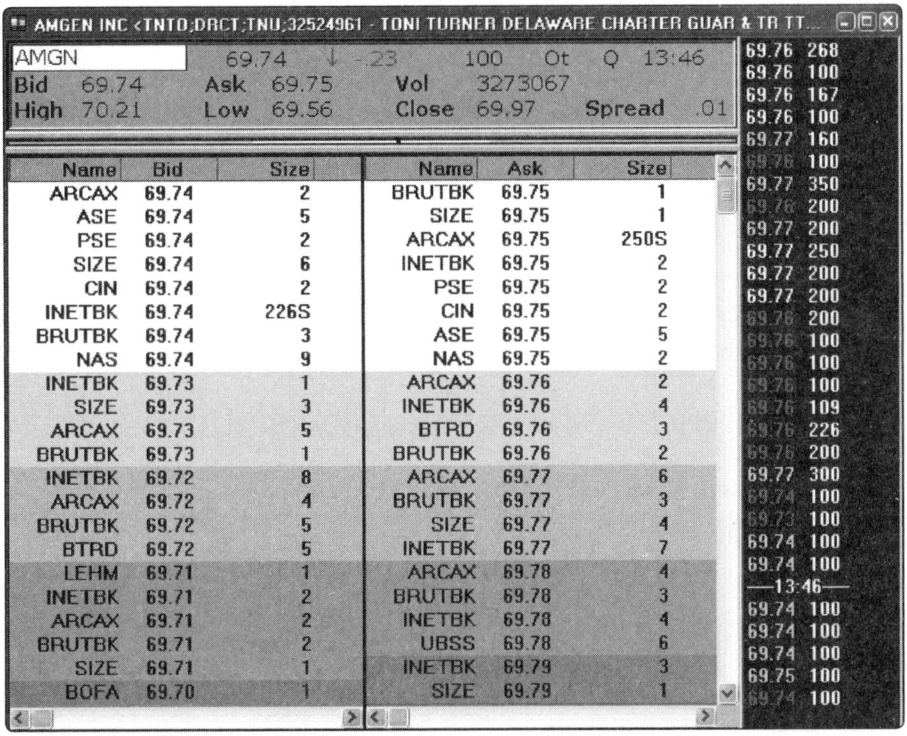

**FIGURE 3-1** | This is a Level II screen of Amgen, Inc. (AMGN). The top portion displays current inside bid and ask prices (Level I quotes), the current day's high and low prices, price change, yesterday's closing price, volume, and spread between the bid and ask. Below, on the left side, you'll see the bid column, with market makers, exchanges, and ECNs lined up, bidding for the biotech stock. If you were to sell shares of AMGN at the market price (69.74), you would sell it to one of these bidders. The column to the right of the bid contains the market makers, ECNs, and exchanges who want to sell shares of AMGN. If you were to buy shares of this stock, right now, at the market price (69.75), you'd buy from these sellers.

RealTick® graphics used with permission of Townsend Analytics, Ltd. © 1986-2007 Townsend Analytics, Ltd.

prints, which are the trades that are taking place, and the time they were executed. We'll talk in detail later about how to read this screen.

Figure 3-1 shows a sample Level II screen for Amgen, Inc. (AMGN), with a Time & Sales screen on the right.

On the far right of the screen, the Time & Sales column posts current trades, with the price and lot size. You can see the time posted toward the bottom: 13:46, or 1:46 P.M., EST. The time is posted in one-minute increments.

If you'd like to look into multi-featured, customizable trading platforms, you have choices: Keep your standard online broker; then custom download the software, pay a monthly fee, and use it as a technical and data analysis tool. Or, you can open an account with a direct-access broker who provides the software;

then you place your orders directly from the screen (a better idea). If you make a minimum number of trades per month, the broker may waive the monthly software fee.

The following is a list of popular trading software platforms.

➤ RealTick *www.realtick.com* 800-827-0141
➤ TradeStation Securities *www.tradestation.com* 800-808-9336
➤ eSignal *www.esignal.com* 800-815-8256
➤ CyberTrader *www.cybertrader.com* 888-2832407
➤ MetaStock *www.equis.com* 800-508-9180

The following is a list of points to consider when checking out a direct-access trading platform.

1. Make sure the order entry system gives you access to all the major exchanges and to more than one ECN. At the present time, the NASDAQ's Total View Level II screens give the most information about market participants.
2. How fast does the system execute trades? Remember, speed is one of your primary weapons. Rapid execution ability saves you money, especially when you need to beat a hasty exit.
3. Are the keystrokes trader-friendly and easy to use? You shouldn't have to type out the order. A click should do it. Are the buy and sell boxes easy distinguish? Learning how to trade on an electronic system can produce enough ulcers, without the system itself adding to the confusion. Just as I did when I was a new trader, you may accidentally sell when you meant to buy, and vice-versa.
4. Is the system reliable? How often does it crash, cutting off your access to the market? This is important because the trading god has a twisted sense of humor: At the exact moment your account is maxed out with volatile semi-conductor stocks, a sadistic analyst will downgrade the entire semiconductor industry. Then, as semi stocks crash and burn, your system will go down! So, grill the system's customer representative: How many customers use the system? How accessible is the company by phone if a problem arises? The best vote of reliability will come from talking to other traders who use the system.
5. Are all your important tools available on a single page? Shifting back and forth between pages to see your account positions and orders, as well as Level II screens and charts, will drive you bonkers.
6. How's the portfolio tracking? You should be able to see your current positions, trades completed, account balance, and real-time profit and loss statistics at

all times. You'll also want your interest list in front of you, including the list of stocks you're watching, their current prices, and changes on the day.

7. Does the system offer a stock index futures feed? Very important. You should have at least the S&P 500 E-mini futures quotes. You'll probably have to pay exchange fees, but they are minimal. Add the mini-sized Dow if you trade Dow stocks, and E-mini NASDAQ 100, if you trade NASDAQ stocks. We'll discuss it later, but for now, know that these stock index futures are watched by every market pro every minute of every trading day.

8. Does the system provide customizable charting features? Charts are pictures that show how a stock is performing. When I'm not watching charts of the stocks I'm holding, I'm skipping through others, searching for the next money-making opportunity. Chart packages differ; some are high, and some are low quality. You don't want bar charts; they don't give you enough info. You want candlestick charts and a full menu of indicators, such as moving averages, Stochastics, Directional Indicator system, Bollinger Bands, MACD, Relative Strength Index, Commodity Channel Index, and more. I'll explain these indicators in upcoming chapters. Just make sure you can change the defaults of the data periods. Also inquire about the available chart time frames. You should be able to access seasonal, monthly, weekly, and daily charts, as well as intraday charts. If all this confuses you, don't worry. These concepts will become clearer as you progress, and its not as difficult as it sounds.

9. When you become a more advanced trader, you may want to create custom scans for a universe of stocks. Will the software accommodate that? Does it have any scans included? (Many trading software programs offer built-in, basic scans.)

10. How does the commission schedule apply—by the number of shares or by trade? Firms charge more or less depending on which market maker or ECN fills the trade. Ask for a comprehensive list of every charge they can levy.

11. Is there a monthly charge for the software? Are you required to execute a minimum number of trades per month? How do the number of trades you make affect the monthly charge?

12. What are the margin rates? Make sure their margin rates are competitive and that they pay you interest on cash balances.

13. Do they require a minimum opening balance? (Remember the SEC's rule about pattern day traders and the $25,000 account minimum. The SEC's rules apply automatically as the broker's rules.)

14. Does the platform offer alarms? If so, can you set them to send alerts, either visual or audio, when specified stocks hit a certain price?

15. Does the platform offer market-related news? How much is the extra charge?
16. How secure is the system? Who, besides you, has access to your account? Are there enough safeguards—codes, passwords, and so on—to assure no hacker will break into your account?

As you download and demo these platforms on a trial basis, you'll see that some are easier for beginners, others cater to tech geeks. And, even if the software is dynamite, you still need to know about the brokerage house where you open an account. Call them on the phone. How fast do they answer? Do they answer at all, or does a canned voice ask you to leave a message? Ask the same questions you'd ask of a standard online broker.

One of the best ways to view different trading software platforms is to attend a trading conference or financial show. You'll see the major platforms displayed, with customer service representatives who know how the software operates. You'll also be able to talk to brokers who offer the systems.

Network with fellow traders and compare notes. Only successful traders, who have been-there, done-that, got-the-T-shirt, will tell you the unvarnished truth. And the truth is important when your money's on the line.

## SHOULD YOU OPEN TWO TRADING ACCOUNTS?

I have always maintained two trading accounts. I keep the first account strictly for day trading, and I trade actively on it. I close out positions before the market closes each day, rarely holding a position overnight.

I maintain a second, intermediate-term account with an online broker for three reasons. First, my online broker allows me to place stop-loss orders on all of my positions, GTC, meaning "good 'til cancelled." (Most direct-access brokers automatically cancel all stop orders at the close of each trading day.) This way, I can take a day off without worrying. I know that if the stock falls, it will be sold if it hits my stop price.

My second reason: Margin calls happen. You can hold a long position overnight that opens way down the next morning, causing a margin call. During market hours, we traders move so fast, and calculate numbers so quickly in our heads, we've been known to make mistakes and slip over margin limits. Some brokers automatically warn you if you try to overshop, and a pop-up will refuse your order.

Recently, though, the automatic system for one of my accounts didn't warn me. It allowed me to place an order that incurred a small margin call. The next morning, when I called the trade desk and asked what happened to the early warning system, the broker admitted, "Sometimes it doesn't work. It's your responsibility not to create a margin call."

The third reason I keep two accounts: Server glitches happen. And, wow, can they be costly. There you are, frantically trying to get out of a position that's going against you and—whap—your screen freezes. After shouting some choice words, you switch to your other account (assuming it's with a different broker) and if the situation's drastic enough, hedge your account that crashed.

Here another bonus for trading in two accounts: When I started trading, I lost money with many of my day trades. Yet, my long-term holds (known as "position trades") made money. At the end of a brutal trading day, I'd turn my weary eyes to my position trading account, and notice that my holdings had

**HOT TIP**

Make sure you have a backup Internet provider. Even cable modems, though fast and efficient, are known to fail once in a while. Consider maintaining an alternative wireless service, or even a dial-up modem— *some* way of getting to the Internet via a different route than your primary cable or DSL line. The extra cost per month equals peanuts if you compare it to losing a point or more, in a 500-share position, because your provider went down.

made money. Those gains bolstered my flagging self-esteem, as well as offset the losses of my day trading account.

The important thing to remember when maintaining two accounts is to keep a separate mindset, or discipline, with each. Don't use your active trading account for long-term holds, or vice-versa. If either account crosses the line into the other, the value of trading two accounts is lost, and you'll have chaos on your hands.

Also, if you decide to go with dual accounts, think about opening an account with a plain vanilla online broker who gives good fills on your orders, but charges low commissions. Remember, the higher commissions you pay, the more bells and whistles you have access to. Your direct-access account should provide you with all the research you need. Plus, there are a truckload of sites on the Internet that offer free stock news and research. Check out the list of financial information sites in Chapter 14.

## SLIPPAGE AND COMMISSIONS: HOW THEY AFFECT YOUR WALLET

Slippage takes place when your order is filled at a different price than the one displayed when you placed the order. Market makers, particularly, use it to pad their pockets when unsuspecting traders and investors issue market orders to buy or sell stocks.

Say you go to your online broker and bring up the price for Igloo Ice Cream. The ask price is $29.50. So you place a market order to buy 500 shares of Igloo at the market (current asking price). When your order is confirmed, you find you bought 500 shares of Igloo at $29.55. What happened? That's five cents per share higher than you intended to buy it. On 500 shares, that equals $25. Repeat that five times a day, and your slippage runs up to $125.

Slippage hurts even more when you're selling at a loss. Say you buy 800 shares of Wacky Widgets at $50 per share.

Suddenly, the trade turns sour and starts to plummet. Within seconds, Wacky hits $48.50, your "sell stop," or the predetermined price you planned to sell the position if the trade went sour.

You throw in an order to sell at the market price (at that moment, $48.50). When your confirmation appears, though, you notice the actual price at which your order was filled: $48.30. That's twenty cents lower than when you placed your order, or an additional $160 tacked onto your already sizeable loss.

I've watched stocks trade quietly at the same price for minutes, even an hour at a time. Keeping an eye on my Level II screen, I've decided to sell a position I'm holding, and for fun, put it in at market. Click. The order is sent. And somebody saw it coming. I watch the price drop ten cents, then my trade confirmation appears. You guessed it. The market maker dropped the bid, or lowered the price he had been advertising on my screen for the past hour. Hmm. A quick profit, at my expense.

Remember when I told you in Chapter 1 that the stock market is sometimes a vicious arena? A dog-eat-dog world? This represents one example, and it happens all the time.

How do you cure the slippage malady? By trading with a Level II system, and/or placing limit orders, where you specify the exact price you're willing to pay for, or sell, the stock. I'll go into detail about limit orders later. Just remember that slippage will gobble chunks out of your profits if you're not careful.

Even though they're a necessary business expense, commissions also absorb profits. Neophyte traders typically overtrade, meaning they trade much more than they should, or need to, then wonder why commissions swallowed their gains.

It's extremely common for an active trader to be "up on the day," but total-out with a loss, after commissions.

Say you're trading 500-share lots of Terrific Truck Lines. You're in and out of the stock all day, trying to buy the pullbacks and sell the rallies. You trade your brains out, and at the market's close, you tally your profits and losses and see you made $600 on the day. Hey, this trading thing isn't so hard after all . . .

You puff out your chest and brag to your friends. Then you glance down at your trade sheet. Oops, you forgot to subtract the commissions. Let's see, you made 30 trades total, or 15 round trips. There's a $20 commission each way, or $40 per round trip. Thirty trades multiplied by $20 each equals $600. Profits are $600. Subtract commissions. You made zero bucks for the day.

When you come out of shock-mode, you can do a little more math. Excepting holidays, there are about 20 trading days in a month. Let's get conservative and say you average 10 trades, or 5 round trips per day at $20 per trade. In commissions, that equals $200 per day. Times 20 days per month, that comes to $4,000 per month! Huh? Really? Yikes!

Want to keep going? You probably don't, but we're going to, anyway. There are about 250 trading days in the year. Multiply that out, and—please sit down before you read this—you're paying $48,000 in commissions per year. Stops your heart, doesn't it? I know it does mine.

What's the cure for paying hefty dollars in commissions every day, month, and year? There isn't one, really, except for a few common sense ideas I'll throw out now.

➤ I mentioned earlier in the chapter that you might consider maintaining two trading accounts. If you do, pay up for speed and accuracy and technical data on your direct-access account, then make sure your other account is with a broker who charges minimum commissions. As of this writing, $5 commissions are being advertised. Every little bit helps.

➤ Don't overtrade. This is one of the biggest, most costly mistakes new traders make. Instead of letting the market "come to them," traders buy anything that moves. They trade during lunch (bad odds), and when the market is going against them. Spastic trigger finger. Big losses. Add commissions to those losses. Ouch.

➤ Keep a realistic attitude. Remember, when you open a trade, you are starting out at a loss (commission) that you have to earn back before you can even begin to make a profit. Unlike you, your broker gets paid whether you win or lose. If you're trading on margin and holding a losing position, the knife plunges deeper: You're paying interest on borrowed money that's shrinking in value.

I hope this dose of slippage and commission reality sobers you enough so you don't overtrade, chase stocks, or have unrealistic expectations of profits when you begin to trade. Please be a wise and cautious trader. Then you'll beat the system and make money despite the odds.

## TRADING ON MARGIN: HOW TO DO IT AND STILL SLEEP AT NIGHT

Margin is a loan given to you by your stockbroker. Just like any bank, your broker charges interest on it. When you open your trading account, you'll want to designate it as a margin account, usually called a "50% margin account." The margin or loan amount (no interest is charged until you actually use the money) matches your deposit amount.

**HOT TIP**

Futures accounts have different minimum opening balances and rules. Contact a registered futures broker for these details.

If you open your stock trading account with $10,000, your broker will give you access to another $10,000. Suddenly, you have $20,000 to trade with. Hey, let's go shopping!

Hold it right there. One of the riskiest things you can do as a new trader is max out your entire trading account, margin and all. Please understand that when a stock you are holding on margin tanks, you lose twice as much money as you would if you were playing with just your own cash. For example, say you're holding 300 shares of a stock worth $50 per share, on margin. The market value is $15,000 of which $7,500 is your equity, and $7,500 is margin (broker's money). The shares slide to $40. Now, the market value of the position is $12,000 or $6,000 of your equity, and $6,000 margin. The position has lost $1,500 of your equity value, and $1,500 of your broker's equity. Had you limited your trade to a smaller lot size using your equity only, the loss would have been half the size.

If you plan to make more than four round trips during the space of five trading days, as mentioned previously, you'll need to open your equities trading account with a $25,000 minimum. You must maintain that balance, or higher, throughout every trading day, no matter what. If that rule is violated, most brokers will freeze your account until you send them the drawdown amount. Common sense dictates that you'd better start with more than $25,000—at least $30,000—to provide a pillow.

Now the good news is, as a pattern day trader, you can day trade with four times your free cash. That means if you have $25,000 in your account, you can day trade $100,000. Your overnight margin, however, is usually double your account value.

Although these inflated numbers look like fun—please—when you first begin trading, forget you have a margin account and use only your original equity to trade with. Keep a portion of your account in cash at all times. Sound boring? Don't worry, no matter how cautiously you trade, the market will provide plenty of entertainment and excitement along the way.

## DEVELOP A SIMPLE BUSINESS PLAN

As the title of this chapter says, trading is a business and should be set up like one. The most successful traders write out a simple business plan before they start. Use the content earlier in this chapter to create guidelines. For example, serious soul searching will tell you whether you are risk averse, or risk tolerant. Match that with your time availability and your principle amount to the trading instrument of your choice.

➤ Budget for a high-quality computer and one or more monitors, Internet service provider, and possible monthly software and exchange fees (pertain to futures markets). You'll also need to expense in research materials and newspaper/magazine subscriptions.

➤ Resolve to never risk more than 2% of your account equity on any one trade. That means if you trade a $10,000 account, you will manage your trades so that you never lose more than $200 on a single trade. Naturally, if that equity amount changes, so does your minimum risk amount.

➤ Decide and write down the maximum drawdown (loss) you'll allow on your account during a trading day. Resolve that once that amount is hit, you'll stop trading and reassess your processes.

Above all, set realistic goals. Many new traders make this mistake: "Okay, I've opened my account with $50,000. I should be able to make $500 per day, trading."

As we'll talk about in the next chapter, it's better to set process-oriented goals, rather than achievement-oriented, or money-making goals. Work on making precision entry/exit trades, and raising your percentage of winning trades. That's a realistic, healthy goal, and one you can write into your business plan.

**REALITY CHECK**

If you make $500 per day, that's $2,500 per week. With 52 weeks in a year, that comes to $130,000, per year, or 260% on your money. The biggest traders in the business don't bring in those numbers—what are the odds a new trader can?

## CREATE A SUCCESS-ORIENTED ENVIRONMENT

The terrific thing about day trading is that you can do it from almost anywhere. Still, no matter what environment you trade from, be it home office, alternate office (some professional types are "close day traders"; they sneak into their offices between patients or clients and trade away), or trading center, certain criteria apply.

To trade properly, you need to maintain a positive mindset, concentrate, and be able to execute trades in a disciplined manner.

We'll start with the home office. Some of the following is obvious, some you may not have considered:

➤ If possible, make sure your office has a window, or natural light. It's psychologically positive and easier on your eyes to have soft, natural light streaming in the windows.

➤ If you trade with high-quality trading software, consider using a second monitor. That way you can watch twice as many charts, market maker screens, and ticker tapes.

➤ Don't forget your backup Internet provider. The extra cost per month is a drop in the ocean compared to the losses you might incur when your main provider goes down.

➤ Install a television and leave it tuned to CNBC or other financial network.

➤ Ignore phone calls. You can't discuss the Mets, give opinions on the new fad in jewelry, and trade well at the same time. I've lost hundreds of dollars by politely talking to friends while trying to trade. Explain to everyone who's likely to call that you can't chat during market hours. Then let your voice mail answer the phone.

➤ Make sure your office is private and quiet. Children running around, a noisy dog, or a well-meaning spouse running the vacuum all interrupt concentration.

➤ Keep your desk cleared, except for your trading log. When your largest position quivers unhappily, it's a real tooth-grinder to push papers around searching for a trading log with the sell stop written on it. Mess causes stress.

➤ Don't leave volatile positions open without automatic stop orders in place, then wander out to the mailbox, or wash your car. Early in my trading career, I lost $500 because I moseyed outside to pet the cat.

## PAPER TRADING: SHOULD YOU DO IT?

Some trading teachers advocate beginners trade on paper—trade without putting real money on the line—for weeks or months prior to placing the first real trade. Others think it's a waste of time.

I believe paper trading can be a valuable tool, as long as you focus as though the money aspect is real. It aids in teaching internal rhythms of the market, and you can become familiar with the personalities of different stocks, indexes, and whatever else you're trading.

You may accumulate a ton of money when you paper trade and mistakenly think real trading is just as easy. One component is missing from paper trading: emotion. Your ability to control your emotions when trading will absolutely, positively define your trading success. In fact, the subject is so huge and so important I've dedicated Chapter 4 to it.

# QUIZ
||||||||||||||||

## Questions
1. Name the two rules that define the money with which you open your trading account.
2. Describe the three levels of quote systems currently at use for trading.
3. Give three advantages to opening two trading accounts.
4. Define slippage.
5. Name three ways to avoid overpaying on commissions.
6. Give one safety measure to avoid margin calls.
7. Is paper trading a good use of time?

## Answers
1. Never trade with "scared money." Trade only with money you can afford to lose.
2. A Level I quote is a stock's real-time inside bid and ask displayed upon demand. Level II quotes are displayed on a screen showing bids and ask of all market participants, and can be used to initiate orders by traders. Level III quotes are used exclusively by specialists and market makers, allowing them to refresh their orders and alter their prices.
3. (1) In case of a margin call, funds to cover it can be accessed from the alternate account. (2) In case of a technical failure, you can hedge one account with the other. (3) The longer-term account may contain core holdings that bolster and hedge losses in the day trading account.
4. Slippage takes place when your order is filled at a different price than the one displayed when you placed your market order.
5. (1) Open two accounts, and keep one account with a good online broker who charges minimal commissions. (2) Don't overtrade. (3) Remember, you have to earn the commission back before you begin to make a profit.
6. Keep a portion of cash in your account at all times.
7. Yes. Paper trading can teach the novice trader how different stocks trade, the relationships between indicators, and help the trader to internalize market rhythms.

## CENTER POINT:
## YOUR VISION: LIFE'S INVITATION TO GREATNESS

*"What would you do if you knew you could not fail?"*

—Dr. Robert Schuller

Deep within you dwells your vision—it's you in the form of your purest potential; your real self. Your true vision is your core being telling you who you really are. It defines your personal greatness.

To see your vision and mold it into a recognizable thought form, you must sweep aside old, limited beliefs of who you thought you were, and see your true self—the self who is made from innate wisdom, power, and intelligence. That self can reach for your highest potential and establish a life built on clear purpose.

Once your vision is clear to you, you may not know how to accomplish it. Few of us do. But just as a seed planted in warm earth and sunlight knows exactly how to grow into a plant, your vision has within it the cosmic wisdom to bring itself into fruition.

In order for your vision to germinate, you need only listen to your inner guidance. Act upon what it tells you. Take one step, then the next. Just as attention from sunlight and rain nourishes the seed into a strong, healthy plant, the more energy you shower onto your vision, the more it will grow. You'll be guided automatically to the right people, places, and situations to move you ahead on your journey.

The vision growing within you is the unlimited you, the powerful you, the wise you. It's the you who has the confidence to step forward with passion and reach for the most challenging opportunities.

Your vision is life's invitation to greatness. Do you accept the invitation?

# CHAPTER 4

# The Winning Market Mentality That Leads to Profits

Experts say good sex is 10% in your body and 90% in your head. Believe it or not, good trading evolves from the same ratios—10% methodology and 90% mental discipline. You can study charts and indicators until your eyes cross, but unless you develop a specific mindset that guides your trades, you'll be walking a tightrope without a safety net.

To start with, let's establish two, etched-in-stone rules to live by the rest of your trading life.

**Rule One:** Protect your principal.
**Rule Two:** Trade to trade well (not to make money).

Do they sound too simple to be true? They're not. They're much easier promised than accomplished, but they can be mastered. Virtually everything you learn in this book points back to these two rules, or imperatives. If you keep them uppermost in your mind, and implement them into every trade, you'll all but guarantee a successful trading career.

## RULE ONE: PROTECT YOUR PRINCIPAL

Successful professionals in occupations all over the world use tools to accomplish their goals.

As a successful trader, your tools consist of market knowledge, mental and emotional discipline, and your trading account. Protect the money in your trading account at all times. Don't abuse it, treat it carelessly, or allow others to take it from you. This money is your most cherished tool, and you must guard it with passion and commitment.

"Yeah, sure, I already know all that stuff," you reply. "You're oversimplifying. You're going overboard with your explanation."

Am I really? I bet we've both heard the same statistics—between 80 and 90% of all traders crash and burn. As you read this, traders somewhere in the world are chasing a stock, ignoring their stops, holding losers, overtrading, taking home dangerous or oversized positions, and buying against a downtrend. Translation? They are treating their precious tool—their trading capital—recklessly.

I work with new traders every day who swear they protect their principal and in the next breath, abuse it by jumping into a careless trade. They get caught up in the thrill of the moment, the excitement of a running stock, the euphoria of buying when everyone else does. We've all done it, and I've been there, too.

Even if you avoid all unnecessary risks, a percentage of your trades will lose money. Don't add to these by careless trades, or you'll wake up one morning with assets that total pocket change.

True trading professionals, who rake in profits of five, six, even seven figures a year, protect their accounts like a mother tiger protecting her cub. They trade cautiously. They look at occasional good-trades-gone-sour as routine business expense. And they don't compound them with losses due to carelessness.

Jimmy Rogers, shrewd investor, frequent guest on CNBC, retiree, and teacher at Columbia University Graduate School of Business, says in Jack D. Schwager's *Market Wizards: Interviews with Top Traders*, "One of the best rules anybody can learn . . . is to do nothing, absolutely nothing, unless there is something to do. I just wait until there is money lying in the corner, and all I have to do is go over there and pick it up."

Rogers, like other financial giants, amassed a fortune by protecting his principal. He knows specific signposts that point to a high probability of success and has the mental and emotional control to wait until they appear. You will, too.

Let's talk about positive mental devices you can use to protect your principal.

➤ During the trading day, repeat to yourself over and over, "At all times, I protect my principal." Say it out loud. Don't just murmur it, shout it with enthusiasm! Sound crazy? Try it. It works.

➤ Before you click on the buy button, ask yourself:

1. Why am I entering this trade? Does my trade coincide with the present market trend? Do primary market indicators support my decision?
2. Is my entry point technically perfect?
3. Do I have a rational, thought-out game plan? What is my exit price if my trade goes sour? What is my profit target if it performs well?

4. What time of day is it? (Certain time slots during the trading day almost guarantee a trade's failure or success. You'll learn these time periods in Chapter 5.)

With practice, you'll soon be able to answer the questions above in five seconds or less. If your answers are quick, concise, and positive, then the trade should be as close to a sure thing as possible. If you fumble or over-justify one of the answers, reconsider placing the trade at all.

Please take a personal oath right now to protect your principal. Print the rule and tape it to your monitor. Tape another copy on your bathroom mirror and refrigerator door. Write it on the back of your hand—whatever it takes to etch these words onto your brain and every fiber of your being. Treat your trading account as any professional treats his or her tools, with concern and respect. Protect your account at all times, and don't expose it to carelessness or neglect. If you care for it properly, it will care for you—and grow at the same time.

## RULE TWO: TRADE TO TRADE WELL, NOT TO MAKE MONEY

It appears to contradict reality, but it doesn't. Traders who routinely rake in big bucks don't mentally count the dollars while they're trading. They don't think, *Wow, I'm up two points in Exxon. Let's see, a thousand shares, times two dollars a share, equals $2,000.*

Nothing blows your concentration and clouds your judgment more than keeping a mental calculator running in your head, tallying up the actual dollars you've made and lost each minute.

While we're at it, let's take this a step further. Please don't get up in the morning and announce to your partner/spouse/children/pet that today, *you "have* to make a thousand bucks trading." Trust me, you're setting yourself up for failure. I've done it. Other traders have done it. It's a losing mentality—guaranteed.

In fact, stating a set goal in dollars you *must* bring home every day, or any day, especially if you're a beginner, assures it probably *won't* happen. The need to make a certain amount of money colors your perceptions of the markets. It pressures you to enter trades that are bad bets because you promised yourself— or worse, someone else—that you would bring home trading bacon.

Besides, the day you make that promise usually falls on the rockiest market you've witnessed in weeks. Indicators warn you'd be best on the sidelines. But your pledge echoes in your mind, so you force trades. Odds are you will lose money. Now you're embarrassed and annoyed with yourself. That punishes your self-esteem, which automatically leads to more losses.

The cure for this malady: From now on, your goal is *not* to make money.

Your trading goal: Trade to trade well. As of this minute, banish money from your mind. As we say in New York, "Forgettaboudit." Think of stock prices as numbers, not dollar amounts.

Good trading is an art form. Throwing a flawless, thirty-yard pass to a moving receiver, performing open-heart surgery, and landing a fighter on an aircraft carrier at sea require "touch," skill, and sheer determination. So does executing the perfect trade. Money represents the by-product of the art of good trading, and you'll have plenty of time to count it at the end of the day.

Funny thing about trading to trade well: The profits add up *much* faster than they do when making money's the primary goal. Why? Traders who trade to trade well cut their losses and let their winners run. They cherish and protect their principal. They leave unnecessary risks to others. They recognize whippy, choppy market conditions and stand aside, content to keep their money safe. They control their emotions. They make no promises to anyone, including themselves, about take-home money.

Traders who trade well "let the market come to them." They insist on entering the trade at the perfect entry point and exiting at the perfect exit point. If those points don't arrive, or are faulty, they automatically discard the trade. If you point to money on the table, they shrug and say, "So what?" They know another opportunity is just around the corner.

Traders who trade to trade well don't trade because they're addicted to the thrill, to get back at someone, or because they're bored. They don't trade when they are exhausted, sick, or hungover. They are calm and confident, but cautious. They keep their list of trading guidelines beside them at all times, and always trade within those guidelines.

To sum it up, traders who trade to trade well are perfectionists about their craft. And wealthy. Make this your goal, too.

## WHY THE STOCK MARKET IS ALWAYS RIGHT

If you've chatted with experienced traders, you've heard, "The stock market is always right." A shortened, Zen-like version sounds even more accurate: "The stock market is."

A macrocosm of collective energy, the stock market expands and contracts with global news, company earnings, government reports, wars, weather, and more. Traders, investors, gurus, and analysts come, participate, and go—and still the self-contained market continues.

Television commentators and journalists judge that the market overreacted to bad earnings, or it underreacted to a war. Does this ball of energy care what judgment we pass on it? Nope. Just like an 800-pound gorilla, it does what it wants to, when it wants to.

Industries within the market inflate and deflate in value, depending on economic fundamentals or the fickle herd-mentality of market participants. Energy stocks are in. Retail stocks are out. Housing stocks are overvalued. Gold stocks are "undervalued."

Think the price of Microsoft is out of line? Too bad. Like it or leave it. Were you sure that small-cap stock you bought would double by now—and instead it fell by half? "Not fair," you mutter. The market doesn't know or care about fair.

What you think, expect, want, or believe should happen carries no weight with the stock market. If you, the trader, show up and find opportunities in the market, you're welcome to them. If you let money slip through your fingers— the market swallows it, then yawns. It shrugs off excuses, complaints, even thank-yous.

As author Mark Douglas writes in *The Disciplined Trader*, "The point here is that right and wrong as you may traditionally think of them don't exist in the market environment."

Just as the market is always right, so are stock prices. Our reasons for buying and selling stocks at certain prices may be biased, insane, bizarre, and crazy. They can be fear- and greed-ridden, or based on the full moon. Doesn't matter. That's the price, and it's right at this moment.

You may contend that you, as a trader, can influence price movement by buying or selling big volume. Sure you can, for a tick or two, but unless you're a major market nabob, you can't change price for any length of time. Soon new forces take over, and with or without you, the price moves depending on the collective mindset of the players involved.

How do you survive and prosper in such an environment? By looking at the market as a field of opportunities based on price fluctuations. You assess the opportunities, and then decide whether or not the reward is worth risking your capital.

Think of the financial markets as a fruit stand. You visit the stand and look over the various displays. If the fruits are ripe and juicy, you buy and enjoy. If they're rotten and overpriced, you shrug and leave with your money still in your pocket.

Please keep in mind the two phrases, *the market is always right*, and *the price is always right*. They cultivate an attitude that's extremely important to successful trading.

## THE TRADER'S MOST FORMIDABLE FOE

Another favorite saying in this business: "Trading is war." It's absolutely true! To emerge victorious, you need to identify your enemies quickly, and go into battle with a tough, winning mindset. My goal is to help you achieve that lofty status of a trader who survives and prospers.

With that in mind, let's drag your most formidable foe into the daylight and get a good look at it. By now, you may have guessed its name: emotion.

As a trader, you can memorize every nuance of technical analysis; equip yourself with the fanciest computer ever built; install the fastest, high-tech software and Level II system available; calculate your own indicators; and still lose a lot of money. How? By allowing the most lethal enemy of all to wield your trades—emotion.

Learning to control you emotions while trading may prove to be the highest hurdle you'll face.

In *The Disciplined Trader*, Mark Douglas writes, "When asked for their secrets of success, [winning traders] categorically state that they didn't achieve any measure of consistency in accumulating wealth from trading until they learned self-discipline, emotional control, and the ability to change their minds to flow with the markets."

I can say, without hesitation, that the first day I traded with composure as my only emotion was the day I became a winning trader. Period.

Before that, I read charts with the best of them. I deciphered intermarket relations, indicators, and oscillators in a nanosecond. I traded on a high-tech trading platform, on a Level II system, and made split-second decisions. And I lost quite a bit of money.

Every day, into every trade, I let greed, fear, the need to be right, anxiety over losses, self-deprecating talk, and a host of other negative emotions accompany me.

The day I started trading from my head—and not my heart—I started making money consistently.

At the time, I marveled at the feeling. I didn't plan it to happen although I'd wished for it long enough! How did it feel? As though an internal shift had taken place. How long did it take to come about from the time I first started trading? A year. Why so long? Because to hone myself into a cool, calculating machine, I had to override the core of my being—my humanness, my emotions.

If you took Psychology 101 in college, you may remember a basic premise: A thought plus a feeling equals an action. That's how humans operate. Try eliminating one of those components and notice how uncomfortable we get.

First, imagine a thought plus a feeling, minus the action—especially if the action relates to pleasure. Thought: I've had a long day at work, and a beer would taste good before dinner. Automatically, you imagine a frosty mug filled with the golden elixir, a foamy top. Feeling: pleasure. Your mouth anticipates the taste of the cool, refreshing, robust liquid. Action: Yes, you'll have a beer. You reach into the refrigerator—but there's no beer. Rats. Now your feeling of expected pleasure turns to irritation. Thought, plus a feeling, minus the desired action.

Thought and feeling also precede automatic actions though they may be lightning-quick, such as sitting down, stepping on the brakes, or kissing a loved one.

You can't eliminate thoughts from the equation; every feeling or action begins with a thought. Feelings were originally installed in humans to tell us those thoughts, if acted upon, would produce pleasure or danger. So to a greater or lesser degree, feelings control our actions. To control those feelings demands superhuman dedication and resolve.

Humans are built to seek pleasure, and the feelings associated with day trading represent the most incredibly thrilling, exciting, breathless, heart-pounding, "I'm gonna be rich," "I was right on the money about this stock," ego-building sensations you'll ever experience. When you make a big score, it's like winning the lottery. Not only did you make big bucks fast, you get to brag about it to your friends. You're on top of the world!

The trade may go something like this. Thought: *Hey, look at that price action in Yahoo! It must be a good buy.* Next, depending on the situation, emotions surge through you:

➤ Thrills: Whoa! Look at Yahoo scream higher. Everybody in the world is buying Yahoo right now. They must know something I don't. I better grab some while I can! Point. Click.

➤ Excitement: I knew it . . . Yahoo's going to the moon and I'm going to go with it! I'll have to carry my profits home in a moving van. Point. Click.

➤ Breathless/heart-pounding: Wait for me, little red Porsche. Yeah, baby. I'm coming to drive you out of the showroom. Yahoo's gonna make me big bucks. Point. Click.

Unfortunately, these emotions don't describe the feelings of most winning traders I know. They do, unfortunately, describe the feelings of the traders who don't make the cut. I remember those feelings many losses ago.

Please don't misunderstand me. After I complete a good trade, satisfaction washes over me, and I give myself a pat on the back. At the end of the day, I feel elated that I came to the market, took winnings from it, and escaped with my capital intact.

The next morning, the emotional slate is wiped clean. New day, new market, new set of circumstances.

For professional traders, the Yahoo scenario goes more like this.

➤ Thought: According to my trading plan, this is the precise entry point to buy Yahoo. Quick assessment of market conditions. Okay, all other systems are a go.
➤ Feeling: calm, confident, and composed.
➤ Action: Point. Click.

To become a winning trader, then, you must leave thrills and excitement to others, and execute your trades in a calm, controlled manner. You'll experience plenty of excitement after the market closes—when you count your money.

In the following paragraphs, we discuss other emotions you'll enjoy leaving behind.

### Confusion

Confusion runs rampant among new traders. And no wonder.

It's like learning how to snow ski. You feel cold and clumsy. The workings of your equipment remain a mystery to you. You're supposed to coordinate brain and body enough to perform an intricate series of movements while falling mach two down a treacherous, icy slope. As if that weren't enough, you're scared spitless.

When you're first learning to trade, the market moves in mysterious ways. You're not yet experienced enough to read signposts that hint at what may happen next. You're trading on a computer, be it online broker or direct-access broker, and you don't understand what to click on next. Stocks shoot up and collapse for no apparent reasons, and you feel ten steps behind everyone else. You've been told that "the best professionals in the business" lurk in every trade, waiting to grab your money. You hate to admit it, but you're scared. When I first started trading many years ago, my hands shook so badly and I got so confused, sometimes I'd buy when I meant to sell, and vice-versa. Soon after I sent a tangled trade into cyber-ether, my online broker would call: "Miss Turner, you bought 300 shares of Igloo Ice Cream. Then you sold 600 shares. Did you really mean to do that?"

Wince. "Um, no. I meant to sell 300. Did I sell it twice? Sorry."

Or "Miss Turner, you just put in a buy order for 5,000 shares of Terrific Truck Lines. That puts you, let's see, $20,000 over margin. Did you really mean to do that?"

Gulp. "Five thousand shares? Twenty-thousand over margin? Rats. I meant to buy five hundred shares. I punched an extra zero by mistake." Wince. "Sorry."

Fortunately, experience will diminish much of your confusion, but catastrophes can occur before experience calms you down. To save time and money, take steps early on to avoid unnecessary confusion.

*Best Cures for Confusion*
1. When you start trading, buy small lots, say, 100 to 300 shares per trade. That way, if the stock tanks, and you accidentally buy more—instead of selling what you have—you won't swallow as big of a loss.
2. Complete one trade before you enter another. Keeping up with one stock in a fast-moving market is difficult enough. If you feel like you're missing out on other opportunities, rest assured that more will come along. And, you'll still have money to trade with.
3. Paper trade until you feel comfortable placing real trades.
4. Thoroughly learn any new system, especially a new broker's system, before you attempt your first trade on it.
5. Learn one trading strategy at a time. Then stick to that strategy, and that one only, one trade at a time. Sound boring? Does making money sound boring?
6. Until you're an experienced trader, don't mix trading time frames, such as putting on a day trade, and while it's still open, diving into a quick momentum trade. Maintaining different time frames is too confusing when things get crazy, and too risky.

### The Need to Be Right

The need to be right about a stock's future direction plagues every new trader I've ever met. It's a major cause of fat losses. Why?

You'll find the need to be right on the flip side of our old nemesis, fear. Insisting that you're right equals the fear of being wrong. Humans in general grow up learning it's important to always be right. Mistakes, and those who make them, we label weak. Successful people are right. Those who fail are wrong. Naturally, we all want to be successful.

The trouble is, being right might be an illusion. We make choices and act on them. One choice produces one result, another choice a different result.

The need to be right in trading causes enormous losses. For example: Tom Trader buys 500 shares of Terrific Truck Lines at $52, the proper entry point. The stock promptly falls to $50.85, hitting his protective stop point. Instead of selling without hesitation, Tom grits his teeth. "I'm not selling at a loss. Terrific Truck Lines is a good company, and just announced fantastic earnings. This will end up being a great trade. I know I'm right."

Terrific Truck Lines continues to fall, sinking toward $45, then $40, and Tom Trader holds. Now if he sells, the loss will seriously dent his trading account, as well as his ego. He's no longer a trader. He's an investor, a term traders use when they knowingly hold onto a losing position. If friends ask Tom why he's still holding, his jaw juts out. "It's a good company. It'll come back."

Maybe it will. Maybe it won't, at least for a long time. Meanwhile, the loss is very real (paper losses are real losses), and even if Terrific Truck Lines struggles back to $52, it may take weeks or even months. During that time, Tom could have used that money to make profitable trades. The need to be right cost him, big time.

### Cure for the Need to Be Right

1. Practice shrugging and saying, "I don't know." Simple yes, funny maybe, but also very powerful. This attitude saves you mega-bucks by alleviating the need to be right syndrome. Listen to Jimmy Rogers on CNBC. When an interviewer quizzes him about what will happen next in the financial markets, the mega-wealthy Rogers usually grins and shrugs. Then he answers, "I have no idea."

2. One of the biggest favors you can do for yourself in this profession: When you enter a trade, don't get attached to the outcome. Banish expectations of which way the stock will go, or any illusions you have of fair. That way, you won't have to be right.

3. Plan your trade and trade your plan. We'll talk about how to do this later, but for now, please understand that planning your trades with exact entry points, exit points, and protective stops is one of the most efficient ways to cure the need to be right. Following your plan assures you limit your risk and keeps your losses small and your profits big.

4. Stop beating yourself up for making silly mistakes. Berating yourself cripples your trading career by paralyzing you when the next good opportunity steps in your path. It will also damage your self-esteem and delay the arrival of that calm, confident attitude you're striving for. You make choices, not mistakes. Different choices produce different outcomes. Each outcome is a learning

experience. Study the thinking behind each trade, your choice, and the result. Learn from every outcome, both winning and losing.

### Greed

Greed motivates new traders and even many experienced traders. As I explained in Chapter 2, "Bulls make money, bears make money, and pigs get slaughtered." Since I discussed this powerful emotion earlier in the book, the following explanation will be brief.

Don't ask me how, but the market sees when greed motivates your trading. Don't believe me? Listen to traders talk about the time they "bet the ranch," convinced a stock was going to double. That was usually the last thing they remember before the stock crumbled.

Greed also comes into play when you chase a stock, or pay too high a price for it. When you chase a stock, odds are good you'll buy at the top of the move—and sell at the bottom!

#### *Cure for Greed*

1. As a new trader, you've already decided to limit your risk by trading small lot sizes. Don't compromise. This alone will temper any notions that more is better.
2. When you see a stock screaming straight up on your quote screen and you're filled with the urge to join in on the fun—sit on your hands. Go get a cold soda. Play with the dog. Leave the room if you have to, but don't touch that mouse! If you insist on staying to watch, notice how rapidly the stock drops when the buyers leave and the sellers rush in. Falls fast, doesn't it? Ouch. Better them, than you.

### Fear

For traders, fear is the Goliath of emotions. Fear, which ranges from mild anxiety to gut-wrenching terror, causes more havoc in the trader's life than any other entity.

Fact: Fear is nothing trying to be something.

As a child, do you remember the still, dark nights you believed a monster lurked under your bed? Your heart pounded, your mouth went dry, and your hands sweated. You curled into a quivering ball and waited for the monster to come and get you.

Of course, no monster lurked under your bed. The sensations of fear were real, but you grew to realize that monsters didn't exist, and your feelings were self-induced.

For a neophyte trader fear takes on many faces, from mild to severe:

➤ Dismay—You enter a trade properly, then watch the S&P E-mini futures dive. Will your stock follow?

➤ Alarm and frustration—Your Internet provider goes out; you have open positions.

➤ Fright—Your stock is falling a point every five seconds, and you can't sell it to anyone.

➤ Outright panic—You held a stock overnight, and this morning it opens down eight points (yes, it happens).

Fear of losing money can cause you to exit good trades too early, and stay in bad ones too long. Fear of losing may also urge you to ignore information that's telling you what the real situation is, and what's truly going on.

### Cure for Fear

1. How do you conquer fear? You don't. You displace it.

Just as a rock displaces water in a bucket, you displace fear with a positive foundation of knowledge, experience, and self-trust. Each of these feeds into the next, creating a symbiotic relationship.

Start by displacing fear with knowledge. Most new traders gain a little knowledge, then stop studying. Yet they continue to trade, repeating the same mistakes over and over, until they blow away their trading accounts.

I remember one new trader who took a three-day course, then dove head-first into the market, buying thousands of shares of anything that moved. When I warned him he didn't have enough trading knowledge to manage so many hefty positions, he replied smugly, "I know enough. I don't think there's a lot more to learn." He went on to crash and burn, losing a great deal of money.

I promise you this—if you study the art of trading until the sun turns purple, you still won't know everything. Still, read every trading book you can get your hands on, whether you agree with the system or not. Study chart patterns until you topple out of your chair. Keep a trading journal; record lessons your trades teach you each day. When a CNBC announcer or journalist explains a financial concept that's new to you, write that in your journal, also. Make it a goal to learn at least one new trading gem each day.

Next, you'll displace fear with experience. Experience constantly reinforced with fresh knowledge crafts a powerful trading weapon. Experience teaches you how to internalize market movements and stock movements. It guides you to the trading style that best suits your temperament. Experience helps you identify techniques that work for you, and those that don't. You discover how you, and other traders, react to certain situations, and the best ways to either profit or escape.

As your knowledge and experience expand, they will present you with a priceless gift: self-trust. When you finally evolve to the point that self-trust guides all of your trades, fear will disappear. Then you will know you've arrived. You will trade with that calm, controlled attitude I mentioned earlier. The market cannot harm you unless you return to your old ways. Self-trust will permeate you with a new sense of inner assurance, and you'll sense that now you're a real trader.

## WHY FAITH AND HOPE SHOULD BE LEFT IN A BASKET BY THE DOOR

We were taught as children to embody faith and hope. Those two attributes add richness to all parts of your life—except trading. Before you enter the trading office each morning, please leave faith and hope in a basket by the door.

> **Faith:** "I know I should get out of my trade, but I'm going to hold it until the market goes back up. The market has an upside bias, doesn't it? By tomorrow everything will be fine."
>
> **Hope:** (in form of prayer to the trading god) "Please, please stop this stock from falling. Please get me out of this trade before I lose my shirt. I promise to never, ever, ignore my rules again!"

If you find yourself muttering those famous words, "It'll come back," or whispering, "Please go up" to your stock, you're trading on faith and hope. This means you're not controlling your trade. Instead, your trade's controlling you.

*Best Cures for Faith and Hope*
1. If you feel a bout of faith or hope coming on, identify it, then try to quickly re-evaluate your trade and take necessary actions.
2. If faith and hope encouraged you to hold onto a losing position, bite the bullet and get out of the trade immediately. The first loss is always the smallest.
3. Remember, faith and hope lose you money. You can't afford them—the price is too high.

## WHY "THE DEVIL" MADE YOU LOSE ALL THAT MONEY

As a new trader, you're about to become very familiar with every personality trait you own. Some traits will aid your quest for success; others will need to be reined in. It's best to identify all of your characteristics that will affect your trading early on. The more you know about yourself, the more it will benefit your trading career.

When you make a questionable move during the trading day, ask, "Why did I do that? Which one of my personality traits caused that to happen?"

Was the answer, "I was impulsive"? Do you feel and act first, then think later? Not a good idea. Replace impulsive urges with thoroughly planned trades. Refrain from trading on whippy or choppy market days.

Was the answer, "I was optimistic"? Did you hope (oops!) for the best? Optimism is a cousin of faith and hope. Rose-colored glasses distort market reality.

Was the answer, "I was stubborn"? Stubbornness is a cohort of the need to be right and will eat into your gains. Replace it with a nimble, go-with-the-trend mindset that knows the market can reverse in a heartbeat. This frees you up to make winning decisions.

## CELEBRATE YOUR POSITIVE TRADING CHARACTERISTICS

Do you embody perfectionism? It drives people around you bonkers, but some aspects of it can enhance your trading. (It can also cause performance anxiety, so be careful not to expect too much of yourself.)

Are you methodical, imperturbable, and nonjudgmental? Great. Stay that way.

Do you trust your instincts? Trading on an instinct or "gut feeling" that's merely a whim can get you into trouble. Trading on a gut feeling sharpened by knowledge and experience can save you money and fatten your wallet.

I absolutely trade from my gut—solar plexus, if you prefer. It's a reliable source for me, and I depend on it. Say all market indicators scream "go," but for reasons I can't see in front of me, my insides tighten, insisting something's amiss. Nine times out of ten, the market will reverse or make an unexpected turn. I've learned to trust my instincts. After a while, you will also.

## REALITY CHECK: WHAT COLOR IS THE STOCK MARKET?

One of the most challenging mindsets in trading is the ability to look at the market, or a stock, and see what is, instead of what you *want* it to be. We all have different perceptions of the same object, and our perceptions are colored by our previous experiences with that object.

Maybe you look at the market as a place of positive possibilities. The trader sitting next to you views it as a terrifying realm of lost money. Guess what? You're both right. The market will be to you whatever you conceive it to be.

How do you perceive the market? Is it an arena of opportunity? Or the opposite? Take a few minutes to reflect. It's important to give yourself an honest answer, because the perception you carry to the market determines the outcome of your trading career. That's an absolute. Count on it.

## DON'T PUSH THE RIVER: SWIM WITH IT AND THE MONEY WILL FLOW TO YOU

Americans are taught to be proactive rather than reactive, and we constantly think of ways to alter our relationships and environments. If you're dissatisfied with the color of your living room, you paint it. If you disagree with your partner, you take action to change things for the better. If your children misbehave, you ask them to redirect their actions.

The stock market flows like a river. You cannot push it in the other direction. You cannot paint it a different color. You cannot disagree with it, or demand it behave differently. You can only control yourself and your reaction to it.

Once you have that concept firmly in place, your goal is to come to the market each day, and regard it with positive objectivity. How does that feel? Like this:

➤ You observe and interact with the market as it truly is, not as you wish it were.
➤ You feel calm, your self-trust is fully intact, and you feel no pressure to do anything except follow your plan.
➤ Feelings of fear, rejection, and mistakes are nonexistent.
➤ You focus intently, yet with a feeling of detachment.
➤ When the market gives you a signal to act according to your plan, you execute the trade quickly and calmly.

## RESPONSIBILITY AND RESPECT: HOW THEY PLAY LEADING ROLES IN YOUR SUCCESS

As a professional trader, you take full responsibility for every action you take during the trading day. Blame is not part of your trading life; it's too destructive. You blame no one, not even yourself, for trades gone bad.

You do, however, assume responsibility. The market did not take money from you, or give money to you. You made choices, and you live with the results of those choices.

If you follow a "hot tip" from a taxi driver and get steamrollered, don't blame the taxi driver. Learn from it. If your trading mentor convinces you to sell a stock, and the next day it doubles, don't rant and rave. *You* clicked on the "sell" button.

Professional traders think for themselves. Sure, they may ask for input, but they apply their own criteria to each and every trade they place.

The world's wealthiest traders respect themselves and their abilities. Your success as a trader will reflect your own self-worthiness.

In *The Disciplined Trader*, Mark Douglas writes, "Taking responsibility is a function of self-acceptance." He goes on to write that the more negatively you think about yourself, the less responsibility you take. The higher your self-esteem, the more positive your thoughts, and the more insight you gain from your experiences.

Along with respecting yourself, to be successful you must respect money. Not just the money in your trading account, but money in general.

Think for a minute . . . how do you treat your money? Do you pay your bills on time? Do you repay personal debts quickly? Do you spend thoughtfully?

In *9 Steps to Financial Freedom*, Suze Orman asks readers to take out your wallet. How are your bills organized? Are they all stuffed together in disarray? Do you have to unravel them to see what they are? If you arrange your bills in order, it serves as a constant reminder of the respect that both you, and your money, deserve.

As Orman writes, "It's very subtle, but the way we treat ourselves and our money touches every aspect of our lives."

# QUIZ
||||||||||||||||||

## *Questions*

1. Name the two etched-in-stone trading rules. Give a brief description of each.
2. True or false? The stock market fluctuates according to exact, economic criteria.
3. As a trader, what represents your most formidable foe? Why?
4. Fill in the blanks. A thought, plus a _____, equals an _____.
5. True or false? You need excitement to make successful, profitable trades.
6. State one cure for greed.
7. Name three important fundamentals that, when achieved, displace fear.
8. Which two "R" words play leading roles in your success?

## *Answers*

1. (1) Protect your principal. As a trader's most important tool, the trading account must be protected at all times and cared for as the valuable asset it is.

   (2) Trade to trade well. The trader's goal is to trade well, not to make money. Good trading is an art form; money is a reward for well-executed trades.
2. False. The stock market fluctuates according to the collective players' opinions as to value at any given moment. That's why the market is always right.
3. Emotion represents a trader's most formidable foe. Negative emotions, such as greed and fear, color perceptions of reality and motivate traders to make losing decisions.
4. feeling, action
5. False. Excitement, as much fun as it is in everyday life, can be lethal when it guides trading habits.
6. Trade small lot sizes, such as 100 shares per trade. Don't chase stocks, especially those rocketing higher on news events.
7. Knowledge, experience, and self-trust
8. Responsibility and respect play leading roles in your success.

## CENTER POINT: EXTEND YOUR REACH

*"The only way to discover the limits of the possible is to go beyond them, to the impossible."*

—Arthur C. Clarke

When we realign our personal beliefs to support our vision and hold that vision high in front of us to light our path, life will call on us to grow. To grasp the good, we have to extend our reach.

When we first imagine our highest reality and own the dreams that have hidden in our heart, there's a sense of excitement—it feels like the perfect fit, right and good. Yet we soon realize that to arrive where we want to go, we'll have to change. We have to go places we've never been before, do things we've never done before, interact with people who are strangers to us. In short, we have to step out of our comfort zone.

With that realization of change, the internal chatter that's held us prisoner inside our comfort zone suddenly speaks out, loud and clear. It tells us we don't deserve that dream, that our dream might be good enough for someone else—but certainly not for us.

If we listen to the doubt instead of the dream, we'll return to that illusion of safety within our comfort zone. Our vision will remain beyond our grasp.

Instead, let's step over our self-doubt and ask, "What must we do to have this? How must we grow and change to be large enough to contain this glorious possibility?"

Affirm your willingness to extend your reach and expand your comfort zone. With purpose, step into new situations that support your goal. Then you will become a vehicle for your magnificent idea, and you will travel the road to realization.

# CHAPTER 5

# Trading Fundamentals You'll Build On

Early in my trading career, I attended a weekend course in commodities trading. The instructor, a well-known veteran in the trading community, said, "The CRB (commodities) Index and Treasury bond yield always run in tandem." Then he'd grin and would add, "Except when they don't."

He also said, "The CRB futures and spot (cash) index always trend in the same direction." Sly smile. "Unless they don't." And, "The price of gold rises during a bear market in stocks. Except when it doesn't."

This man drove me bonkers. No matter what financial market he discussed, or which chart pattern he described, he'd start by saying, "This always happens," then hedge with, "except when it doesn't."

Now that I'm thousands of trades wiser, I ask you to etch the following on your mind for all of your trading days. If you forget, the market will remind you in a hurry.

The wealthiest traders know this. And it's true now, more than ever, as global communities affect each other's financial markets on a twenty-four-hour basis.

**HOT TIP**

Nothing "always happens" in the financial markets. The only absolute in the market or stock behavior is constant change.

## THE MARKET HAS NO PRICE OR TIME LIMITS

Do the Dow Jones stocks, the NASDAQ 100, or the S&P 500 have limits as to how high they can soar? Or how low they can drop before they reach zero?

In Jack D. Schwager's *Market Wizards*, world-renowned investor/trader Jimmy Rogers is quoted as saying, "The market is going to go higher than I think it can and lower than I think it will."

Besides having no defined limit on price, the financial markets have no time boundaries. Every minute of the day, as markets open and close around the globe, someone, somewhere is trading in financial markets, be it stocks, bonds, currencies, or commodities.

Here in the United States, bond futures and stock index futures trade almost around the clock. Many financial gurus insist that in the not-too-distant future, our stock market will stay open twenty-four-hours a day.

Even if U.S. market hours remain as they are, stocks that close at one price Thursday don't necessarily open at the identical price Friday morning. This happens for a couple reasons.

First, specialists and market makers adjust the price of their stocks each morning according to the orders waiting to be filled.

Second, human opinions change constantly. Say on Friday just before the market's close, you sold the position you were holding in Halliburton (HAL). The oil service stock had waffled for days, and you wanted to free up the cash. Over the weekend, however, talk of war between Middle Eastern countries simmered and gathered steam.

Now it's Monday morning, and rumors bubble that irate governments are readying attack planes to hit the oil-rich nations. Fears of oil shortages mushroom, and by the time the market opens, HAL is rocketing.

In little more than forty-eight hours, fueled by world events, the prevailing opinion of stocks like HAL reversed from apathy to enthusiasm. While the oil service company's fundamental data did not change over the weekend, the perception regarding its share value changed. Emotions and opinions change the value of a stock. Now, do you have a clearer idea of what I mean by the statement, "The market has no time and price limits"?

## FUNDAMENTAL VERSUS TECHNICAL ANALYSIS

Two basic sectors of reasoning constitute the way investors and traders go about choosing stocks: fundamental analysis and technical analysis. Those who strictly adhere to one method usually sneer at the other, much like the Republicans and the Democrats.

Fundamental analysts enjoy telling anyone who will listen that they've never met a rich technician. Technical analysts laugh at the fundamentalists' insistence that P/E ratios really do matter in a stock's ability to gain value. (P/E ratios are price-to-earnings ratios. These are calculated by dividing the stock's price by its earnings-per-share figure.) Much like the Republicans and Democrats, both points of view have their good parts.

In very broad terms, investors, both private and institutional, use fundamental analysis as their basis for stock purchases. Short-term traders use technical analysis. Since the risk–reward ratio between investing and trading is very different, and of course, the time horizon for long term versus short term is so diverse, it makes sense that two different methods are employed. By the way, that's also the reason why many people who invest successfully imagine they can jump easily from investing to day trading—then find themselves swimming in troubled waters. Investing and trading are two different animals!

### Fundamental Analysis

Fundamental analysis relies on economic supply–demand information in the overall picture, and a company's financial health in the smaller picture. It includes such statistics as a stock's annual growth rate, five-year, one-year, and quarterly earnings records, and P/E ratios.

Investors who rely on fundamentals are more interested in a stock's performance year to year than they are in market behavior. They don't care that the Dow Jones plunges one day and soars the next. They are satisfied with steady, conservative growth, and their goal is the end result—that their investments eventually provide for their children's college fund, retirement nest egg, or a condo in Florida. That's why, when the market falls hard, or even soars skyward, and CNBC interviews Joe Public for comments, Joe invariably says, "I don't care how the market acts today. I'm in it for the long haul."

Besides long-term investors, many commodities brokers and traders—especially those who trade agricultural futures, including corn, sugar, and pork bellies—rely on fundamentals such as the weather and global shortages. An event as predictable as the arrival of winter can dictate the balance of supply and demand—and so ultimately, the price. Example: winter = cold weather = more natural gas usage = higher demand. Result? Energy and energy services prices usually rise in autumn months, just before winter arrives and demand increases.

One reason stock traders don't delve into fundamental analysis is the time challenge. Although it provides highly valuable information, the research consumes too much time. Most of us don't have time to spend researching a single company's new product potential, along with earnings as compared to past earnings.

One fundamental statistic, however, that I do use whenever time permits is a proprietary ranking shown in Investor's Business Daily (IBD) stock tables. Called the SmartSelect Composite Rating, it's displayed in the first column next to each stock listed and represents a composite rating of the company's fundamentals. You can also use the rating to compare stock's fundamental strength, one to another. Ratings range from 1 to 99, with 99 rated highest.

When I target stocks to trade, especially for longer-term holds of days to a week or more, I first choose industry groups that are in an uptrend, or breaking into an uptrend, on their daily and weekly charts. Then I narrow my focus to a few of the most promising component stocks in that group. From the best of those, I glance at their current IBD Composite Ratings, and usually buy the final choice if the ranking is 70, or better. If the market gets a case of the hiccups, as long as the stock doesn't hit my sell stop, I relax knowing my stock has good fundamentals, along with a strong technical outlook.

### Technical Analysis

Technical analysis is the alternate method of researching stock. It is the study of time, price, and sentiment. The tool used most often by technical analysis is a chart. Charts show a stock's price history, and with practice, we can see everything we need to know about a particular equity in a matter of seconds.

The prices on charts don't get there by themselves. Remember our discussion on supply, demand, and price? Price patterns on charts reflect the collective mindset of the stock's participants. Patterns repeat themselves because those buyers and sellers operate from memory. They may have never seen a stock chart in their lives, but even Ivan Investor remembers that when he bought Simple Software, it was $50 a share. It fell soon after he bought it. When it finally climbed back to $50 a share three months later, Ivan, along with many other investors, sold it to get even and avoid another possible loss. Those actions form chart patterns.

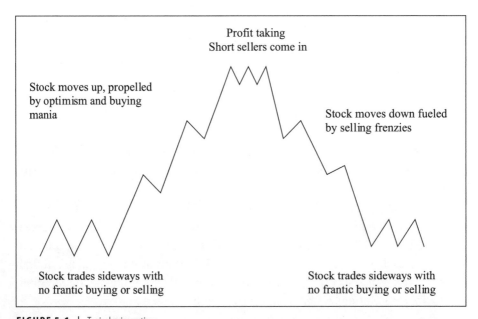

**FIGURE 5-1** | Typical price action.

Figure 5-1 shows how you can recognize excited buying mania, uncertainty, panic, and selling frenzies in charts. When up or down energy dissipates, the stock may meander in the same price range for a while because the numbers of buyers and sellers level off, and neither emotion rules.

Along with time, price, and volume, charts can display different indicators and oscillators (overbought/oversold indicators). Every trader has his or her favorites. (We'll talk more about various indicators and oscillators in upcoming chapters.) Volume spikes on charts tell how many shares have been traded on a particular day, week, or month. Moving averages indicate a stock's strength by averaging the closing prices during a certain time period. Don't worry—indicators sound confusing, but by the end of this book, you'll be interpreting them with ease.

Traders also depend on technical analysis to retrieve up-to-the-second information about equities and market indicators. Unlike investors, who may ignore daily market gyrations, most traders pay close attention to major market indices, including the Dow Jones Industrials, Standard & Poor's (S&P) 500 Index, NASDAQ 100 and NASDAQ Composite, and more. Charting these indices and other indicators gives insight into which direction the market may move next.

## DIFFERENT TRADING TIME FRAMES: WHAT THEY MEAN TO YOU

Traders enter and exit positions within the parameters of four basic time frames. Each time frame has its own expected risk–reward ratios.

1. Position trade—Stock may be held from weeks to months.
2. Swing trade—Stock may be held for two to five days.
3. Day trade—Stock will be bought and sold (or the reverse) the same day.
4. Momentum and scalping trades—Stock will be bought and sold (or the reverse) within seconds or minutes, to hours.

Most traders engage in the last three trades—swing trades, day trades, and momentum plays. I added the first, position trade, for a reason.

In Chapter 3, I talked about maintaining two trading accounts, one for day trading, and the other for swing/position trades. In the second account, you may mimic what many seasoned traders do, which is to have a core holding or two that you hold for one week or longer. (The usual criterion is that the stock is held as long as the stock is in an uptrend (or downtrend, if short) on a daily chart. Just as shopping malls have anchor stores—large, well-known department stores that ensure the mall's success—so you may decide to have an anchor stock or two in your account that you hold for a nice, profitable ride.

This *does not* mean you hold onto Igloo Ice Cream because you bought it as a swing trade and ignored your sell stop. Then, after it fell like a rock, you were too embarrassed to sell it at a big loss, so you designated it as a "core holding," or "investment."

It *does* mean that you find a stock, preferably with strong fundamentals; like a Dow "blue chip." Or, perhaps you buy an entire index, like the S&P Depository Receipts (SPY). (Because of their acronym SPDR, these receipts are known as "spiders." Spiders mirror the S&P 500 and trade just like a stock on the Amex, under the symbol SPY.) You buy the core holding at a good entry point and hold until its current uptrend weakens, or is broken.

Swing trades are positions that you intend to hold for two to five days. In a perfect world (read: bull market), a nice, easygoing stock may rise for three to five days. Then, it will then pull back to "rest." In order to catch most of the rise, or upswing, you enter the stock using the criteria you'll soon learn, hold it overnight for a few days, and sell it just as it approaches its next point of resistance, or pullback area.

Many traders refuse to hold positions overnight. Their reasons are certainly valid. Still, I've made a great deal of money spotting brawny stocks that close on their high for the day, and then "gap open" (it opens at a higher price than it closed at the preceding day) the next morning, literally handing me a sweet profit overnight.

The downside is you may hold a stock that opens lower because an analyst chooses that morning to downgrade it, or because the market itself opens lower. Holding stocks overnight is risky, but can be profitable. You decide.

The most common trade executed is a day trade, where we enter the position in the morning, and exit before the market closes the same day.

Momentum and scalping plays are performed with lightning speed and precision. Momentum players typically enter stock with the intention of riding it up for the current leg of the move; the time frame is usually measured in minutes. Scalpers jump aboard with the intention of making a fraction of a point per trade; expected time duration of a scalping trade is seconds to minutes.

In the late 1990s, I knew scalpers who executed hundreds, even thousands of trades a day. With decimalization reducing the bid-ask spread—and thus the profit traders could make by trading it—many of those traders left the trading scene.

Yes, that style of trading is still viable. And yes, you can jump in and out of volatile stocks and mini stock index futures multiple times during a day. Still, I don't recommend this trading style for new traders. The pros taking the other side of your trades love to see new traders come in. It makes them drool, and they're very clever with a knife and fork.

This is a good time to reflect on your personal risk tolerance. Some people thrive on stress, some buckle under it. All traders endure a certain amount of stress, but you can choose the potency of your poison depending on the time frames you trade in.

Patient plodders enjoy intermediate-term holds and swing trades. Adrenaline addicts prefer day trades, momentum plays, and "scalps."

Experienced traders with guts of steel and superhuman powers of concentration make the best momentum players. They watch a host of indicators out of one eye, and the stock's chart and Level II screen out of the other. If the stock so much as breathes funny, they're out.

If you're in a momentum or scalping play and aren't using automatic stop orders, you cannot get up to use the bathroom, or get a cup of coffee or a sandwich. You cannot talk on the phone or to someone standing behind you. So, if you're a social animal, have to eat the minute you get hungry, or aren't blessed with the bladder of a camel, consider leaving these plays to hardier souls.

As a novice trader, it's best to postpone scalping plays until you learn how to properly execute swing and day trades. Otherwise, instead of being the scalper, you could end up getting scalped.

## TRADING WITH THE CLOCK FOR PROFITS

Now that I've hammered home the point that the market is unlimited, unstructured, and timeless, I'm actually going to tell you that key time periods during the trading day do show up with a degree of regularity. *Degree* is the operative word here. Market reversals and shifts according to the clock fall under the "This always happens, except when it doesn't" premise. The following times are all Eastern Standard Time.

**9:30 A.M.:** Equities market opens
**9:45 A.M. to 10:10 A.M.:** First reversal period
**11:20 A.M.:** Beginning of lunchtime lethargy
**1:30 P.M.:** Lunchtime lethargy begins to clear—some stocks start to edge up for the afternoon session
**2:30 P.M.:** Stocks break out (or down) in a more definitive manner
**3:00 P.M.:** Treasury bonds stop trading; market breathes a sigh of relief, possible shift in direction
**3:20 P.M.:** Active traders begin to close out positions for the day
**3:30 P.M.:** Mild reversal possible
**3:55 P.M.:** Additional reversals possible as more positions closed
**4:00 P.M.:** Equities market closes

These times don't play out exactly each day, but they give you a good idea of the general ebb and flow of a typical market day.

If the market opens in a bullish mode and the indices trend up, by 9:45 A.M., they begin to retrace, or pull back. Why? When stocks opened up with strong buying, specialists and market makers were forced to take the other side of the longs and sell short. They have no intention of riding those losing positions all day. So they start "dropping the bid" (lowering the price at which they'll buy the stock for), about fifteen minutes or so after the market opens. That way, they can cover their shorts at a profit.

If the market opens down, or in a bearish mode, when traders sell, specialists and market makers have to buy. Around 9:45 A.M., or so, many stocks that have been trending start to turn upward. You guessed it—specialists and market makers are selling at a profit.

At about 10:10 A.M., give or take a few minutes, strong stocks that have pulled back slightly on a bullish day will again turn up. Bearish stocks on a negative day resume their growling.

Lunchtime lethargy ambles in about 11:20 A.M. On an extremely bullish day, the apathetic period may hold off till closer to noon. At that time, institutional managers and the majority of players leave their desks for lunch; stock and overall market movement quiets down. Stocks tend to fall off, or slide down slightly or even steeply, depending on their morning's activity and strength. On a bearish day, I've found weaker stocks fall hard at lunchtime. Many active traders take profits, partial or all, before 11:30 A.M. in order to lock in gains.

**ESCAPE STATEMENT**

Yes, occasionally lunchtime rallies come into play and stocks jump higher. Mostly, though, it's a dangerous period to play in.

Experienced traders avoid entering positions during lunchtime. Stock movement, if any, can be whippy and erratic. The majority of breakouts fail. I've known many a trader, myself included, who's made nice profits in the morning and given it all back at lunch. This happens nine times out of ten.

Moral of the story: Go out for lunch. Get out of your office. Take a walk and eat a light, healthy meal. This will clear your head, soothe your eyes, and prepare your body for a productive afternoon.

A few stocks start to perk up around 1:30 P.M. Still, if you stay away until 2:00 P.M., you probably won't miss that much. (I'm assuming you didn't leave a bunch of volatile stocks in your account during lunch—that's a bad idea.)

By 2:30 P.M. on a bullish day, stocks decide where they'll go for the duration of market hours. Later, I'm going to show you some chart patterns that form at lunch and that can give tidy profits for the afternoon.

Treasury bonds stop trading at 3:00 P.M. Bond prices affect the stock market, so when they cease trading, the market breathes a sigh of relief as though it's shooed a cranky child outside.

During the last half-hour of the day, institutions tend to reshuffle their positions, and individual traders do the same. So, look for another shift in the 3:20 P.M. and 3:30 P.M. time period.

The technique for recognizing when directional shifts, or reversals are initiating is to watch leading indicators that we'll talk about soon, such as the E-mini S&P futures, the TICK, and the TRIN. These indicators act as guides, and most stocks follow their lead.

## INTRODUCTION TO CHARTING TECHNIQUES

Basically, traders use three types of charts: line charts, bar charts, and candlestick charts. They each tell the same story with a different spin.

### Line Charts

Line charts are drawn from the closing prices each day (or designated period), and so form a single line across the chart. Figure 5-2 shows a daily chart in line format, of Halliburton Co. (HAL).

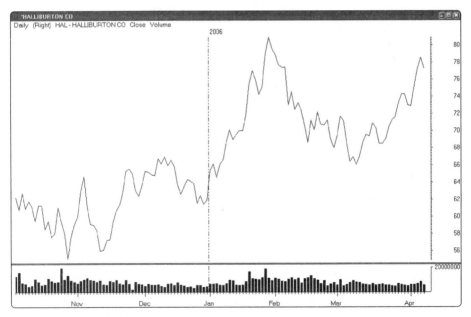

**FIGURE 5-2**  |  Line chart of the Halliburton Co. (HAL).

RealTick® graphics used with permission of Townsend Analytics, Ltd. © 1986-2007 Townsend Analytics, Ltd.

Line charts can be helpful tools to see the big picture, particularly when you use them to overlay on top of each other. For instance, some analysts overlay a line chart on the Transportation Index on top of the S&P futures to note when these indices move in tandem, or when they diverge. The Advance-Decline Line, which I talk about in Chapter 13, is generally shown as a line chart.

For our purposes as traders, bar charts, and more especially candlestick charts, offer more information, faster.

### Bar Charts

Bar charts are used by many traders. On a daily chart (see Figure 5-3), the vertical bar shows the price range the stock has traded in during that day. The protruding, horizontal bar on the left designates the opening price. The horizontal bar on the right indicates the closing price.

Figure 5-4 shows a bar chart of the Halliburton Co. (HAL). The oval in the chart isolates the bars for January 26 through January 30. Notice how this oil services company fluctuated nearly ten points in a three-day period.

Figure 5-5 is the same chart of HAL previously shown in bar format (Figure 5-4), but this time it's in a candlestick format.

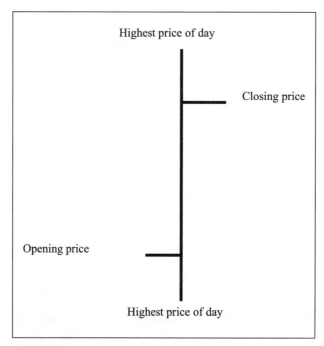

**FIGURE 5-3**

**FIGURE 5-4** | Bar chart of the Halliburton Co. (HAL).

RealTick® graphics used with permission of Townsend Analytics, Ltd. © 1986-2007 Townsend Analytics, Ltd.

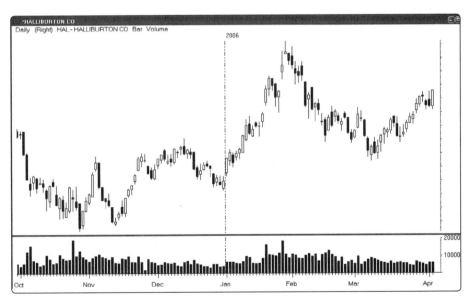

**FIGURE 5-5** | Daily candlestick chart of the Halliburton Co. (HAL).

RealTick® graphics used with permission of Townsend Analytics, Ltd. © 1986-2007 Townsend Analytics, Ltd.

### Candlestick Charts

Bless a seventeenth-century Japanese rice broker, whose trading principles evolved into candlestick charting techniques. The black-and-white "real bodies" make chart reading quicker and clearer than bar charts. If you spend the day staring at charts, as do most technical analysts, you'll realize how much easier candlestick charts are on your eyes. Candlestick charts also interpret stock movement in more detail and give more signals about possible future movement, offering an extra dimension to your analysis. In other words, candlestick charts save you from going blind and broke.

First, let's look at the basics. Like bars, candlesticks use bar forms to designate price range. Then they fatten the bar with a vertical rectangle to indicate opening and closing price comparisons, which the Japanese believe are very important. At those times, traders and investors are most likely to buy or sell their position with the most emotion.

A clear or white body denotes the closing price was higher than the opening price. A black body means the closing price was lower than the opening price. Say, Igloo Ice Cream opened at $23, the low of the day. It closed at $27, which happened to be the high of the day. The candlestick representing that day would look like Figure 5-6(a).

If Igloo Ice Cream opened at the day's high of $27 and closed at the low of $23, the candlestick would look like Figure 5-6(b).

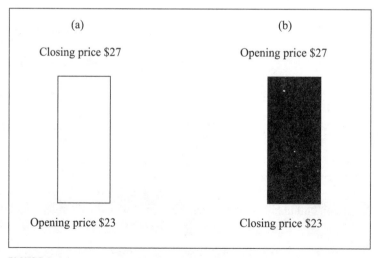

**FIGURE 5-6**

Let's modify it: Igloo's low for the day is $23 and the high is $27; it opened at $24 and closed at $26. The body is still white because it closed higher than it opened, but now you can see two shadows that indicate the price range, as in Figure 5-7(a). The shadow above the real body is called the *upper shadow*; the shadow below is called the *lower shadow.* If the stock opens at its low and stays above it, the white body will have no lower shadow. That's referred to as a *shaven bottom.* If it closes at the high, and has no upper shadow, it's referred to as a *shaven head.*

If Igloo's price range remains, but it opens at $26 and closes at $24, again, the body is dark, as in Figure 5-7(b).

If Igloo's price range remains the same, but it opens and closes at the same price, for instance $25, the real body is reduced to a line, as in Figure 5-7(c). This candlestick is called a *doji.* The plural of doji is *doji.*

Candlestick patterns are valuable trading tools for traders because, interpreted properly, the candles show market psychology (bullish, bearish, or indecisive), forecast reversals or changes in trend, and can be used as a decision support tool in your money management strategies.

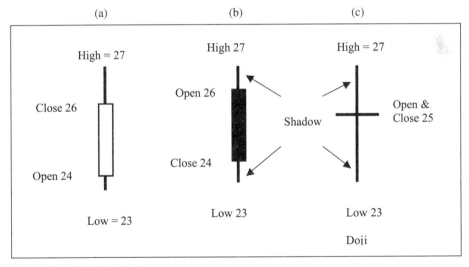

**FIGURE 5-7** | Candlestick configuration.

Now, we'll look at some basic candlestick patterns. The hammer and the hanging man are good indicators that a trend change may occur (Figure 5-8).

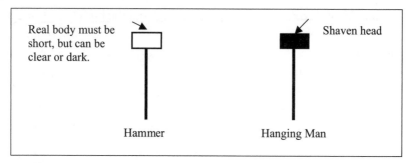

**FIGURE 5-8** | Hammer and hanging man.

For both hammer and hanging man:

➤ The real bodies are at the top of the day's trading range, the lower shadow should be twice the height of the real body, and it should have a shaven head.

➤ A "hanging man" appears at the top of an uptrend. A "hammer" appears at the bottom of a downtrend.

➤ Their appearance during a downtrend or uptrend signals the prior move may be broken.

As you can see in Figure 5-9, either real body can be white or black, but it is slightly more bullish if the hammer is white and slightly more bearish if the hanging man is black.

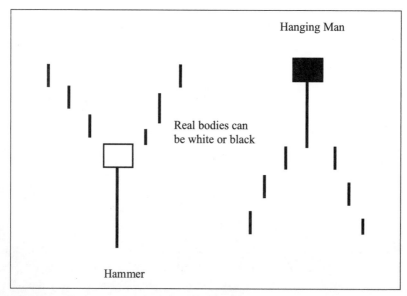

**FIGURE 5-9** | Hammer and hanging man in chart patterns.

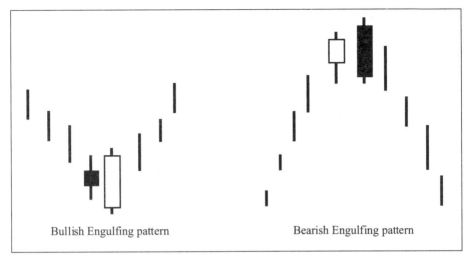

Bullish Engulfing pattern            Bearish Engulfing pattern

**FIGURE 5-10**

Engulfing patterns use two candlesticks to prophesy a major trend reversal. Figure 5-10 shows how a bullish engulfing pattern reverses a downtrend, and a bearish engulfing pattern reverses an uptrend. In *Japanese Candlestick Charting Techniques*, Steve Nison writes, "The bearish engulfing pattern can be viewed as a total solar eclipse blocking out the entire sun."

### Characteristics of Bullish or Bearish Engulfing Patterns
➤ The stock has to be in a definite uptrend or downtrend, even if short term.
➤ The second real body should be the opposite color of the prior real body.
➤ The second real body has to engulf the first real body although it need not engulf the shadows. This pattern becomes even more accurate when the first real body is quite petite, and the second very long.
➤ If the second real body engulfs an additional body, the signal grows stronger.

Dark cloud cover is a bearish reversal pattern illustrated in Figure 5-11. It appears when an uptrend has run out of steam, or at the conclusion of a congestion move. Again, the pattern consists of two candlesticks.

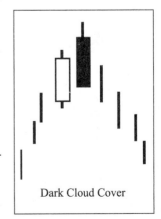

Dark Cloud Cover

**FIGURE 5-11**

### Characteristics of Dark Cloud Cover

➤ First candlestick is a strong, white real body.

➤ Second candlestick's price gaps open above the top of the white body and its shadow, if any.

➤ By the end of the move, though, the second body closes well into the white body and near its own low. The more the second, black body moves into the lower part of the first, white body, the higher the probability that the bears are taking control and the uptrend is weakened.

➤ If a long, white real body closes above the highs of either the dark cloud cover or the bearish engulfing pattern, it suggests the start of another rally.

The reverse of the dark cloud cover is the bullish piercing pattern shown in Figure 5-12.

This pattern forecasts the reversal, or change, in a downtrend.

### Characteristics of the Bullish Piercing Pattern

➤ The first real body is a black body in the context of a falling price move.

➤ The second is a white real body, in which the stock gaps open lower than the previous candlestick's low.

➤ Then the price rises higher, and the real body closes more than midway into the prior black real body. Now the bulls have wrested control from the bears, and the downtrend is broken.

➤ If the real body doesn't close at least halfway or more into the black body, it negates the signal and indicates the downtrend may continue.

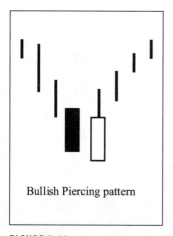

Bullish Piercing pattern

**FIGURE 5-12**

Note: If the white real body opens lower than the previous day's low and closes higher than the previous day's high, Western technical analysis defines it as a "key reversal day."

Stars also warn of reversals, or shifts, in price movement. Basic star patterns are very powerful warning signals. They include the evening star, the morning star depicted in Figure 5-13, and the doji evening and doji morning stars illustrated in Figure 5-14.

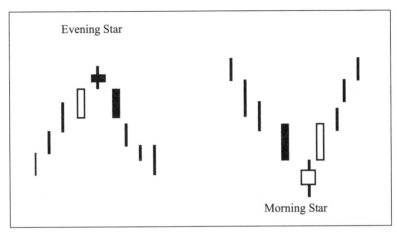

**FIGURE 5-13**

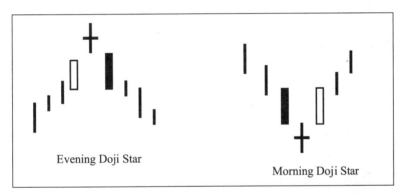

**FIGURE 5-14**

➤ In each case, the star itself can appear as black or white.

➤ Technically, the star must gap away from the preceding candlestick, meaning the star's real body must not overlap the previous real body.

➤ The star's real body is small, indicating a stock that's had a strong surge up or down is now slowing, and the bulls and bears are deadlocked in battle.

The evening star, Venus, signals the arrival of darkness. In candlestick charting, the appearance of an evening star denotes a bearish reversal in an uptrend. Three candlesticks create the evening star pattern:

➤ The first two are composed of a long, white real body, followed by a star with a small body, which can be white or black. The star suggests the top of the uptrend.

➤ The third candlestick is a black real body that drops low into the range of the first, white candlestick. Now the bears are in control, and the uptrend is weakened.

The morning star derives its name from Mercury, which appears just before the sun rises. It foretells a bullish reversal in a downtrend. The pattern is the opposite of the evening star and shows three candlesticks in a complete pattern.

➤ The first two are composed of one, long black body, followed by a star with a small body, which can be white or black. The star gaps open lower than the previous real body's close, then the price rises. This move indicates buying pressure has begun.
➤ The third star is a white real body that moves into the price range of the first, black real body. Now the bulls have taken control, and the downtrend is weakened.

Doji are created when a candlestick opens and closes at, or very near, the same price; only a lateral line forms the real body. As you can see in Figure 5-14, doji resemble crosses. Doji stars are doji that gap open either above or below the previous real body in an uptrend or downtrend. They represent powerful reversal indicators and should be respected when they appear in a strong trend move. It means, once again, that the bulls and bears are at a stalemate, and the next move is up for grabs. The candlestick following the doji should confirm the trend reversal and the winner of the power struggle.

An evening doji star warns of a potential top in an uptrend.

➤ It gaps open above the white real body prior to it.
➤ The next candlestick is a black real body that descends into the white real body of the candlestick formed prior to the evening dog star. This confirms the bears gained control, and the uptrend is broken.
➤ If the next candlestick after the evening doji star is a white real body, the doji warning is negated.

A morning doji star indicates a possible bottom in a downtrend.

➤ It gaps open below the black real body prior to it.
➤ The next white real body opens higher, and the price rises into the area of the black body prior to the morning doji star. Now the bulls are definitely in control, and the move down is broken.

➤  If the next candlestick after a morning doji star is a black real body, the doji downtrend reversal is negated.

Our last star of this discussion is the shooting star. This one-candle (from now on, I will use "candle" and "candlestick" interchangeably) pattern consists of a small real body, either black or white, with a long upper shadow. It derives its name from the shooting star blazing across the night sky, which the Japanese say suggests trouble overhead. You can see the analogy in Figure 5-15(a). The shooting star appears at the top of moves up, warning that the bull's buying power is deteriorating. Think of it this way: the long upper shadow shows sellers are gaining power.

A variation of the shooting star forms the gravestone doji, another powerful topping candle. As Figure 5-15(b) displays, the gravestone doji also has a long upper shadow, but the candle opens and closes at the low of the day—an ominous sign.

Remember, both the shooting star and gravestone doji patterns act on the negative pattern only when the next day's candle opens lower and moves lower, confirming the weakness in the prior move up.

On my charts, I configure the white real bodies to appear green, and the black real bodies to appear in red. This coincides with most Level II software systems' formats that display upticks in green and downticks in red, thus reinforcing a stock's price action at a glance.

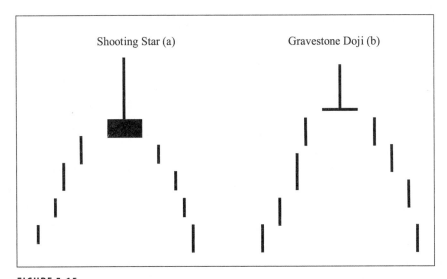

**FIGURE 5-15**

If you'd like to study candlestick patterns further, I strongly suggest you read Steve Nison's books; they're comprehensive and easy to understand: *Japanese Candlestick Charting Techniques, Second Edition* (NY: New York Institute of Finance, 2001), and *Beyond Candlesticks: New Japanese Charting Techniques Revealed* (NY: John Wiley & Sons, 1994). For even more information on candlestick charting techniques, go to Nison's Web site: *www.candlecharts.com*.

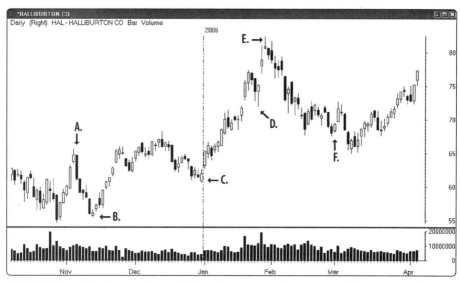

**FIGURE 5-16 |** This daily chart of our buddy HAL, which we've taken all the way through this lesson, shows how chart interpretation can be built from a simple line chart, all the way through to candlestick chart patterns. Note how the candles gave powerful warning signals that the trend had potential to change, or even reverse.

**A.** Bearish engulfing pattern: On this dramatic top after a breakout, note how the white candle gapped open to form a small real body. The next day's candle opened even, then swiftly dropped to engulf the prior day's white body . . . then dropped even more dramatically to the downside.

**B.** Morning star: This morning star fell to near the prior low, then stopped, signaling that bulls were buying. The next day gapped up and closed higher, indicating that the bears had been shooed back to their caves.

**C.** Bullish engulfing: This pattern is a bit difficult to see, but notice how the white bottoming candle's real body engulfed the black real body of the prior day, indicating that the move down had potential to reverse.

**D.** Hammer: The move down ended in a hammer, suggesting buyers were offering support. The next day HAL's price gapped open to the upside dramatically, and the bulls took total control.

**E.** Shooting star: After HAL's ballistic run, a shooting star formation signaled exhausted buyers. The next day ended in a long black candle, confirming the shooting star's warning.

**F.** Bullish piercing pattern: This quick move down ended in a long black candle, and a quick reversal to the upside in a variation of a bullish piercing pattern. While the white piercing candle didn't gap open below the prior day's low, as some insist is necessary (in fact, it gapped up), the white real body "pierced" the black candle's real body, and closed on the high of the day. That suggested the bulls had taken control, at least for the time-being.

The charts shown in Figures 5-16 and 5-17 illustrate examples of the patterns described in this chapter. Please study them so you can learn to spot the patterns quickly.

Remember, combined with other technical indicators, candle patterns enhance your ability to recognize potential trend reversals—and that's extremely valuable trading information.

**FIGURE 5-17** | This daily chart of Lennar Corp. (LEN) shows the wild swings made by the homebuilder's stock, especially in January, 2006. Several candle patterns warned of upcoming reversals in the price moves.

**A.** Dark cloud cover: Both of these up-moves were halted by dark cloud cover patterns. The dark cloud cover is very reliable.

**B.** Morning star: Although this white real body did not gap down, this morning star, or variation on a hammer (without a shaven head) tells you that the bulls are wresting control from the bears after a brief price move to the downside.

**C.** Yikes! No, there is no "yikes" candle pattern, but there probably should be. As you can see on this long, black candle that gapped open big-time, then fell rapidly to close on the low of the day—the breakout failed. Please know that when you see these candles on a daily chart, they usually portend at least short-term doom.

**D.** Hanging man: Great example of a hanging man—the poor guy certainly got hung up at the top of LEN's dramatic slide to the downside.

**E.** Hammer: A variation on the hammer theme (no shaven head). Just as a long upper shadow on a candle denotes sellers, the long lower shadow indicates buyers.

**F.** Doji: Although this doji did not gap open to form a legal "star," it still exuded strength as a topping bar. Remember to wait for the following candle to form, to confirm the pattern and reversal.

**G.** Shooting star: Great example of the shooting star's ability to stop an up-move in its tracks.

**H.** Bullish piercing pattern: Here, the long white bullish piercing candle halted LEN's fall.

**I.** Morning stars: Both bottoming patterns were reversed by star formations.

# QUIZ

IIIIIIIIIIIIIIII

*Questions*

1. "The only absolute in the market or stock behavior is _____."
2. Give a brief explanation of fundamental analysis. Who uses it most?
3. Give a brief explanation of technical analysis. Who uses it most?
4. Name four trading time frames.
5. True or false? During market hours, lunchtime is the best time to trade stocks.
6. Describe the candlestick pattern known as a bullish engulfing pattern.
7. What designates a doji?
8. What makes a doji a star doji?
9. True or false? Doji stars are highly potent indicators of a possible trend reversal.

*Answers*

1. constant change
2. Fundamental analysis is the study of supply and demand, as well as statistics such as a company's growth rate, quarterly earnings, and P/E ratios. It is used primarily by long-term investors.
3. Technical analysis is the study of time, price, volume, and sentiment as it relates to the financial markets. This analysis is used primarily by traders.
4. Position trade: one to two weeks or longer; swing trade: overnight to five days; day trade: position opened and closed during the same day; momentum/scalp: trade duration is usually minutes to seconds.
5. False. Lunchtime (11:20 A.M. to 1:30 P.M.) is the worst time of the day to trade. Stocks either don't move at all or become highly unpredictable.
6. The current stock pattern is a definite downtrend. The first real body is black. The next, white real body opens lower and closes higher than the black one, thus "engulfing" it. If the next candle moves higher and confirms the bulls are in control, the downtrend may reverse and the stock may break out to the upside.
7. A doji is formed when a stock opens and closes at the same price.
8. A doji becomes a star doji when it gaps open above the prior candlestick's real body in an uptrend, or gaps open below the prior candlestick's real body in a downtrend.
9. True. Doji stars are potent trend reversal indicators.

# CENTER POINT: THE MIRACLE OF GIVING

*"He who loves others is constantly loved by them. He who respects others is constantly respected by them."*

—Mencius (4th–3rd century, B.C.)

Would you like to be on the receiving end of prosperity and abundance for the rest of your life? You can be if you expand your experience of giving.

Our world operates through the universal law of cause and effect. Nothing stands still. Life moves continually as energy flows through us and circulates to the rest of the world, then returns to us once more. Your relationships with your spouse, boss, children, and friends constantly revolve in a circle of giving and receiving.

Your career, your health, your spiritual community, your family, and yes, even your bank account, require an energy flow of give and take. If you stop giving to one area of your life, be it knowledge and enthusiasm, food and rest, quest for inner harmony, love and nurturing, or financial support, that part of your life suffers—returns little to you. Why? You've blocked the energy flow, the circulation. Like a stream, energy must keep circulating to stay alive and vital. Otherwise, it grows stagnant.

Giving and receiving forms a circle, and a circle has no end. For each area of our lives to thrive and grow, we need to give freely and receive with gratitude.

Begin the process of circulation by giving what you most want to receive. Would you like more abundance in the form of money? Give what you can, with kind intentions, and no thought for its return. Would you welcome more attention and appreciation? Give honest compliments, do someone an unexpected favor. Give of your time, your caring.

In *The Seven Spiritual Laws of Success*, author Deepak Chopra writes, "Make a decision to give wherever you go, to whomever you see. As long as you're giving, you will be receiving. The more you give, the more confidence you will gain in the miraculous effects of this law."

Remember, whatever you send out will return to you. So, give for the sake of giving, and your life will overflow with abundance and prosperity.

# CHAPTER 6

# Technical Analysis 101: The Trend Is Your Friend

As we begin our study of charts, you'll notice that stock prices move in one of three directions: up, down, and sideways. *Sideways* means the prices change very little, and so move between an upper and lower price area in what we call a *trading range.*

The up, down, or sideways price movements are the only directions prices can take. This is always true. No other movements are possible. Stock prices cannot move backward because time moves forward.

Note that I said always true. This is one of the rare times you'll see *always* appear in connection with the financial markets because, as I stated in Chapter 5, there are precious few times that *always* applies.

The up, down, and sideways price movements take place whether we're speaking of a macrocosm of months to a year in a stock's life, or a microcosm of seconds to minutes.

Just as each crystal of sand represents a single unit that connects with other units to form an entire beach, each minute, hour, and day of a stock's price movement connects with the next, forming an overall cycle that repeats itself through time.

## STOCK CYCLES: HOW THEY HELP YOU PLAN YOUR TRADES

Our world is made up of cycles. Planets orbit our sun on a precise course. On Earth, cycles occur in every aspect of nature. The four seasons follow each other predictably. Tides ebb and flow. Birds migrate. As part of this system, we humans tend to think in cycles, or patterns, whether as a collective mindset or as individuals.

Our tendency toward cycles reflects in the financial markets. Because the markets and their internal components—whether commodities, options, industry indexes, or individual stocks—are fueled by human expectations, recognizable cycles emerge.

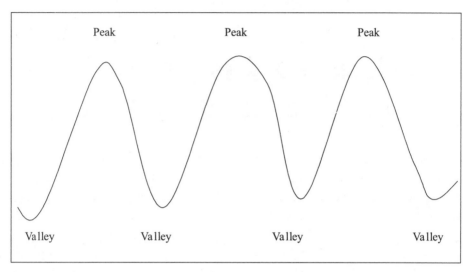

**FIGURE 6-1** | Three complete cycles.

As traders, we attempt to recognize those cycles and use them to our advantage. Look at a dozen stock charts in a row. See the cycle presented in Figure 6-1? A series of peaks and troughs, resembling a mountain range, stretches across the time line of a chart like the Rocky Mountains stretch along our Western states.

Formations on charts are analogous to mountain ranges. When you stand at a distance, you see only the outline of the major peaks and valleys against the sky. Move in closer, and you notice that smaller hills and dales form that mountain. Start hiking up the mountain, and you encounter rock formations and gullies at each rise. From the big picture to the small picture, the cycles evolve, one into the next.

An extended stock cycle may take years to complete. Within that cycle, smaller cycles take place in months, weeks, and days. Within a single trading day, miniature cycles evolve. These cycles, no matter the time frame, can form predictable patterns. Why are they predictable? Because people's emotions—our emotions—are predictable.

Some traders do not use charts to trade. To me, that's inconceivable. Trading without charts would be the same as getting into my car and backing onto the street blindfolded. Trading is hard enough. Attempting to do it without charts accelerates risk immeasurably. Why chance it? High risk equals lost money. No thanks.

When the stock is in a valley, or touch, we say it is "basing," or "bottoming." You could say the stock is resting. This basing area in a stock's cycle is one of those times brokers call their clients and tell them to buy.

"Remember that high flyer, Igloo Ice Cream? It used to be forty bucks a share, but it's melted down to twenty." The broker chuckles, then his tone turns serious. "We oughtta' pick up some for your account today. It's a heck of a bargain."

Maybe. Maybe not. Trouble is, if Igloo has fallen that far, and institutional money managers and investors are ignoring it, it may take weeks or months to rise again. In the meantime, that same capital could have bought a stock catapulting in an uptrend and making money—fast.

**HOT TIP**

When you're considering a stock for a swing, day, or scalping trade, develop the winning habit of checking out the stock's weekly chart, or a year's worth of price action on a daily chart. This gives you a picture of the stock's true personality and shows how it behaves relative to the overall market.

### Uptrends

When a stock breaks up and out of the valley, then climbs higher while maintaining a steady course upward, we call it an uptrend. As a trader, the uptrend is the most prevalent pattern you'll search for as you look for stocks to buy. For bulls, this is when the most profits are made. A "breakout" designates the exact point where the stock rises over the valley and leaves the foothills behind to mount that steady course upward.

To remain in an uptrend, a stock's price must make a series of higher highs and higher lows.

Remember, as we discussed before, stocks move according to supply, demand, and the mindsets of the market players involved. If buyers believe the stock's value will increase and pay higher prices as the sellers elevate the price, the stock moves up. The more volume (number of shares traded) that comes into the move up, the more powerful the move.

Greed and, finally, euphoria (when buyers convince themselves "this baby can rise forever") propel uptrends. At higher highs during the uptrend, and particularly at the final expansion high of the cycle, we call the stock "overbought."

The nature of cycles, though, dictates that nothing goes up forever. When an uptrend starts gasping for breath because buyers close their wallets, the sellers step in. Many of these sellers are previous buyers from the stock's upward move who take profits. Others are short sellers, or bears, who bet the stock is ready to retrace or pullback; they want to profit from the drop. During the price pullback, volume typically decreases, indicating a momentary loss in the stock's popularity. Now, buyers wait in the wings for the perfect time to return to the game.

As long as the price retracement, or pullback, does not drop lower than the previous low in the trend, the stock technically remains in an uptrend. If,

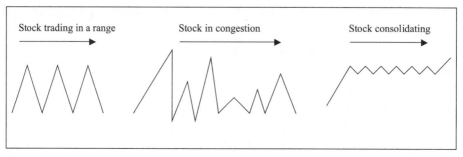

**FIGURE 6-2**

however, the previous low price on the trend is penetrated and broken decisively, technically speaking, the uptrend is over.

When the uptrend concludes, buyers and sellers even out in strength, and the cycle arcs into a sideways pattern. Traders call this movement "rolling over."

The stock may now move sideways for a period of time. Anytime a stock moves sideways, it makes one of three basic patterns. Each tells a different story. You can see the different patterns in simple line drawings in Figure 6-2.

If a stock "trades in a range," it fluctuates between higher and lower price areas in a somewhat predictable, horizontal channel. When it dips to the bottom of the range, or channel, buyers step in and support the price from slipping into a downtrend. When it reaches the top of the range, sellers step in and push the price down once again. Sellers who short at the top of the range "cover" their short positions (buy the stock back to close the trade) when it nears the bottom of the range, knowing buyers will surely step in and reverse the stock to higher prices.

Although most traders hot-foot it to stocks rocketing in uptrends to capture dramatic buying opportunities, or to downtrends to grab shorting opportunities, you may want to consider playing stocks trading in an orderly range. You can make nice chunks of change buying the dips and selling the rallies.

### Congestion

The second horizontal pattern—or lack of it—we call "congestion."

Say you have a cold, and your head feels miserable and congested. You can't breathe because your nose is all stuffed up. Stocks trading in a congestion pattern feel the same way. No uptrend or downtrend emerges (stock can't breathe) because buyers and sellers won't make up their minds which way this stock should go. Daily price ranges fluctuate from wide to narrow as the stock flounders unpredictably. It gaps open to the upside one day, then gaps to the downside, the next. Tactic: Stay away. You don't kiss your friends who have colds, and you don't trade stocks that trade in congestion patterns, unless you want your trading account to get sick.

### Consolidation

The third sideways pattern we label "consolidation." Learn to spot the pattern easily. Whether it appears on daily charts or intraday charts, it will become one of your best friends.

A consolidating stock is doing just that. It marches sideways across a chart in a compact, linear fashion. The price range for each candlestick is short, tight, and orderly. To you, as a trader, it means buyers and sellers are in an even heat, and pressure is building within the compressed price range. When it blows, the stock will move up or down in a fast, furious manner. That volatility can earn sweet profits for traders.

### Downtrends

When a stock tires of trading sideways, buyers jump ship. Short sellers attack like hungry sharks, and the stock tumbles into a downtrend.

A stock in a downtrend makes lower highs and lower lows. The trend remains lower until price closes above a prior high in the downtrend.

Stocks can slide into downtrends on lack of interest alone (low volume). But if volume picks up as the stock falls, that stock has problems. High volume on a falling stock means fear just escalated to panic. Everybody's dumping and heading for the door.

Whether the downtrend is orderly or panic-driven (long, black candlesticks), bears control the helm, and we say the stock is headed south. If you're like most traders and investors, you look elsewhere for greener pastures. Only grumbling, long-term investors and happy short sellers hang around a stock in a downtrend. For the shorts, (those holding short positions), the farther the unhappy stock tumbles, the richer they get. During the downtrend, and particularly near the bottom, we call the stock "oversold."

Nothing goes down ad infinitum. Well, almost nothing. I know of a handful of stocks that dropped to almost zero, but they gave early warning signs, and as a savvy trader, I'm sure you wouldn't have been within shouting distance of them.

If a stock represents a decent company that's fallen from grace because of poor, but fixable, fundamentals, or because it's a laggard in its industry group, it usually drops to the levels of its previous valley. There, we hope, sellers have mercy and buyers start nibbling again. It bases, or bottoms, then trades sideways until/if it gathers enough momentum to begin another uptrend. Then the cycle repeats itself.

Please understand, with the volatility so prevalent in today's market, high-flying stocks can go from an uptrend to a downtrend in a matter of minutes, nearly wiping out any sideways move. Likewise, they can reverse from a nasty downtrend to an exuberant uptrend quicker than you can say "ticker tape." It's still important, though, to understand the complete cycle so you can identify general pattern and trend changes as you study charts.

Point to remember: On charts, each candlestick represents the indicated time frame. When you look at a weekly chart, each candlestick represents one trading week. On daily charts, each candlestick represents one trading day. Intraday charts are the same: On 5-minute charts, each candlestick represents five

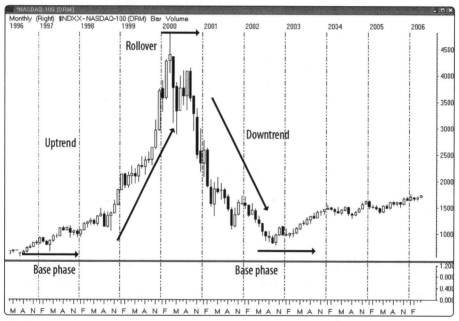

**FIGURE 6-3** | As you can see by this monthly chart (each candle represents one month) of the NASDAQ 100 Index, equities—and so the indices they form—move in cycles. Many times, full cycles are easier to see on long-term charts, such as monthly charts. Although variations in the cyles occur—valleys can be higher than the last, or lower—the theme stays the same:

1. A trough, or valley, where the stock/index bases; also called the accumulation phase.
2. The uptrend, or markup phase, consisting of higher highs and higher lows.
3. A topping formation, wherein the stock moves in a sideways pattern, and trades in a range; also called the distribution phase. This can last from days to months.
4. The downtrend, or mark-down phase, containing a series of lower highs and lower lows. After the downtrend completes its move, the stock begins another basing formation and the cycle repeats itself.

minutes; on thirty-minute charts, each candlestick represents thirty minutes; on
one-hour charts, each candlestick represents sixty minutes; and so forth.

Figures 6-3 through 6-10 illustrate examples of index and stock cycles. They
also show stocks trading in uptrends, downtrends, and the three basic sideways
patterns.

**FIGURE 6-4** | This monthly chart of the S&P 500 Index shows the completion of a cycle and the onset of a new one.
Most cycles form in approximately four years. When you study this chart, note the many candlestick patterns that formed at
the bottoms and tops of price moves and warned of reversals.

RealTick® graphics used with permission of Townsend Analytics, Ltd. © 1986-2007 Townsend Analytics, Ltd.

**FIGURE 6-5** | This daily chart of Varian Semiconductor (VSEA) shows the technology company making a relatively quick price cycle. The base formed in the last quarter of the year. In January, VSEA broke out to higher lows and higher highs. Note the shooting star in mid-February, which marked the end of that uptrend. VSEA capsized in late February, falling to lower lows. The downtrend continued until late March, until the bulls finally showed up and propelled the market higher, once again.

RealTick® graphics used with permission of Townsend Analytics, Ltd. © 1986-2007 Townsend Analytics, Ltd.

**FIGURE 6-6** | This daily chart of Google, Inc. (GOOG) displays a wild and wooly price cycle that spanned 180 points in six months. Note that the Internet information provider did not return (yet!) to its $300 price area. Cycles don't always form perfect parabolic curves. Many times price retraces only a percentage of the prior move up, or uptrend.

RealTick® graphics used with permission of Townsend Analytics, Ltd. © 1986-2007 Townsend Analytics, Ltd.

**FIGURE 6-7** | This daily chart of AmerisourceBergen Corp. (ABC) displays a stock in a strong uptrend. During the course of this uptrend, the pharmaceutical distributor gained 30%, without so much as a hiccup. This presents a good argument for including core stocks as position trades, or short-term investments in your second trading account.

RealTick® graphics used with permission of Townsend Analytics, Ltd. © 1986-2007 Townsend Analytics, Ltd.

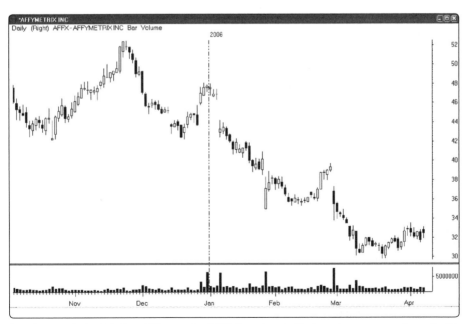

**FIGURE 6-8** | This daily chart of Affymetrix, Inc. (AFFX) shows the scientific electronics systems manufacturer in a big slide south. A couple of times during its tumble, poor AFFX gathered the energy to spike to the upside, creating "bull traps." Make a mental note not to get caught in these false breakouts by buying and holding a stock that's legally in a downtrend.

RealTick® graphics used with permission of Townsend Analytics, Ltd. © 1986-2007 Townsend Analytics, Ltd.

**FIGURE 6-9** | This daily chart of the American International Group, Inc. (AIG) shows the insurance giant trading in a horizontal trend, or range, between $65 and $70, from November through April. Except for a couple of jolts where traders might have gotten stopped out, a "buy the rallies, sell the dips" strategy, properly implemented, would have earned dandy profits.

RealTick® graphics used with permission of Townsend Analytics, Ltd. © 1986-2007 Townsend Analytics, Ltd.

## SUPPORT AND RESISTANCE: WHAT THEY ARE, HOW TO RECOGNIZE THEM

Support and resistance are perhaps the most widely used of all trading applications. As a trader, it's important you understand these concepts thoroughly. Every time you look at a chart—any chart—be it a one-minute chart or a daily chart, a chart of the E-mini S&P 500 futures, or the NASDAQ Composite, the first two questions that should pop into your mind are: Where is support? Where is resistance?

Support and resistance form an integral part of supply and demand. As you know, stock prices don't rise and fall of their own volition, or at the whimsy of an erratic computer or capricious trading god. Market players virtually draw price movements on charts as they buy and sell. Furthermore, these market players, you included, have memories. Human memory coupled with emotion and fundamental factors creates support and resistance.

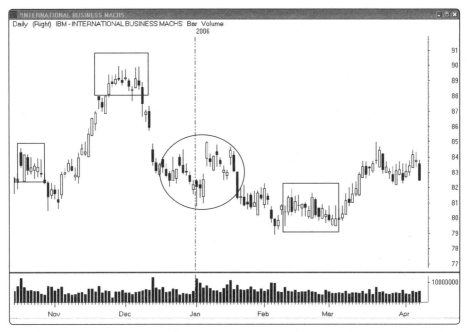

**FIGURE 6-10** | In this daily chart of International Business Machines (IBM), the candlesticks within the circle form a congestion pattern. As you can see, no discernible pattern emerged during this sideways movement. Savvy traders, especially those contemplating overnight holds, stay away from these disorderly price moves.

In the rectangles, IBM's price forms consolidation patterns. These tight sideways moves build up steam. When price breaks out to the upside or downside, the movement can be dramatic—or traumatic—depending which side of the trade you are on.

While we're looking at this chart, have you already spotted the dramatic price cycle that took place from November to January? If you examine the chart further, you'll see more mini cycles in the price pattern.

RealTick® graphics used with permission of Townsend Analytics, Ltd. © 1986-2007 Townsend Analytics, Ltd.

The stock in Figure 6-11 forms peaks and valleys as it trades in a range between $50 and $60. The pivot points created by price reversal form support and resistance.

Support and resistance are zones, or areas, not exact prices. Imagine you're standing on a tennis court, next to the net. Lean on the net and feel it stretch. Prices that form support zones or areas are like the net on a tennis court; they stretch a little, both ways.

Another way to think of support and resistance: You are standing in a room on the first floor of a two-story building, holding a large ball. The ball represents "price." You toss the ball up, and it hits the ceiling—resistance. Then it falls, lands, and bounces up from the floor—support. See Figure 6-12.

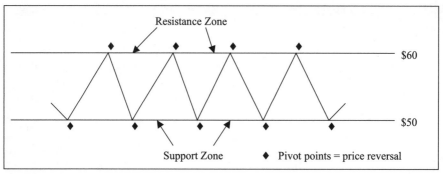

**FIGURE 6-11**

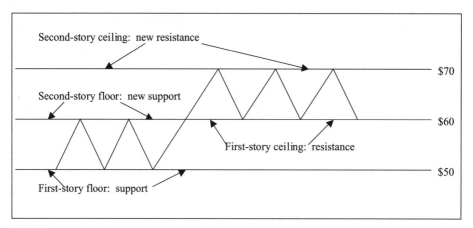

**FIGURE 6-12**

After the ball bounces from the floor to the ceiling a few times, you catch it and throw it up with all of your strength. It soars upward and flies through a hole in the ceiling, into the story above you. It continues to soar, then gradually loses velocity. When it falls, it lands on the floor above you and bounces up from that. The floor where it lands is the new support for the ball.

Notice how once the ball soars through the ceiling and finally falls, the ceiling becomes the new floor. Former price highs, formed by previous pivot points at $60, are now support. When, or if, the stock moves through the second-story ceiling at $70, $70 (give or take a point or two) becomes the new floor, or support.

Imagine the movement reversed, as in Figure 6-13. The ball bounces from the first floor to the ceiling a few times. Then you catch it and throw it down, through a hole in the floor. It falls into the basement. When it lands on the basement floor, it bounces. It rises back up toward the floor where you're standing, but it's too weak to propel itself any farther than the basement ceiling, which represents resistance.

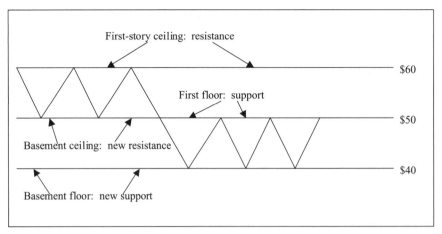

**FIGURE 6-13**

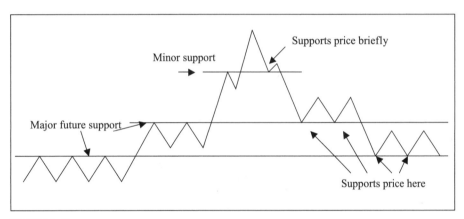

**FIGURE 6-14**

Figure 6-14 exhibits how, when a stock breaks below a major support area to sink even lower, it's usually in deep trouble. If it tests the support area only a couple of times during a short period of time and then violates it, that, in itself, is a negative signal. But if it bounces off the support many times during a long time period, and finally falls through it, that's an ultra-negative signal, and the stock's probably in for a deep decline. The more times it tests its support area, and the longer the time span it tests it, the more negative the signal if it does fall. (Think of a perpetual law-breaker. The first few times he's caught for his crimes, he's fined and put on probation. But if he continues to break the law, he's sent to prison.)

If the stock does fall into a deep decline, or downtrend, it will test previous support areas as it falls; it will also form new support areas.

Resistance is the mirror image of support. Resistance is also called "supply," and in trading rooms, the terms are used interchangeably. You already know why. It's the price where a stock's been before, then reversed. It's where all the previous buyers said, "If this doggoned stock ever crawls back up to what I paid for it, I'm selling!" Supply = resistance = lower prices.

Resistance is the "ceiling zone," where a stock will meet with sellers, at least temporarily. Yet a strong stock will keep bouncing up to that ceiling zone until it gathers enough velocity (buyers) to accelerate through it.

The more times a stock tests resistance, and the more extended time period it does so, the more bullish it is when it breaks through it.

Of course, as the stock advances, it forms more resistance along the way, either succumbing to previous resistance areas or creating fresh resistance by pulling back due to overall market conditions, news, or the reason that always wins, more sellers than buyers.

Figures 6-15 through 6-18 indicate support and resistance levels. Please study them and other charts from your own source in different time frames (weekly, daily, intraday), until you recognize support and resistance areas automatically.

**FIGURE 6-15** | On this daily chart of Marvell Technology (MRVL), notice how support and resistance play an important role in price movement. As you study the chart, note how price rises, and then pulls back. The top of the move forms resistance for the next move up. Once price moves above that resistance, that resistance formed new support.

Also take note of the candle pattern that culminated MRVL's three-month uptrend of 40 points—a shooting star. As the semiconductor stock moved down, it used prior support for a few days at a time—support that then formed resistance.

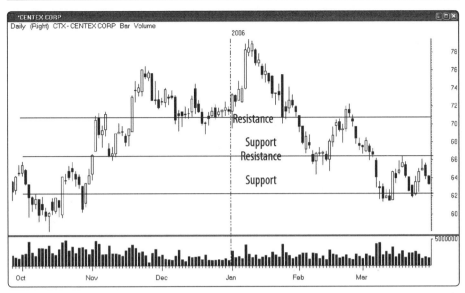

**FIGURE 6-16** | This daily chart of Centex Corp. (CTX) displays how the homebuilder moved in a complete price cycle from November to March. Note how the stock rose in an uptrend from late in October, and each time it pushed through prior resistance, and stepped above it, it then used that price as support for the next leg up. Poor CTX rolled over quickly in January, and though it held previous support (buyers) from November and December, the buyers refused to hold it up into February. CTX fell through that support period and fell to prior support from October. When that didn't hold, the stock fell to an even lower level of support.

RealTick® graphics used with permission of Townsend Analytics, Ltd. © 1986-2007 Townsend Analytics, Ltd.

**FIGURE 6-17** | This daily chart of Cisco Systems, Inc. (CSCO) displays the tech behemoth shooting from its January lows of about $17.75, to its current March highs of $22. Strong support areas worked to keep the stock moving higher. Now, though, CSCO has rolled over, and it remains to be seen if buyers will offer support, or if the networking and communications giant will slide even lower.

RealTick® graphics used with permission of Townsend Analytics, Ltd. © 1986-2007 Townsend Analytics, Ltd.

**FIGURE 6-18** | This daily chart of General Electric Co. (GE) shows the blue chip stock in a relatively undecided pattern, with definite moves to the downside and upside at various stages over the six-month period. Support and resistance, however, still play a role in how the stock behaved.

RealTick® graphics used with permission of Townsend Analytics, Ltd. © 1986-2007 Townsend Analytics, Ltd.

## MONEY-MAKING BREAKOUTS AND BREAKDOWNS: HOW TO IDENTIFY THEM

Breakouts and breakdowns in price can occur as continuations in uptrends or downtrends, or as trend reversals. These continuations, or reversals, are where the most momentum (price expansion) usually comes into play. As traders, we want to buy (or sell short) just before, or as the momentum begins, and take profits before, or as, it slows.

### Breakouts

When a stock breaks out, it turns upward from a sideways move or pullback and rockets through resistance to a new high. It's the same move shown in Figure 6-12 when the ball shoots through the hole in the ceiling. You'll find that breakouts create excellent buying opportunities for all trading time frames, from momentum and day trades to initiating core trades.

### *Breakout Steps*

1. The leading breakout: the moment the stock moves above key resistance (when the ball shoots through the hole in the first-story ceiling). If the

resistance is at $60, you buy when the stock trades—not when it's shown at the ask on a Level II screen, but when an actual trade takes place—say at $60.05 or $60.10. The first strong move above resistance—some traders wait for an actual close—is the breakout point. The best leading breakouts are fueled by strong volume.

2. The pullback: As profit-taking sets in, the stock hits resistance (second-story ceiling) and reverses, pulling back toward the breakout price. When the selling recedes and buyers jump back in, the price pivots (reverses) and heads north (up) again. The moment the price recovers from the pullback and moves up again, it initiates the second entry, or buying point. This is the safest place to buy because the leading breakout established the stock has buyers.

3. The secondary breakout: Now the stock shoots up again, past its former pivot point (second-story ceiling). It accelerates through a hole in the second-story ceiling and flies into the third story. For day traders trading on intraday charts, this point may come late in the afternoon, and price momentum may be slowing. Swing traders using daily charts can buy the third leg or swing up in a trend, although momentum may slow, as well.

> **HOT TIP**
>
> When stocks move through a whole number, and especially a round number, such as $60, they will sometimes scoot above the number and stay there for a few minutes, only to tumble back down through it, again. So, don't jump the gun. If you trade on short-term intraday charts (5 to 15 minute charts), wait for the candle to close above the round number before you jump in.

Figure 6-19 show the three steps in a breakout. When the breakout steps complete the pattern shown in Figure 6-19, the stock has moved out of a trading range and into an uptrend.

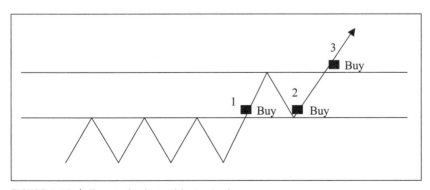

**FIGURE 6-19** | Three step breakout with buying signals.

Figures 6-20 through 6-23 show examples of breakouts in the 1, 2, 3 pattern on daily and intraday charts. Remember, whether you apply it to a daily chart, or an intraday chart, the entry points on the pattern stay the same.

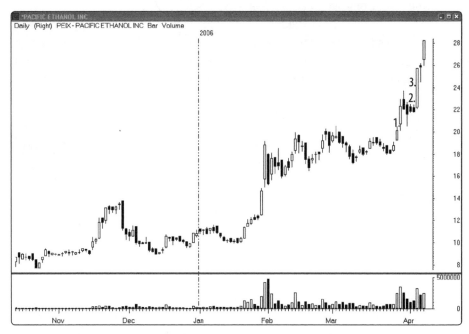

**FIGURE 6-20** | On this daily chart of Pacific Ethanol, Inc. (PEIX), you can see a perfect 1, 2, 3 breakout in the month of April, although the producer of renewable fuels had broken out of its earlier base in January. The nearly perfect breakout pattern that's good to recognize is the spectacular April pattern.

1. PEIX broke above its consolidation—a buy signal at $20. As you'll learn in later chapters, the immensely strong volume would have told traders to buy a few cents before.
2. The stock flew to 23, then neatly pulled back to 22. When PEIX started to rise out of that pullback, it initiated another buy signal.
3. When PEIX penetrated resistance created at the top of the first leg up (23), the position could be added to, if conditions warranted.

There are other breakouts on this chart that initiated nice moves up (hint: January). Notice the support and resistance levels, and decide where you might enter and exit trades.

RealTick® graphics used with permission of Townsend Analytics, Ltd. © 1986-2007 Townsend Analytics, Ltd.

**FIGURE 6-21** | On this 15-minute chart of Psychiatric Solutions, Inc. (PSYS), the breakout pattern emerged halfway into the trading day on 4/06.

1. After lunch, the operator of psychiatric inpatient hospitals stock broke out of its intraday base and gave a buy signal at about 30.60.
2. The stock stopped to rest and consolidate at 30.90
3. PSYS broke out again in the last half-hour of the day to close on the high of the day (31.20) on high volume.

If you hold stocks overnight, you'd be glad you held this one. On an intraday trade, if you bought at 30.60 and sold at 31.20, you would have earned about .80 per share. While that's a tidy profit, traders who held the stock overnight (the dotted line marks the close of one day, and the open of the next) and rode the opening leg up would have made about .50 more per share. Clue: When a stock closes at the high of the day on strong volume, many times they will move higher at the next morning's open. This is especially true if the stock market is in a bullish mode and the industry group where your stock resides is moving in an uptrend on a daily and/or weekly chart.

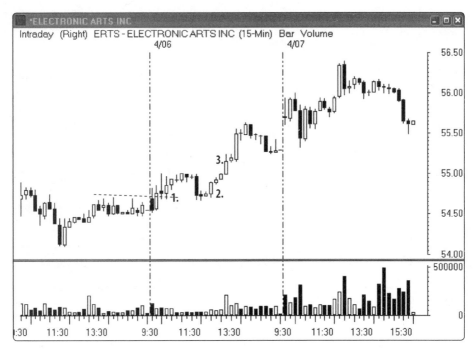

**FIGURE 6-22** | On this 15-minute chart of Electronic Arts, Inc. (ERTS), you can see how this maker of interactive software games broke of its prior day's lethargy during the first half-hour of 4/06.

1. The break above resistance was the buy signal, at 54.68. ERTS rose to 55, then pulled back to 54.67 on low volume.
2. Although the pullback was orderly and on low volume (we'll learn more about volume signals, later), it surely made traders nervous who held their shares as a day trade. ERTS held on the top of prior support, though (see dotted line). And, as the lunchtime doldrums came to an end, ERTS woke up and resumed its move higher.
3. At about 1:45 p.m., ERTS broke above its 55 intraday high, to rise to 55.63 at 2:25 p.m. With a point profit (per share) firmly in hand, wise day traders would take profits.

I extended the chart so you could see how volatile stocks can become when they diverge, or move in the opposite direction, from their "home" index. On 4/07, the NASDAQ fell hard. Notice how ERTS managed to climb all morning, then gave into the tech index's bad mood in the afternoon. Many times a stock that is trading against the intraday market trend will have the energy to buck that trend in morning hours, but will then succumb to the larger trend in the afternoon session.

RealTick® graphics used with permission of Townsend Analytics, Ltd. © 1986-2007 Townsend Analytics, Ltd.

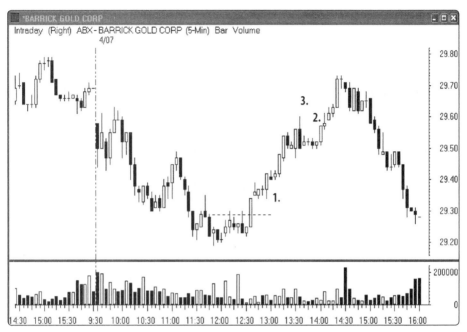

**FIGURE 6-23** | In this 5-minute chart of Barrick Gold Corp. (ABX), you can see a momentum trade on a small time frame (each candle represents five minutes), using a textbook 1, 2, 3 breakout pattern.

1. The gold mining and refining stock moved in a steep intraday downtrend, to stop and create a quick base. ABX then started rising at 12:30 P.M., and broke out of its base at 29.28. It ripped through the prior high at 29.50 and stopped to consolidate right at 29.55.
2. At 2:25 P.M. ABX started up again, and traders could have added to their position.
3. Soon after the breakout of the pullback, the gold stock broke above the consolidation highs at 29.58. Additional shares could have been added. By 2:30 P.M., ABX hit 29.75 (the prior day's closing price), and created a doji followed by a dark cloud cover. Savvy momentum traders took profits.

**Breakdowns**

Breakdowns are the opposite of breakouts. When a stock breaks down as it does in Figure 6-24, it penetrates its support base from its trading range or rally, and tumbles to a new low.

Breakdowns create excellent shorting opportunities. We'll talk about exact shorting techniques later in the book, but for now, here's a quick definition of selling short: If you think a stock is going to head lower and decrease in price value, you can "short" a position. You sell shares on the open market and then buy them back at (hopefully) the lower price. Your profit is the difference between the price you sold the shares, and the price at which you bought them back (covered the position).

*Breakdown Steps*

1. The breakdown: the moment the stock moves below key resistance (when the ball drops through the hole in the floor). If the resistance is at $60, you sell short the stock right as it trades below $60.
2. The stock may decline to its next support area, then bounce, or rally. This rally is the same as a pullback in a breakout, only in the opposite direction. Soon the bears regain control, the bulls surrender, and the stock resumes its downward fall. This is the safest point to short a falling stock.
3. When the price drops below the last support, or pivot point (basement floor), it may be too late to enter for a day trade, but swing traders can still sell short here.

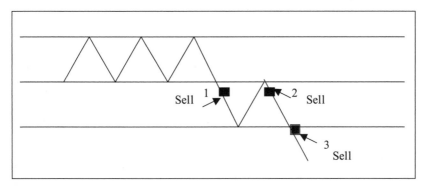

**FIGURE 6-24** | Three step breakdown with sell-short signals.

Figures 6-25 through 6-28 show breakdowns on daily and intraday charts. Despite differences in the time frame, the pattern is always the same.

**FIGURE 6-25** | This daily chart of Vertex Pharmaceuticals, Inc. (VRTX) shows the stock in a dandy uptrend from October until March—in fact, it doubled in price. Then the drug manufacturer weakened and started to tumble.

1. It fell through support (and gave a sell signal) on March 23, at 36.95 (long, black candle). In the next three days, VRTX fell to 34.68.
2. The pharma (current nickname for pharmaceutical companies) stock rallied back to prior support zone at 37, which had now become resistance. After six days of consolidating, it headed south again, issuing another sell (short) signal.
3. On the same day (4/06), it quickly slid below its prior low of 34.68, issuing yet another sell-short signal. In the next two days, the stock plunged to 31.

Know, please that pharma and biotech stocks can be highly volatile, so holding a short position more than 2–3 days can cause heartburn. Manage these positions carefully. Biotechs, especially, tend to hop up or fall down according to the clinical trials being conducted on their products. That's why you'll notice that many times their price patterns diverge from their own industry group as well as broader market action.

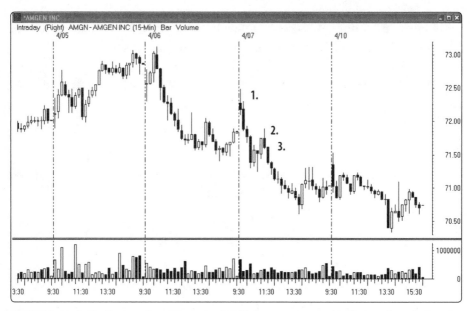

**FIGURE 6-26** | This 15-minute chart of Amgen, Inc. (AMGN) shows many opportunities for day trades to the short side. If you studied a daily chart of this global biotech company—which you would do before you entered a trade on any time frame—you'd see that AMGN is currently falling in a downtrend.

1. After skidding dramatically the day before, the biotech managed to gap open higher on this day (4/07) at 72.28 and fly to a high of 72.49. But sellers quickly came in and pounded the stock back to the prior day's close at 71.85, and even lower to 71.25.
2. AMGN rebounded to the prior day's close, but it was a classic bull trap, and the bears once again pounded the bulls. In this case, you'd add to your position to short AMGN below the low of the high candle (the black one).
3. AMGN plummeted below the first low of the day (71.25) that represented the only support. But buyers put their hands behind their backs as the bears took control and continued to push lower. Smart traders covered their short positions when the biotech stock hesitated at 70.60, then headed higher.

RealTick® graphics used with permission of Townsend Analytics, Ltd. © 1986-2007 Townsend Analytics, Ltd.

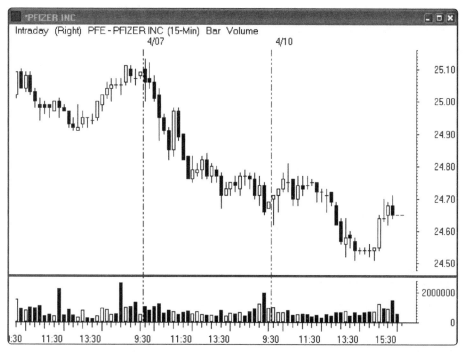

**FIGURE 6-27** | This 15-minute chart of Pfizer, Inc. (PFE) shows the stock in a well-defined downtrend. If you looked at a daily chart of this manufacturer of pharmaceutical and consumer healthcare products, you'd see that it's in a downtrend in that larger time frame, as well. On 4/07, PFE etched a nearly perfect 1, 2, 3 breakdown pattern on its intraday chart. An aside on pharmaceutical stocks: Pharms are "defensive" stocks. During economic downturns, many investors will run to the Consumer Staples sector, which includes health care (pharmaceuticals, biotechs, and medical equipment), food, household goods, personal care, and cosmetic companies.

RealTick® graphics used with permission of Townsend Analytics, Ltd. © 1986-2007 Townsend Analytics, Ltd.

**FIGURE 6-28** | This 5-minute chart of the mini-sized Dow, which is the small version of the standard Dow Jones Industrial Index futures contract, traded on the Chicago Board of Trade. We'll talk more about the "mini Dow," as traders call it, in upcoming chapters. For now, let's look at the breakdown that occurred during the course of this trading day.

1. The mini Dow rose to its intraday high of 11,242, then it chopped sideways into the lunch period. At 12:30 P.M., it began its breakdown, falling through the support zone established by the consolidation top, and sliding to prior support from earlier that morning.
2. Note how quickly the mini Dow surrendered and slipped off this "consolidation cliff" at 11,215, then held again for another 5-minute candle at 11,210.
3. When the mini index approached the prior support area, it fell past it. Still, with upcoming support perched just below, wise traders wouldn't have added many more contracts to this short position. As you can see, by 2:30 P.M., buying came back into the futures contract.

RealTick® graphics used with permission of Townsend Analytics, Ltd. © 1986-2007 Townsend Analytics, Ltd.

## HOT TIP

Some traders insist that if a stock corrects sideways—as opposed to falling back toward the breakout point—it's stronger and odds are the move up will be powerful. Others say it doesn't matter. Just be aware that when the price moves sideways, the buyers are supporting it by holding—not selling—which in itself is a positive signal.

A stock corrects itself in one of two ways: (1) by moving sideways, or consolidating, or (2) by pulling back. In the case of a downtrend, we call the pullback a "rebound" or "rally."

Either way, if the stock pulls back without falling through support at the breakout point, then turns back up, this is an excellent time to add to your position.

If, however, when the stock pulls back it drops below support, all bets are off. This signals you to exit—fast.

**HOT TIP**

Things that go straight up come straight down. That includes stocks. If you hang on to a stock that zooms toward the moon for more than two days, the return trip straight down—with no buyers in sight—will make a much more exciting trip than you had planned!

## HOW TO DRAW TRENDLINES
## OR WHERE TO CONNECT THE DOTS

It's important to get into the habit of automatically establishing trendlines. You can draw them mentally by eyeing the chart, or physically, by drawing the line with your trendline charting tool.

Officially, you can draw a trendline on a chart by connecting two lows or two highs, using the same technique we use to identify support and resistance on sideways moves. We're going to be more explicit, though, with our uptrends and downtrends, so they are even more exact.

Properly drawn trendlines are fundamental to technical analysis and essential tools for every trader and investor.

➤ They act as uptrend support lines, or downtrend resistance lines. They demonstrate where a stock's current trend is expected to go if it continues, and give you a boundary of trend breaks, or rising, or falling angles.

➤ Trendlines can make excellent, if somewhat tight, stop-loss points.

➤ Channel lines are parallel lines drawn along the tops of uptrend price patterns, and along the bottom of downtrend price patterns. Traders also use channel lines (if they can be applied to an established trend with an orderly price pattern) as profit-taking points, when the price touches it. (You'll see examples of this in upcoming charts.)

To draw a trendline for an uptrend, find the lowest low near the bottom of the trend. Next, look for the major low prior to the highest high. Connect the pivots, as in Figure 6-29.

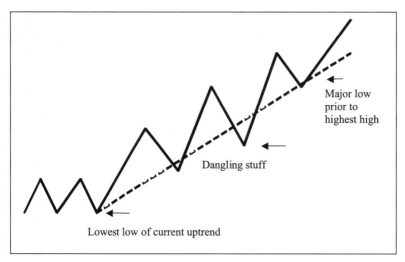

**FIGURE 6-29** | Draw an uptrend line.

If the price bounces off your advancing trendline three times or more, regard the trendline as a major trendline, and highly significant support (uptrend) or resistance (downtrend). When, or if, the price penetrates the rising trendline and closes below it, that's obviously negative and could predict an upcoming shift or reversal. When price slices through a falling trendline and closes above it, it's positive; the stock could gather strength for a shift in the downtrend, or even reversal to the upside.

Trends can change angles and still remain trending up, or down. A typical example would be a trend that rises out of a base and continues higher at a 45-degree angle for days to weeks, pulls back or consolidates, then resumes at a 60-degree angle—shooting higher on euphoria. During those trend shifts, you'll need to draw new trendlines for your analysis.

Sometimes you'll have to draw a trendline through a bit of dangling stuff. "Dangling stuff" is my technical term for a temporary price drop in an uptrend, or spike up in a downtrend that violates the trendline for a candlestick or two. You'll note that on a few charts, I've drawn trendlines right through some candle shadows that interfered with more consistent prices.

In cases like these, learn to step back and observe the big picture. The more volatile stocks become, the more you take errant price spikes into consideration.

Note that in Figure 6-29 even though the dangling stuff prices defied the trendline, both times the lows were still higher than the previous lows. That's the criterion to remember. Since the definition of an uptrend is a stock making higher highs and higher lows, a trendline like the one in Figure 6-29 is not officially broken until a previous low is surpassed. When that happens, the trend is at an end.

While you're looking at trends, remember, an uptrend is an uptrend, whatever time frame you're trading in. Are you looking through binoculars at a weekly chart, or a microscope on a one-minute chart? It doesn't matter. An uptrend has the same definition.

For a valid uptrend, the candlesticks must advance with higher highs and higher lows. Three or more touches to the trendline make the line more important. If the stock breaks below its uptrend line and that's where you've placed your stop—sell and beat a hasty retreat.

For position trades and some swing trades, the best-behaving stocks trend up at about a 45-degree angle on a daily chart. Those that trend up steeper than 45-degrees are great for some swing trades, or day and momentum trades. Since you pay close attention to these trades, you'll follow your plan with profit targets and stop-loss orders.

The sleepy stocks that trend up somewhere between horizontal and below 40-degrees don't appeal to most traders because the low volatility doesn't deliver profits quickly. On the other hand, if you're busy with other occupations, these slow-rising stocks can be reliable for steady gains, minus the heartburn that goes along with trading missile-like stocks.

To draw a trendline on a stock in a downtrend, find the highest peak, or pivot point above the lowest low. Next, locate the highest peak at the top of the trend. Connect the dots as in Figure 6-30.

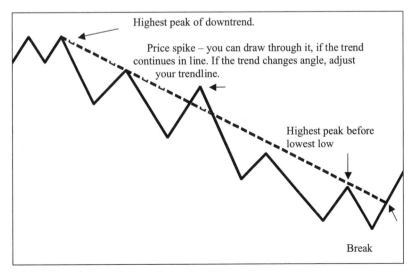

**FIGURE 6-30** | Draw a downtrend line.

Notice that when the stock tried to break above the trendline, but couldn't sustain it, that false breakout high was still lower than the previous high. Since the definition of a downtrend is a stock making lower highs and lower lows, a trendline like the one in Figure 6-30 is not officially broken until a previous high is surpassed. When that does happen, all short sellers should beat a hasty retreat.

Figures 6-31 through 6-37 show a selection of stocks in uptrends and down-trends, with trendlines drawn. You will want to draw more lines, perhaps adding channel lines, and horizontal support and resistance lines.

After you study these, go to your own chart source. Flip through, identifying stocks in uptrends and downtrends. Pinpoint stocks trading in a range, as well as moving in congestion and consolidation patterns. Locate stocks breaking up, and breaking down. Where will you draw support and resistance lines? Up or down trendlines?

Analyze charts until the preceding concepts are firmly etched in your brain—or you start to snore—whichever comes first.

**FIGURE 6-31** | On this daily chart of the Centex Corp. (CTX), you can see an example of an entire price cycle that took place from October through April, and isn't over yet. We drew an uptrend line from near the lows of the uptrend (I don't always count single candle shadows as lows, when many lows line up in a row (dotted line). The homebuilder fell though its uptrend line in late November, and drifted down into the end of the year. In January, CTX again started a euphoric rise, shooting nearly straight up to its high of $79.40. But euphoria has its price, and poor CTX has fallen ever since.

To avoid confusion, I've drawn only a single uptrend line, and a single downtrend line. Many more support and resistance lines can be drawn on this chart. Since it's your book, you can draw all over it.

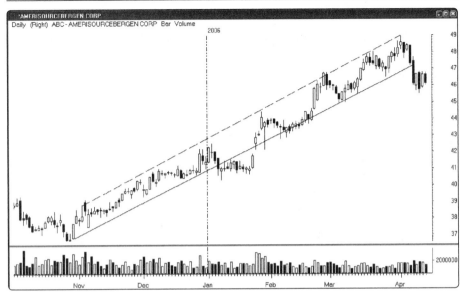

**FIGURE 6-32** | On this daily chart of AmerisourceBergen Corp. (ABC), the pharmaceutical distributor moved in a near perfect uptrend from November to April. Then the neighbors called the cops on the merrymakers, and the party was over, at least for the time being. This chart shows you how uptrends can hesitate (January) and consolidate sideways for a period of time without actually breaking the trend. (ABC did not make a lower low at this point.) Some swing traders use the top channel line as a sell signal: when the price touches it, and doesn't go through it, they sell their position.

RealTick® graphics used with permission of Townsend Analytics, Ltd. © 1986-2007 Townsend Analytics, Ltd.

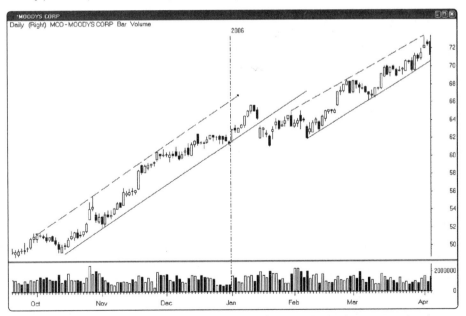

**FIGURE 6-33** | This daily chart of Moody's Corp. (MCO) shows how the provider of credit ratings stepped neatly up an uptrend for six months, and is still going to date. Note how uptrends can shift slightly, due to pullbacks. While the uptrend, itself, wasn't broken dramatically, in the January/February pullback it caused new trendlines and channel lines to be drawn.

RealTick® graphics used with permission of Townsend Analytics, Ltd. © 1986-2007 Townsend Analytics, Ltd.

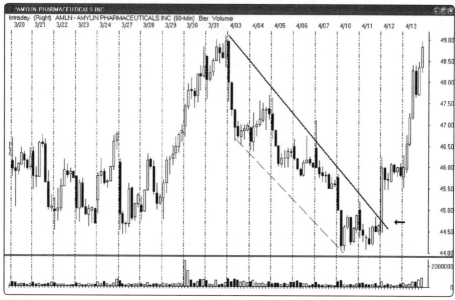

**FIGURE 6-34** | On this 60-minute (each bar represents one-hour) chart of Amylin Pharmaceuticals, Inc. (AMLN), you can see how the temperamental biopharma company chopped sideways for a few days, then rose in a missle-like uptrend from 44.50 to 49, where it topped out and fell to 44. It formed a short-term base, then popped back up from support at 44—back to 49 once again (and who knows where, from here). Note how you can use trendlines for entry signals: When AMLN broke its downtrend line (arrow) and began to move above resistance, short-term traders could have bought and held, keeping profits intact with a trailing stop. (We'll talk about trailing stop orders in upcoming chapters.)

RealTick® graphics used with permission of Townsend Analytics, Ltd. © 1986-2007 Townsend Analytics, Ltd.

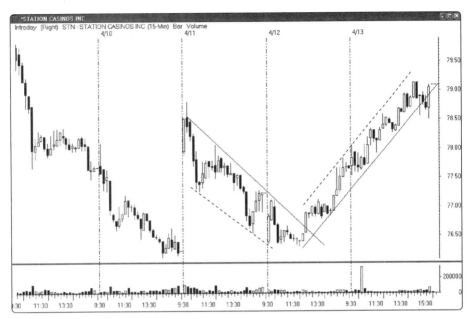

**FIGURE 6-35** | This 15-minute chart of Station Casinos, Inc. (STN) shows the volatile stock moving down in a nasty four-point downtrend (4/09 – 4/10). You can draw the trendline on this one. Then, the next day (4/11), the wild and woolly hotel/casino operator gapped open nearly two points, scaring the daylights out of the bears. But on the second candle into the day, STN once again started falling and slid back to 76.25. On 4/12, the stock rattled around all morning, then reversed direction, breaking its short-term trendline. The bears lumbered off for good, this time, as the energetic bulls grabbed the reigns and took STN back to 79. Note: Observing the break of the downtrend line on 4/12 would have warned you to close any short positions, and possibly enter a long one.

RealTick® graphics used with permission of Townsend Analytics, Ltd. © 1986-2007 Townsend Analytics, Ltd.

**FIGURE 6-36** | This 5-minute chart of the mini-sized Dow futures contract shows it moving into an uptrend shortly after the equities market opened at 9:30 A.M., ET. (This futures contract trades nearly around the clock.) The "Yummy," as we sometimes call it (the contract's root symbol is YM), moved up smartly and we could connect two lows (lowest and next higher low) by 10:45 A.M. The contract moved up until about 11:15, created a shooting star, and then started down. Important: Trendlines act as support while price is in an uptrend, but if price falls below that trendline, the trendline then acts as resistance. Notice how the uptrend line—extended—acted as resistance after the mini Dow contract moved below it. Just remember to check with trend positioning and support and resistance levels on a daily chart before you jump into any stock on an intraday level. The longer the timeframe, the stronger the signal.

RealTick® graphics used with permission of Townsend Analytics, Ltd. © 1986-2007 Townsend Analytics, Ltd.

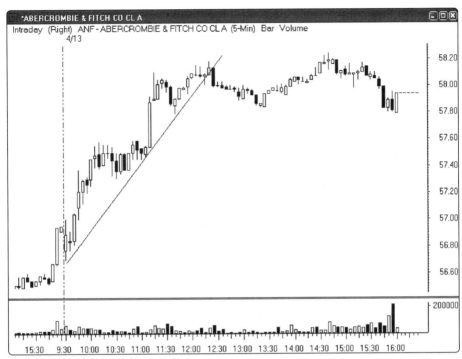

**FIGURE 6-37** | This 5-minute chart of Abercrombie & Fitch Co. (ANF) shows the stock gapping down a few cents at the open on 4/13, then turning to fly up in a strong uptrend for the first half-hour of the trading day (momentum traders would have closed positions, here, with a profit of .70 per share). From that high, the clothing manufacturer consolidated until 11:30; then it took off again, until noon. If you'd drawn an uptrend line from the opening low to the lows of the consolidation, and then extended it, you could have used it as a "sell signal" for a day trade, when ANF finally violated it at about 12:30 P.M. From this illustration and those previous to it, you can see how trendlines are extremely valuable trading tools, both on long-term timeframes, such as daily and weekly charts, and short-term timeframes or intraday charts.

# QUIZ
||||||||||||||||||

*Questions*

1. What three directions can stocks move?

2. Define the conditions of an uptrend.

3. What human emotions motivate an uptrend?

4. What three basic chart patterns come into play when a stock trades sideways? Give a brief definition of each.

5. What trading technique works successfully with stocks trading in a reasonably orderly range?

6. What trading tactic do you use when a stock is in a congestion pattern?

7. Define a stock price in a downtrend.

8. True or false? Support and resistance prices are firm, exact numbers, and must be treated as such.

9. If a strong stock rises through a resistance level and trades above it, then that resistance level automatically becomes _____.

10. If a stock rises off a support area several times during an extended period of time, and then tumbles below it, is this a positive or a negative signal?

11. Describe the three steps of a breakout.

12. When a breakdown occurs, what type of trader starts drooling? What trading tactic will that trader use?

*Answers*

1. Up, down, and sideways
2. A stock in an uptrend makes higher highs and higher lows.
3. Optimism, greed, and euphoria
4. In a range, congestion, and consolidation. Trading in a range means the stock trades in a fairly predictable pattern, rising and falling between upper and lower, horizontal channel lines. Congestion means no definable trend emerges. The price gaps up and down, price is helter-skelter, and traders should stay away. Consolidation means the stock trades in a tight, orderly price range and may be preparing to initiate a strong move either up or down.
5. Stocks trading in an even, orderly range are prime candidates for the trading tactic known as buying the dips and selling the rallies.
6. The trading tactic we apply to stocks forming a congestion pattern is to *stay away*.
7. A stock in a downtrend makes lower highs and lower lows.
8. False. Support and resistance prices denote areas or zones that must be allowed to expand according to stock's volatility.
9. support
10. Negative. The more times a stock bounces off support, and the more extended the time period, the more negative the signal when or if it falls below that support.
11. (1) The leading breakout occurs when the stock pushes up and out of a base and above previous resistance. Strong volume makes this move more powerful. This is the most profitable time to buy. (2) The pullback is when sellers come in to take profits and price consolidates or drops (pulls back) in an orderly fashion, and stays above the prior base area. Soon, though, the bulls take over again, and the stock resumes its upward climb. This is the safest time to buy. (3) The next breakout occurs when the stock trades above the prior high created by the first breakout run.
12. Traders who drool over breakdowns are bears. They make money by selling the stock short and betting on its subsequent fall in price.

## CENTER POINT: COINCIDENCE OR SYNCHRONICITY?

*"The basics of belief in synchronicity are that every single life has a purpose and a deeper meaning than we are generally aware of. Behind all form is an intelligence that is exquisitely perfect, and that works in synchronized fashion. Everything happens for a purpose, and the puzzle pieces of life fit together perfectly. When you trust and know these thoughts, you will daily recognize evidence for your belief in synchronicity."*

—Wayne Dyer, *You'll See It When You Believe It*

How many times have you lifted the telephone receiver and suddenly known who was on the other end of the line before you said, "Hello"? Or how many times have you thought of someone you've not seen in a while, only to have that person appear in your life the same day?

At a deeper level, have you ever looked back at your life and realized that at the moment you struggled most in a difficult situation, the right person or occurrence appeared out of nowhere to help you over the rough spots? Or have you endured a tough situation that ultimately led to new and surprising opportunities?

Some of us call incidents such as these "coincidence." Maybe they were. I believe they occurred through the process known as "synchronicity."

Carl Jung first described synchronicity as "the simultaneous occurrence of two meaningfully but not causally connected events."

The Earth orbits perfectly around the sun; it does not fly off on a path of its own to destruction. Gravity holds each of us on the planet equally, not in spotty chaos. When left alone, nature operates in exquisite synergy, totally synchronized.

If our environment is so perfectly arranged, is it possible our lives are also? Is it possible that each of our lives has an intrinsic purpose? And that each life is orchestrated by an intelligence that works through perfect synchronization to bring about our progression according to a grander plan?

To understand the phenomenon of synchronicity, most of us have to suspend some of our old beliefs that life is random and chaotic. The next step is to become aware of the synchronous events that take place in our lives, welcome and enjoy them as supportive occasions, and trust in them as a wondrous component of our existence.

# CHAPTER 7

# Choose a Stock to Trade

One day, very early in my trading career, the market was in dire shape. To capitalize on this, I found a weak stock sliding into a breakdown. Then, I sold it short at the perfect entry point. Sitting back, I watched with satisfaction as the market continued its freefall, dragging the stock with it.

Suddenly, with no explanation, my stock suddenly made a U-turn. It reversed, shot straight up, passed key resistance, screamed through the day's high and headed for the stars. In shock, I covered the position.

I traded in an office in New York with a group of traders, so I jumped up and ran over to Greg Capra, a great technical analyst.

I tapped Greg on the shoulder. "I just shorted the ugliest stock in town. It fell like a sack of rocks. Then, for no reason, it recovered. Now it's making new highs. Could you please look at it and tell me what happened?"

As other traders crowded behind me, Greg brought up the stock chart on one of five computer screens he stared at all day. He studied the chart, and we all waited expectantly. Surely he'd give us an explanation of intricate technical rhetoric, laced with indicators and oscillators that would explain this stock's bizarre behavior.

Finally, Greg looked up at me, his brown eyes twinkling behind his glasses. "More buyers than sellers."

"Huh?" Traders standing behind me echoed my keen reply.

"That's it," he said, turning back to his monitors. "More buyers than sellers."

Oh.

His message: Keep it simple.

With all the computerized information we have at our fingertips, it's easy to get caught up in the "paralysis of analysis." If you apply too many chart tools to a stock or market index, you can analyze yourself into a corner.

In this chapter and those that follow, you'll learn different indicators and oscillators that have great predictive value. Still, don't cram them all onto one chart. As you begin to trade, choose two or three—at the most—that work for you, and leave the others to experiment with at a later time.

## 🔥 HOT TIP

You're scanning daily charts. Suddenly, you notice one of your favorite stocks. It's in a basing period, but just grew a volume spike so tall, you nearly trip over it. More mysterious, the high-volume day didn't push the price higher. You check news sources to justify the volume, but no announcements have been made. Translation: "Big volume/little price rise/no news" days may mean institutions are quietly accumulating, rumors leaked of pending news, or insiders (the company's corporate officers) buying. Whatever the reason, watch it closely and be prepared to enter quickly if it meets your breakout criteria. When nudged by buying support, these stocks tend to skyrocket—fast.

In other words, keep it simple. If you get confused and find yourself tangled in a maze of information, stop. Back up and look at the big picture. What are the bare essentials? Are there more buyers than sellers? The stock will go up. Are there more sellers than buyers? The stock will go down. Ninety percent of the time, to trade well, one of those answers is all you'll need to know.

## VOLUME: A SIMPLE INDICATOR THAT SAYS A LOT

As you've seen in previous charts, volume is displayed in bar form at the bottom of charts. The bars show the number of shares traded for each corresponding candlestick above it.

Level II screens don't tell all. Only a percentage of actual orders in play line up in the bid and ask columns. Institutions make behind-the-scenes trades with each other frequently.

As well, if broker Goldman Sachs receives a large order from one of its institutional clients to purchase a large block of stock, Goldman doesn't post the entire order on the bid screen at one time, for everyone to see.

Instead, the broker slips in and out of the market. He slowly purchases small blocks of the stock, careful not to alert the other market players; he doesn't want them to raise their prices. Now, while Goldman can hide his true intentions momentarily, he cannot hide his accumulation of this large order from the volume bar.

Volume is a fantastic indicator of momentum, or lack of it. It's one of the only predictive tools we have that is not a derivative of price. And, that's valuable information. Moving averages, momentum indicators, oscillators, Fibonacci retracements, and indeed most charting tools come from calculating price action in different formulas. Volume does not. Volume is a separate "voice" in and of itself. Think of it as getting a second opinion on future price direction. The more I've learned to interpret the signals volume gives and to correlate them with price action, the more that knowledge has increased my bottom line.

Reading volume is a skill you can only acquire over time. While you can quickly grasp and use basic volume concepts and signals, only time and experience—and staring at boatloads of charts—teach you how to absorb the fine distinctions volume displays.

Volume Rule: When volume expands, price expands higher or lower. When volume contracts, price contracts. When volume expands and price does not, it's referred to as "price/volume divergence." You can expect that volume expansion to show up shortly in upcoming price movement.

In the last chapter, we emphasized that high volume powers successful breakouts and breakdowns. When you notice increased volume on a chart, the higher the bar spikes, the more emotion (greed) you're looking at. If it accompanies a strong breakout above key resistance, voracious buyers are gobbling as many shares as possible. If increased volume coincides with a breakdown that penetrates support, then glutinous short sellers are having a field day, and terrified "longs" are dumping and heading for the door (fear).

**HOT TIP**

Joe Granville, a well-known technician who created the popular On-Balance Volume indicator, said, "Volume precedes price."

A stock experiencing a robust uptrend shows steady volume on positive days. The breakout day may be the highest volume day of the price swing. The following days in the upswing can still soar higher, but on a little less volume. Why? Because, as the stock rises in price, traders are less likely to sell their shares. That means fewer shares for sale—so demand easily chews through supply.

If it's a healthy uptrend, as seen in Figure 7-1, you'll see volume shrink on consolidation or pullback days. Apply this to the time frame you're trading in— if you're trading from an intraday chart, strong volume fuels the white breakout candlestick(s) and the upswing candles that follow. Lower volume should allow the subsequent candles to form an orderly pullback, or consolidation.

Warning: When you see high volume on the pullback days (or intraday candles) in the context of an uptrend, it means the stock is being sold as heavily as it was accumulated on the breakout day.

Here's another warning that applies many times to small-cap stocks, although it's true in larger-cap stocks, as well. When you see a stock shoot higher on big volume, then reverse and implode on equally large volume, this action typically

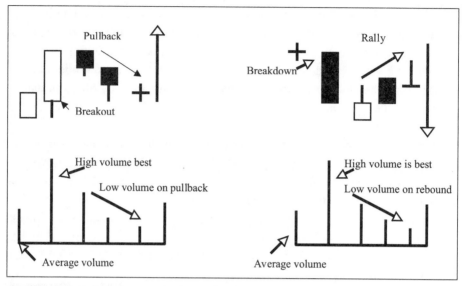

**FIGURE 7-1** | Ideal volume setups on breakouts and breakdowns.

comes into a quiet stock inflated by a single electric news item (think earnings, upgrades, downgrades, buyout rumors). Traders buy fast, run it up, then snatch profits and run. Those asleep at the wheel (no stop-loss orders), who thought they had a sweet swing or core trade in place, go slack-jawed when the pullback continues to slide downhill and tumbles below the original breakout point.

Beware of low-volume breakouts. Odds are they will fail. Why? Light volume on a breakout means it's not supported by an increasing amount of buyers. Even though it breaks to the upside over resistance, the stock still doesn't have the power to rise (buyers are not committed) and follow through to the upside. If you accidentally jump into a breakout with low or average volume on the breakout candlestick and the stock looks wobbly, immediately take a quick profit and look for greener pastures.

This scenario applies to intraday trades, especially those made during the lunch period: Stock is in an uptrend on the day, and now consolidating in a tight, sideways price pattern. Buying comes in, and the stock breaks out on low volume, spiking a fraction of a point higher. Now, though, market makers sell it short. This instantly deflates the breakout. They pound it down, below the consolidation area and through the zone where most of the stop-loss orders are set. Traders panic and sell their shares to market makers. Seconds to minutes later, the price spikes higher, usually right back into the consolidation zone where it started. How to avoid this: Avoid trading during lunch hours (11:30 A.M.–1:30 P.M. EST). Enter breakout trades with a small initial lot just as the stocks begin to breakout, then add more shares if the breakout continues. If you miss the original breakout, don't chase it. For breakdowns, reverse the preceding guidelines. Volume should be on the breakdown day (or long, black candlestick), and negative down days, hereafter.

### Volume Signals in Uptrends and Downtrends—How They Differ

Here's a differentiating factor between volume signals in uptrends and downtrends: Although strong volume accompanies the ugliest breakdowns, price can fall abruptly on minimal volume and continue into a downtrend.

If a stock falls on strong volume, negative feelings drive it down, and fast. Average to decreased volume on a breakdown translates into apathy or negative market conditions—but a stock can slide downhill rapidly in this event, as well.

Just as pullbacks follow breakouts, rallies or rebounds follow breakdowns. When the price rallies after a breakdown, it should bounce on condensed volume. Huge volume accompanying a rally indicates a shift or reversal in the downtrend.

Another volume signal applies to uptrends in all time frames: A climactic volume spike that appears in the context of a highly extended uptrend signal means a reversal may start soon. It's caused by the euphoria of novice traders chasing stocks and the pros coming in to take profits—lots of activity! When you spot this and you're in a trade, take your profits. If the trend gathers more steam and continues, you can reenter. Otherwise, you have the satisfaction of knowing you took profits at exactly the right price.

The same climactic signal in a downtrend can reverse the trend, *or* just slow the falling price action. Know that when you see a climactic volume spike on an intraday chart on a stock that's crashed fast and furiously—if you're short, cover (close) some or all of it. The extreme spike usually indicates that buyers are coming into picture.

Figures 7-2 through 7-6 display breakouts and breakdowns with their volume signals. Note how the pattern remains the same whether you're looking for a core trade, swing trade, day trade, or momentum trade.

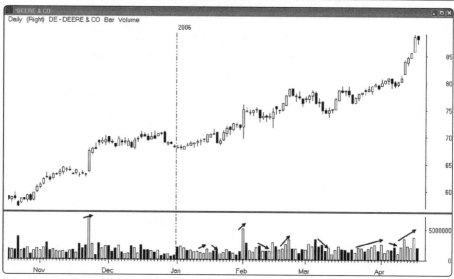

**FIGURE 7-2** | This daily chart of Deere & Co. (DE) shows the stock moving in an uptrend. I've color coded the chart's volume spikes to correlate with their candlesticks. Note the huge volume spikes that powered up the farm and construction equipment manufacturer to higher highs. In January, you'll notice that although no huge volume spikes appeared, DE drew seven consecutive higher lows on the chart, with steady volume. In March, you can see how DE moved slightly higher, then fell nearly back to the prior low on heavy volume. Learn to think of volume as an emotionally driven indicator.

RealTick® graphics used with permission of Townsend Analytics, Ltd. © 1986-2007 Townsend Analytics, Ltd.

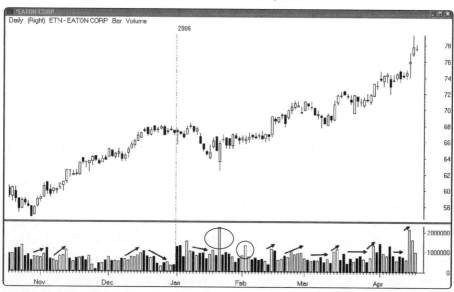

**FIGURE 7-3** | This daily chart of the Eaton Corp. (ETN) shows the global industrial manufacturer tacking on nearly 20 points in a little more than 6 months. You can see how several spikes of steady volume in a row produced nice price upswings. Notice the big price spike toward the last week in January (circled). As you can see, that morning ETN gapped much lower, but buyers swooped in to grab shares and support it, and pushed it right back into its price range. Another spike on February 2 looked like it might cause a breakout, but the stock continued to consolidate for another week before it broke to the upside.

RealTick® graphics used with permission of Townsend Analytics, Ltd. © 1986-2007 Townsend Analytics, Ltd.

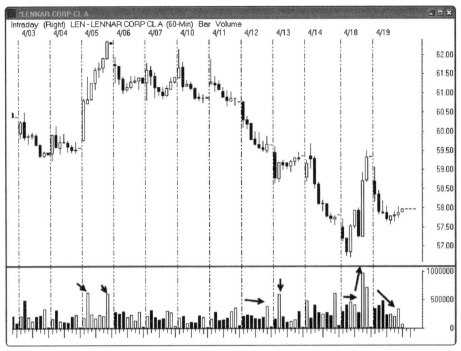

**FIGURE 7-4** | This hourly chart of Lennar Corp. (LEN) shows the stock in a downtrend most of the time. However, note the third day from the left (4/05). LEN gapped slightly open on this day, then extreme volume propelled it higher. The next six hours, the homebuilder rose dramatically. Although the volume spikes that took it higher were not as dramatic as the initial spike, you'll note they are steady. On the final hour of the day, LEN was overextended. That high volume spike told you that even though enough demand pushed it higher, additional trading activity included sellers taking profits. The next morning, 4/06, LEN gapped down at the open. On 4/12, note how steady selling volume took LEN lower. Also note the upper shadows on the last four candles of the day. Remember, upper shadows indicate sellers. On 4/13, a strong volume spike sent LEN higher for one hour, but demand could not outweigh supply enough to push LEN up to its prior day's open. On 4/18, climactic selling came into the stock, taking it two points lower. When you see strong volume coming into a stock that's oversold, no matter the color of the candles, know that in time, strength may show up and reverse the trend. On 4/18, the homebuilder gapped down, then found support and a truckload of buyers for the second half of the day. Note how quickly the stock reversed, and, after a quick pullback, shot up, missile-style, into the close. On 4/19, equally potent volume sent this volatile stock back down again. What a wild ride!

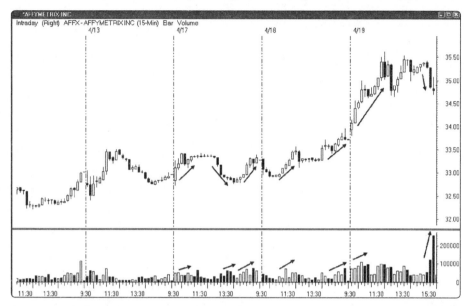

**FIGURE 7-5** | If you could see a daily chart, you'd see Affymetrix, Inc. (AFFX) breaking to the upside, out of a base. This 15-minute chart zooms in for a close-up on the final part of the price action and breakout. Notice the indecision on the part of the bulls and bears as this manufacturer of systems for genetic analysis grinds up and down, especially on 4/17. The next day, 4/18 shows progress in a potential breakout. Notice how the first breakout held its ground, and the noontime consolidation did not return to prior daily lows as the previous ones did. AFFX closed very near the high of the day on strong volume, indicating bulls were out in force. On 4/19, AFFX rocketed a point higher on mega-volume. It pulled back, started up again, refused to follow through, then gave up more than half a point into the close, on extremely high volume, as traders closed positions.

RealTick® graphics used with permission of Townsend Analytics, Ltd. © 1986-2007 Townsend Analytics, Ltd.

### Predicting Breakouts or Breakdowns

Okay, we've talked about volume in breakouts and breakdowns. It all looks simple on charts that we can Monday-morning quarterback, but how do you spot them when the breakouts or breakdowns are about to happen?

For position and swing trades on the long side, monitor daily charts from a selection of high-quality stocks that are basing, or moving sideways at the bottom of a cycle. The best candidates are industry leaders that have been beaten down because of sector rotation. That means that their sector, or industry, has not been in favor in the present economic environment. Or, perhaps the company has dipped due to poor fundamentals that are being fixed.

Note the average daily volume and watch to see if it begins to build, or suddenly spikes.

For added information on when industry leaders may start to rise, monitor charts of the industry index it correlates to. Many charting systems will let you chart

**FIGURE 7-6** | This 5-minute chart of Armor Holdings, Inc. (AH) shows a perfect example of the volume signal that indicates how climactic volume can slow an overextended trend. This signal is extremely useful when you're day trading on the short side using short-term intraday charts (5–15 minutes). The manufacturer of armored vehicles gapped open slightly up, and then reversed sharply. A spinning top forms the topping candle. Then poor AH tumbled nearly three points like a rock tied to a brick in water. Note the volume increase at 10:30 A.M., when volume activity began to heighten. The volume spike at 10:50 A.M. traded 30,000 shares. It warned traders that panic selling was now coupled with buyers coming in. AH recovered slightly, but soon started skidding downward again. The two black volume spikes warned remaining short sellers to cover their positions. Bulls roared onto the scene, and AH rallied to make a higher high. At about 1:45 P.M., any residual short sellers felt pain as the stock headed up. Heightened volume appeared in the last 45 minutes of trading, which is usually the case in most large-cap stocks.

indices such as the Amex Oil Index (XOI), the Philadelphia Bank Sector Index (BKX), the Philadelphia Gold/Silver Sector Index (XAU), the Morgan-Stanley High Tech Index (MSH), the Amex Pharmaceutical Index (DRG), and more.

You can also go to my Web site, *www.ToniTurner.com,* and click on the Sectors & Stocks tab. The page lists major industry groups and important stocks within those groups.

If you don't have access to these indexes through your trading software or broker, you can refer to sector exchange traded funds (ETFs), Select Sector SPDRs, at *www.spdrindex.com.* Next, go to *www.holdrs.com* for Merrill Lynch

**HOT TIP**

If you further investigate the rapidly growing world of ETFs, you'll discover additional examples of these investment tools that closely mimic sector and index movement. In Chapter 14, you'll see a selection of ETF Web sites.

HOLDRS, which are ETFs that represent industry groups. ETFs don't track correlating indices exactly, but they'll give you a good indication as to the group's direction.

Also, pay attention to CNBC announcers when they make statements like, "The oil index is finally waking up," or "Analysts finally upgraded the down-trodden disk drive makers."

And now, let's return to our hunt for position and swing trades using volume signals, only this time, to the downside. For breakdowns, look for a stock that has concluded a strong uptrend and has rolled over. It should be moving sideways across a potential cycle top, either trading in a range or in a congestion pattern (not in consolidation—that's positive). If strong volume appears for several days, and the price continues to move sideways, it may mean distribution (selling) is taking place and a breakdown is imminent. In Chapter 11, we'll discuss other criteria you will use to consider shorting a stock.

With day trades and momentum trades, volume signals tell the same stories, but at a much faster pace. If you're trading from a three-minute or 5-minute chart, strong volume either propels the breakout candlestick or it doesn't. If it does—good. If it doesn't, forget it. On the times the stock shoots higher on minimal volume and keeps going, shrug it off. As a savvy trader, you're playing the odds.

My rule is this: If I see a possible breakout pattern forming, I get all ready for it—order entry screen up, and finger on the mouse ready to pounce. If market internals are positive and the pattern is a tight consolidation, I many times buy an initial lot within the consolidation. During the seconds the breakout takes place, if volume doesn't spike, all bets are off. Why? It's probably a false breakout.

A false breakout, one that breaks over resistance for a few seconds or minutes, then comes back in—meaning it drops back to its breakout price—usually comes in fast, with few buyers to take up the supply. Remember, the pros are using individual traders to test the strength of breakouts.

**HOT TIP**

A stock in an overextended uptrend that makes a new high on low volume could be ready to topple. This indicates bulls have lost interest. A shooting star that appears in the context of a ballistic uptrend on low volume warns traders to take partial or all profits, or at least tighten stop-loss orders.

Failed breakouts mean lost money. Even if you break even on the trade, you're still paying the commission.

Keep-it-simple-rule: Low volume on the breakout, no trade. Period.

To short intraday breakdowns, you don't have to have strong volume, although it confirms your decision. You can short successfully just as the stock falls through resistance and profits from a gradual meltdown to the next support level.

### "Thin" Is Good for Waistlines, Not Stock Volume

I avoid day trading or momentum trading stocks that trade fewer than 300,000 shares per day, average daily of volume. I prefer not to swing trade stocks that trade less than 100,000 shares, per average day. They may be suitable to hold for investments, but they make for dangerous trading. First of all, a low-volume stock—we call it "thinly traded"—may not move very much.

Second, the more active a stock (the more shares per day it trades), the safer you are. Why? Because when the sky falls in an actively traded stock, some fool will likely buy your shares from you.

In a thinly traded stock, when times get rough, you can't always find that fool someone to dump your shares on—especially if you're desperate. The market makers on a low-volume, crashing NASDAQ stock just lower the bid and turn their backs. When you scream, "Aaack! Take it at the market—anything to get me out!" they snicker and hand you a rock-bottom price. NYSE and Amex specialists don't turn their backs, but you'll still have to sell at the market price to get out fast. In other words, you're not exiting where you want to, but rather where you're forced to.

#### *Volume Guidelines*

➤ Strong volume on breakouts or breakdowns means the price will potentially continue in the current direction. Volume equals emotion, and propels price moves.

➤ Weak volume on breakouts indicates potential breakout failure.

➤ Climactic volume in the context of an overextended uptrend or downtrend may reverse or stall the trend.

➤ High volume on a doji, evening star, morning star, shooting star, or spinning top (also has a narrow real body, or price range from open to close), when appearing in the context of an overly extended uptrend or downtrend, can indicate an upcoming price or trend reversal.

➤ It sounds contrary to the last statement, but it really isn't. When a highly overextended stock (uptrend only) makes a new high on obviously low volume, it signals a potential price reversal. Again, it indicates disinterest on the part of new buyers and buying exhaustion.

➤ Stocks that trade volume of fewer than 100,000–300,000 shares average daily volume result in dangerous short-term plays.

Figures 7-7 through 7-11, both daily and intraday charts, note how volume acts as a great decision support tool in signaling entry and exit points. When you get a practiced eye at spotting volume opportunities, go to your own charting source and scan for instances of high volume, which if acted upon, would have reaped rewards.

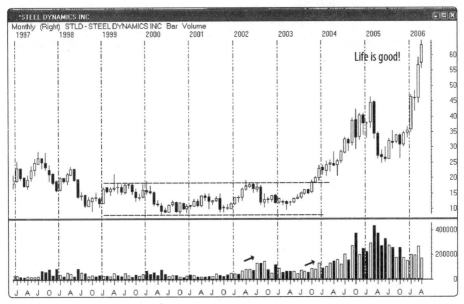

**FIGURE 7-7** | This monthly chart of Steel Dynamics, Inc. (STLD) that dates back to 1997 shows how important it is for traders to back up and evaluate the big picture. Note how in 2002, even though the steel manufacturer closed about where it opened, at about $11.70, in comparison to prior years, volume began to swell. That volume indicated interest flowing into the stock—it's the action you want to see in a basing period. If you were to be fortunate enough to notice it in early 2003, you would have gotten in on the ground floor, when STLD traded at $11–$15 per share. It broke out in November, at about $18. By now you would have made nearly 400% on your money. So, keep in mind that weekly and even monthly charts can be very useful in giving you an overall volume picture that can lead to profits.

**FIGURE 7-8** | This is a weekly chart of the Oil Service HOLDRS (OIH), an ETF representing the oil services industry group. Space constraints limited the chart, but the OIH carved an orderly, tight base in 2003. You can see how volume came into the ETF, supporting it from its breakout price of $65, all the way to its current price of $162. Naturally, the economic environment propelled this commodity-related ETF to nosebleed territory. Oil prices rose and took the oil service companies with them. Know that rising oil prices are a harbinger of inflation. (Oil is a commodity, as are other raw materials such as aluminum, steel and paper.) Conversely, rising inflation usually has a negative impact on non-commodity equities.

RealTick® graphics used with permission of Townsend Analytics, Ltd. © 1986-2007 Townsend Analytics, Ltd.

**FIGURE 7-9** | This daily chart of Monster Worldwide, Inc. (MNST) illustrates the stock shooting through its base at about 33, and creating a dandy 1, 2, 3 pattern. In late October, note volume coming into this temporary staffing company (arrow).

Those side-by-side candles each opened and closed within just cents of each other, and each closed near the high of the day on strong volume. That's extremely positive news. MNST broke above its base resistance and continued higher into the close of the year. Note the volume spike in December. As MNST shrugged it off by continuing sideways, we must conclude that end-of-the-year accumulation or distribution took place. In the beginning of 2006, you'll see other volume signals play out. The gigantic, 10-million-share spike on February 1, which took MNST from a low of 42, to a high of 50.45, may have related to earnings. Subsequent volume dried up and then expanded, as MNST's price followed suit.

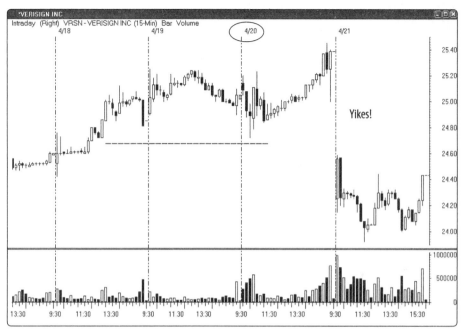

**FIGURE 7-10** | This 15-minute chart of Verisign, Inc. (VRSN) shows a great reason that traders should remain aware of company earnings' reports, and when those reports are issued. Earnings season (when companies announce their quarterly earnings) takes place four times per year, in the weeks following each quarter (March, June, September, December). In this case, VRSN's earnings came out before the opening bell on 4/21. Note the volume and price action on the prior day, 4/20. In anticipation of earnings, the Internet software and services company gapped open, then fell hard to previous support (dotted line). The hammer-like candle, with its long lower shadow and expanded volume, told short-sellers to look for a rebound. The next long white candle jettisoned the stock in a quick reversal—then quickly failed. These kinds of whipsaw movements are typical with volatile stocks, the day before earnings' announcements. Novice traders should wisely stand aside. Now—look at VRSN's close on 4/20: at the high of the day on strong volume. Those are greenhorn traders buying into the close and hoping VRSN will come out with good earnings the next morning. Not smart. VRSN came out with disappointing earnings, opened nearly a point lower, and did not recover that day.

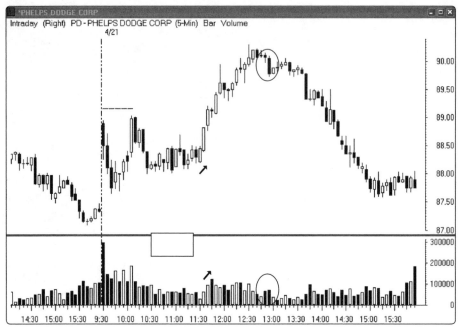

**FIGURE 7-11** | If you could see a daily chart, you would see how Phelps Dodge Corp. (PD) etched an incredible uptrend during the last couple of years. Had you decided to day trade or momentum trade the copper mining and manufacturing stock on 4/21, the day shown on this 5-minute chart, you would have noted that while it closed on 4/20 at $87.34, it opened on 4/21 at $88.90, more than one and one-half points higher—on strong volume. PD filled a good portion of the opening price gap, then the first white candle of the day indicated the pullback might reverse. Indeed, strong volume soon shoots PD higher. Note however, that the stock could not overcome the opening high (dotted line). The dark cloud cover indicates temporary weakness, and PD drifts down to consolidate into lunch. PD experienced a rousing lunchtime rally, and your early clue to buy was increased volume coming into the consolidation (arrows). The next move shows why stop-loss orders are important. Weakness came into PD with the two black candles on strong volume. This was your signal to at least tighten your stop-loss order. The overall market weakened fast on this Friday afternoon, and savvy traders took profits when they saw the market selling off. Others became painfully aware of how a complete cycle can form on a 5-minute chart.

## MOVING AVERAGES: WHAT THEY ARE, HOW TO USE THEM

Moving averages rank next to volume for being dependable chart tools. I think of major moving averages like my favorite uncle—consistent and reliable. They form strong support and resistance zones—support when trending under price patterns, resistance when trading above them.

These price average lines, figured over a designated time period, are known as "lagging" indicators. Moving averages lines rely on price action that's already taken place for their calculations.

### How Moving Averages Are Calculated

On a daily stock chart, a twenty-day moving average represents the closing price each day for the last twenty trading days, divided by twenty. With each succeeding day, the last price is dropped and the current one added. When you apply this moving average to a chart, it comes out as a single line, similar to a trendline.

Many times, you'll find that a major moving average moves in lockstep with the stock's trendline. That tells you that the moving average confirms the trend, which is valuable information.

Major moving averages used by most traders are the 10-, 20-, 50-, 100-, and 200-period lines.

The period is the time frame you're looking at. If you're looking at a 50-week Moving Average (MA) on a weekly chart, it's averaged to draw the last fifty Friday closing prices. On a 60-minute chart, a 50 MA averages the fifty closing prices of the last 50 hourly candlesticks. On a 5-minute chart, a 50 MA forms the last fifty closing prices of each 5-minute candlestick, averaged, and so forth.

 **HOT TIP**

As you will see, a 10-period moving average, known in trading jargon as the 10 MA, hugs the price pattern on the chart more closely than the 20 MA, and certainly more than the 50 or 200 MA. The shorter the time frame used to calculate the MA, the more closely it will follow the price pattern.

Every trader uses his or her favorite moving averages, and you can try different lines, or moving averages, on different time frames.

Different stocks dance to different moving averages, especially on their daily charts. In a perfect world, you'd apply the moving average that the stock favors for support, rather than the MA we impose on it. For example, in the old days (1990s) Cisco Systems (CSCO) preferred the 30-day MA. Many stocks consistently bounce off of their 20-day or 50-day moving averages.

➤ Try the 39-week moving average on your weekly charts, along with the 20 and 30 MAs. The 39-week MA on a weekly chart compares nicely to the 200-day MA on a daily chart. That means the 39-week MA falls the same place on the price pattern on a weekly chart as the 200-day moving average falls on the price pattern on a daily chart. If this confuses you, tuck it away for further reference.

➤ Many position and swing traders use 20-, 50-, 100-, and 200-period moving averages on daily charts. Some add the 10-day MA.

➤ Moving average preferences on hourly charts vary, with the dependable 10-, 20-, 50-, and so forth remaining popular. I use the 65- and 130-period moving averages on my 60-minute charts. If we transferred these to daily charts, they would fall in nearly the same place as the 10- and 20-day moving averages. That way, it's like imposing long-term (daily) information onto my shorter-term chart (60-minute), which offers great information. To calculate these moving averages, I multiply the number of hours in the trading day, (six and a-half), by the moving average. So the 10-day MA on a daily chart becomes the 65-period MA on the hourly chart. The 20-day MA on the daily chart becomes the 130-period MA on the hourly chart. Of course, using 10-, 20-, and 200-period averages on your hourly charts works well, too.

➤ Day traders use the 10-, 20-, and 200-period MAs on short-term intraday charts, although preferences vary widely. My favorites: the 20 and 200 MAs on 15-minute and 5-minute charts. For momentum trades, which take advantage of single, intraday price moves, I add the 10 MA.

If you have a direct-access trading platform or good trading software, you should be able to specify as many MAs as you want to overlay on your charts. Don't pile them too high, though. Remember to keep it simple. Especially for novices, two or three MAs on one chart are plenty. More than three resemble a wad of tangled spaghetti.

When I get confused, I delete them all except for the 20 MA. I find it one of the best storytellers.

Moving averages act as "multiuse" indicators. They're like ketchup—you can put them on everything, including volume spikes. And, like volume, their message tells it like it is. If the stock behaves properly depending on where the MAs appear on the chart, enter the play. If it doesn't, don't.

**HOT TIP**

The moving averages referred to in this text are "simple" moving averages. You may want to explore exponential or weighted moving averages on your charts. Basically, they weight the most recent price action more heavily than the price action prior to it.

### How to Use Moving Averages

One school of market players claims stock prices make random movements, with no set pattern. To them I say, give me a daily stock chart with 20- and 50-day MAs applied to it, and I'll bet you my mouse I can show you a stock with a memory. It's positively uncanny how stocks bounce off these support and resistance lines.

Of course, we know that much of that action takes place because traders agree that moving averages form valid support and resistance boundaries.

For example, say a stock broke out and is climbing nicely in a healthy uptrend. It's above its 20 MA on a daily chart, and whenever it pulls back, it bounces up off of the moving average line. Experienced traders will buy anticipatory lots when a stock edges down to its 20 MA, anticipating the bounce. (Of course, if the stock falls through the 20 MA, experienced traders high-tail it out of their position.) I don't recommend this strategy for new traders; it's safest to buy when the stock actually starts to spring higher.

Position and swing traders should buy stocks trading above their rising 20 MAs on a daily chart, and hopefully above the rising 50 MA.

Exercise caution when buying a stock that's fallen below its 200-day MA on a daily chart, or trading just under it. Mathematically, it makes sense. There are approximately 245 trading days in a year. The 200-day MA uses 200 days of closing prices, averaged, to calculate the stock's current strength in relationship to it. If the stock's price is trading below the 200-day MA, it's floundered for a long time.

That's why this line is an extremely powerful indicator. On a daily chart, especially, it weighs a stock down.

Unless you're bottom fishing, and you're aware of moving averages overhead, you'll want to enter stocks on the long side that ride just on top of a moving average. For instance, if you see a stock on a daily chart in an uptrend, and it's bouncing off its rising 20 MA or 50 MA in orderly waves, you can plan your entry point for the minute it bounces on strong volume.

If, however, the stock is flying high above the MA, especially the 20 MA, we say the stock is "overextended," "toppy," or "frothy." Chances are it's ready to pull back soon. Wait for the pullback and a confirming bounce before you enter.

For the safest short trades, short sellers should trade stocks trending down and trading below their declining 20 MA, and better yet, below their declining 50- and 200-day MAs.

On intraday charts, day traders find success buying stocks that bounce off their rising 200-period MA on a 15-minute chart. I like the 20-period MA on a

5-minute chart for support areas. Short sellers jump in when stocks fall below support areas and under declining moving averages.

Sometimes, when you're day trading to the long side, you'll see the 200 MA above your stock's price, maybe the 100 MA below that, then the 20 and 10. In other words, the moving averages are layered from the slowest to the fastest. This is common in negative markets and is usually a good warning to keep your money in your wallet.

Say the market just opened down, and the bears are in control. You're day trading and looking at a 5-minute chart of your favorite stock, Simple Software. On the day chart, it looks ripe for a breakout. But on your intraday chart, it's fallen below the opening price.

Even though the market is down, you believe a reversal to the upside will take place at the 9:45 A.M. reversal period. You're watching a 5-minute chart of Simple, and it appears to be bottoming. At the current price of $21.10, it's sitting on the 10 MA, which is just starting to turn up. That's positive.

On the downside, the 200 MA, which always slopes more gradually than the others, looms like a dark cloud above Simple's attempt to move higher. Note the illustration in Figure 7-12. Even if the stock rises on a market bounce, when it reaches the declining 200 MA, it may run into strong resistance and fall back down. In a situation like this, you quickly assess the risk–reward odds. Is it worth it? Think: If I enter this play, am I protecting my principal? If the answer is no, then you know to wait for a better opportunity.

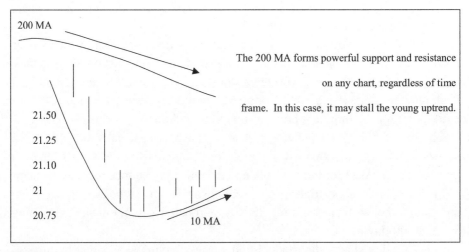

FIGURE 7-12

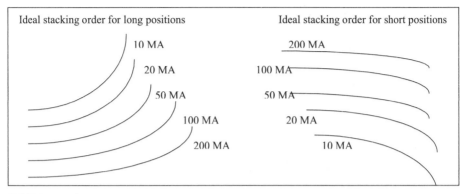

**FIGURE 7-13** | Moving averages.

It's always safest to enter a long position, regardless of the time frame you're trading in, when the moving averages support the stock in the most positive order, as shown in Figure 7-13. You won't have all these averages on the same chart at once, but if you did, the ideal stacking order is the 10 above the 20, the 20 above the 50, the 50 above the 100, and the 200 below all of them. Reverse that order for shorting.

Moving average crossovers issue very important signals. Traders call them "golden crosses."

### Moving Average Crossovers

A crossover takes place when a faster moving average, which has been trading above (or below) a slower moving average, penetrates and crosses below (or above) the slower line. For example, the 20-day MA falls below the 50-day MA. Or, the 50-day MA rises through the 200-day MA. These crossovers signal a potential price move, or continuation of the price move, in the same direction as the shorter-term MA.

Many traders add crossovers to their setup and entry criteria. One shorting setup I like involves the 20-day MA piercing the 200-day and falling below it. At the point that happens on the daily chart, I'm watching for the remainder of my signals to line up and give me a short entry signal.

Direct-access software platforms, such as RealTick, include simple scans that will alert you when moving average crossovers take place. This is handy information that can aid you in entering, or managing, your trades.

Now that you're an expert on moving averages, the next bit of information falls into the "this is always true, except when it isn't" category. Moving averages work best with a trending stock, that is, a stock moving in an uptrend or downtrend. When a stock is moving sideways, if the MA moves in a horizontal line with it, the MA becomes ineffectual as a storyteller. When the MA moves laterally, it looses much of its predictive value.

Figures 7-14 through 7-17 show the relationships between stocks and their moving averages. Study them and note how trending stocks use the potent lines for support and resistance. Also, know that we'll apply these relationships to virtually every stock from now on, so by the time you finish this book, you'll become thoroughly acquainted with a variety of them.

**FIGURE 7-14** | This weekly chart of the QQQQ spans more than two years. It shows the tracking stock (ETF) for the NAS-DAQ 100 lumbering above, then slipping below, its 39-week moving average. Many investors use the price cross and two consecutive closes above the 39-week MA as a buy signal, and penetration to the downside with two consecutive closes below it as a sell signal. While that system worked well some of the time, the Q's tumble in the first two-quarters of 2005 made traders grateful for the ability to read charts!

**FIGURE 7-15** | This daily chart of the ETrade Financial Corp. (ET) shows the online broker in a picture-book uptrend. Just so, it's 20-, 50-, and 200-day moving averages are moving in concert with it. Notice that in this six-month+ time span shown on the chart, ET stayed mostly above its 20-day line, and definitely above its 50-day line. In the last week or two, however, you can see the price pattern losing steam. Today, ET closed below the 20-day MA. If the broker breaks below the 50 MA, that's bearish, and some institutions may lose interest and sell. Also note: The rising 50 MA coincides closely with ET's pullback low of 25.35 (arrow). If both price support and moving average support are broken simultaneously, as you can imagine, the signal is double-negative. These reasons help you see that moving averages can team up with price support/resistance to form important predictive tools.

RealTick® graphics used with permission of Townsend Analytics, Ltd. © 1986-2007 Townsend Analytics, Ltd.

## THE FINAL TOUCH: MOMENTUM INDICATORS

Popular momentum indicators such as Stochastics, CCI (Commodity Channel Index), the MACD (moving average convergence-divergence oscillator), RSI (Relative Strength Index), ROC (Rate of Change), Momentum indicator, and more, are displayed in scales above or below the price patterns on our charts. These indicators tell us whether the stock is overbought or oversold. They also imply when a stock may be ripe for a reversal.

The term *overbought* suggests a stock or index is trading at a lofty price in comparison to its recent price activity. *Oversold* means that compared to recent price activity, a stock or index has fallen to a low price.

We also call overbought/oversold indicators "oscillators." They oscillate, or fluctuate, between their high and low readings like a snake in a pipe.

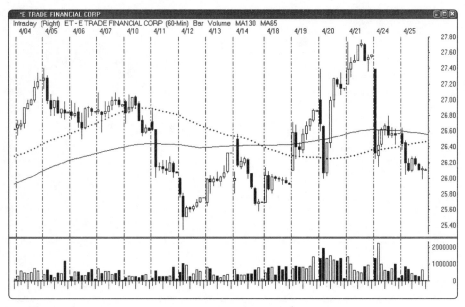

**FIGURE 7-16** | On this hourly chart of E Trade Financial Corp. (ET) I've plotted the 65-period (dotted line) and 135-period (solid line) moving averages. As I explained in this chapter's text, these MAs closely match the 10-day and 20-day moving averages on the daily chart. This chart displays the 15 most recent days on ET's daily chart in Figure 7-15. And, you can see how the 20-day moving average on that chart falls in approximately the same place on the price pattern, as the 130-period MA does on this chart. If we'd plotted the 10-day MA on Figure 7-15, it would match, as well. You may prefer to use the standard intraday 10-, 20-, and 200-MAs on your 60-minute charts. Still this is a nifty trick for pinpointing entries and stop-loss points for swing and day trades.

Interpreted properly, momentum indicators act as decision support tools that confirm our decisions to enter, exit, and manage risk.

When we use these chart tools as overbought/oversold indicators, we call them "lagging indicators." Since they are calculated from price action that's already taken place, they "lag" the current price.

These indicators can transform, however, into "leading" indicators—meaning they may "lead" the price. When they diverge in direction from price, the operative theory says price will soon follow the direction of the indicator. Example: A stock keeps making higher highs, but the Stochastics indicator makes lower highs. That's called a "bearish divergence." Traders interpret that to mean that price is weakening and will soon reverse to the downside. Or, a stock consolidates sideways in a basing formation, but the CCI heads higher in a "bullish

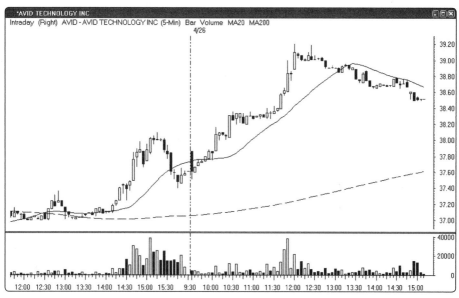

**FIGURE 7-17** | This 5-minute chart shows 20-period (solid line) and 200-period (dotted line) moving averages. Note how Avid Technology, Inc. (AVID) gapped open slightly on 4/26 (black candle), then quickly rose over its 20-period line and drew a nice 1, 2, 3, pattern. Remember the volume rule that states climactic volume on an overextended uptrend can reverse it? It works well on 5-minute charts, as well as longer time frames. Also note that you could have used the 20-period MA on this day to enter AVID with a long day trading position. You could have closed the trade when AVID broke the 20-period line.

divergence." At that point, the CCI predicts the stock will soon move higher and acts as a leading indicator.

If you'd like to learn about additional indicators, go to *www.toniturner.com* and click on Tutorials.

When we move into momentum indicators such as these, created from complicated formulas derived mainly from price history, we also approach the area where traders launch the most diligent searches for the "holy grail." Everyone longs for a magic indicator that can broadcast—instantly and with conviction—the perfect signal as to where the stock, or index, will travel to next. Sorry, but there is no holy grail. No single indicator can tell you for sure where price will move next—or for how long.

The signals oscillators give—indeed, the signals any indicator gives—are just that—signals. These indicators are useful and fickle. They change direction in a heartbeat.

We analyze price using a combination of signals, such as candlesticks, volume, and moving averages. Then, we unite them with momentum indicator signals to arrive at a buy, sell, or risk management decision.

Some traders do not use momentum indicators on their charts. Others swear by them. This is a personal choice you'll make as you study these tools and decide which do, or don't, resonate with your style of trading.

Stochastics, the CCI, and the MACD are popular indicators that can be found on most trading software packages. If set on their standard defaults, Stochastics and the CCI are the most temperamental. The MACD draws slow, smooth, even-tempered lines.

### Stochastics—What It Is, How to Use It

Stochastics is a powerful momentum indicator that consists of two lines. The main line is referred to as the %K line. The signal line, which is really a moving average of the %K line, is the %D line. If you use "slow Stochastics," which I recommend, the signal line is called the "%D slow." The slow %D is actually a 3-period moving average of the %D.

If you're a novice trader, this description may give you the urge to throw this book across the room. Please stay with me a little longer. Stochastics is easier to read than it sounds.

Range: 0 – 100. Stochastics lines move on a scale between 0 and 100.

Default or look-back periods: The main line, the %K, has a standard default of 14. The signal line, the %D has a standard default of 3. If you wish to make your signal line "slow Stochastics," the "%D slow" line is set at a default time period of 3. (If you're not sure what I'm talking about, just leave your software settings as they are. They're probably already set to these defaults.)

### Why It's Important

Stochastics tells us where a security's price closed relative to its highs over a designated time period. That's important information.

Typically, strong uptrends are built from many candles closing near their highs. That pushes the Stochastics lines higher. When the trend and the bulls who supported it get tuckered out, even if prices inch up or start to consolidate, closing prices begin to shrink toward their lows. (The closing price is the most important price of the period, or day.)

Stochastics "sees" the closing prices weaken. It alerts you by hooking the %K line down and crossing below the %D slow line in a sell signal. The sell signal may simply warn of a pullback, or it could mean the bulls' party is over for a while.

On the flip side, a downtrend develops with candles closing at or near their lows. When the bears get tired, bulls sneak in and start to nibble. Bullish nibbling causes closing prices to edge up. Again, the Stochastics indicator detects price closing nearer to its highs. This time, the %K comes from under the %D slow, crosses it to the upside, and issues a buy signal.

> ### 🔥 HOT TIP
>
> Warning: Stochastics has an annoying quirk: it issues overbought signals very quickly. That means if your stock breaks out of its base and runs higher, Stochastics will read "overbought" within days. If the stock continues to shoot upward, the lines bump up against the upper scale at 100, reissuing overbought signals. We call this head bumping action "Stochastic pops." When it happens, the indicator loses its effectiveness as a predictive tool, until it hooks down and gives a firm sell signal.

*How to Use Stochastics:*

➤ Overbought signal: The lines rise above 80.

➤ Sell signal: The signal line (%D slow) hooks down over the %K line from above 80.

➤ Oversold signal: The lines fall below 20.

➤ Buy signal: The signal line hooks up and rises through the %K line from below 20.

➤ Divergence examples: The stock makes a higher high(s), while Stochastics %K line trends lower. Or, the stock etches a base or consolidates, but Stochastics trends higher.

➤ Time frames: You can apply Stochastics to all time frames. Although some traders use it on intraday charts, I apply it to weekly, daily, and 60-minute charts as confirmation for entry, exit, and risk management decisions.

Figure 7-18 shows an example of Stochastics on a daily chart of F5 Networks (FFIV).

> ### 🔥 HOT TIP
>
> When you apply momentum indicators to short-term intraday charts, keep in mind that large opening gaps skewer these indicators and their signals for the initial candles.

**FIGURE 7-18** | This daily chart of FFIV displays the 20-day MA (solid line), the 50-day MA (dotted line), and the 200-day MA (dashed line), along with Stochastics in the middle scale. The %K line is solid, and the %D slow line, which is also the signal line, is dotted.

1. FFIV consolidates just under its 20-day MA, while Stochastics etches a bullish divergence. Shortly thereafter, the networking provider ran higher.
2. FFIV scooted up to prior January resistance. Stochastics soon issued overbought signals above 80. Then, unimpressed with FFIV's run, it made a lower high. FFIV soon followed it down.
3. In a classic case of a Stochastics bearish divergence, FFIV climbed into a dandy run from its mid-February 50-day MA bounce. It made a breakout high, and then another. Stochastics, however, specified "no dice" and skidded into lower highs. FFIV dissolved into a pullback shortly thereafter.
4. Here's another bearish divergence. In March, FFIV jettisoned higher, again rose to two highs, but Stochastics warned bulls not to stay around. FFIV tumbled hard in an ugly fall of 13 points. By the way, the big gap down resulted from a disappointing earnings announcement. Traders who sold FFIV were wise to exit before earnings came out.

RealTick® graphics used with permission of Townsend Analytics, Ltd. © 1986-2007 Townsend Analytics, Ltd.

### The CCI—What It Is, How To Use It

The CCI is a single-line overbought-oversold oscillator that originated as a tool for use in commodities trading by Donald Lambert. The CCI oscillates (fluctuate) between 0 and 100.

*Why It's Important*

The CCI acts as a gauge, measuring a stock's current price in comparison to its statistical mean.

*How To Use It*

You can use the CCI as for overbought/oversold readings, as well as bull and bear price divergences. The standard default is 14 periods.

**HOT TIP**

Carry overbought-oversold information signals on daily charts into your day trades. If during the trading day, you know that your target stock is overbought or oversold, that's good information as to why it sells off—or takes off—in the afternoon session.

➤ Overbought: When the line rises above +100, the CCI reads "overbought."
➤ Sell signal: The line hooks down from +100.
➤ Oversold: Readings below −100 signal the stock is oversold.
➤ Buy signal: The line hooks up from below −100.
➤ Alternative buy-sell signal: When the line rises above (falls below) the zero median line

Like Stochastics, the CCI is a temperamental indicator, so I prefer to use it in longer time frames, such as daily and weekly charts, to confirm setups. That said, I know many traders who use it for entry signals on intraday charts. Whatever your trading time frame, team it up with your other tools to obtain strong buy/sell signals.

Figure 7-19 shows a daily chart of health care product manufacturer, Johnson & Johnson (JNJ), with the CCI plotted in the middle scale.

### The MACD—What It Is, How To Use It

The acronym MACD ("the mack-dee") translates into the "moving average convergence-divergence oscillator. " It is a technical chart tool developed by renowned technician Gerald Appel.

The MACD derives its formula from moving averages, so it's a steady, non-hysterical tool that's used a lot by investors, as well as traders. We use this dual-line chart component as decision support for entry and exits.

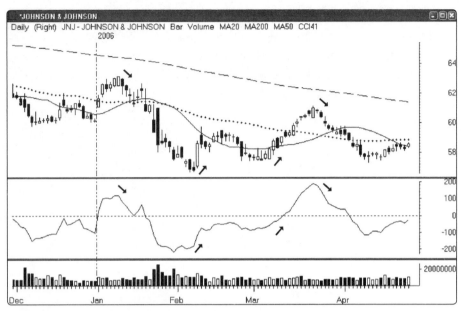

**FIGURE 7-19** | This daily chart of Johnson & Johnson (JNJ) shows the CCI plotted in the middle scale. On extremely vola-tile stocks, the CCI jumps up and down like an over-caffeinated kangaroo; traders who follow each signal it issues can—and will—get whipsawed. On a lumbering stock like JNJ, however, the CCI's early bullish and bearish divergences add good value to your entry and exit decisions. Study each overbought and oversold signal, its bearish or bullish divergence, and its corre-sponding price move. The last move to the upside in April is still up for grabs, as JNJ may get bopped on the head by its 50-day moving average. As well, the DRG, which is the Amex Pharmaceutical Index of which JNJ is a component, is in a downtrend. We'll watch the CCI, 50 MA, and other chart indicators for new signals before entering.

RealTick® graphics used with permission of Townsend Analytics, Ltd. © 1986-2007 Townsend Analytics, Ltd.

### What It Is

The MACD is plotted as two lines on your chart, the MACD line and the sig-nal line. As with other oscillators, your software will plot them in a panel above or below the price pattern. The MACD line represents the "fast" line. The for-mula is calculated by subtracting the difference between the 12- and 26-period exponential moving averages (EMAs).

The signal line represents the "slow" line. It's the 9-period EMA of the MACD. Most trading software settings adhere to these defaults.

You may prefer the MACD displayed as a histogram; some software pack-ages offer dual-line or histogram options.

*Why It's Important*

The MACD is a steady, reliable trend-following oscillator, and as such makes a great confirmation tool. I use it on weekly, daily, and hourly charts to confirm entry and exit decisions, thus keeping me on the right side of the trend.

I also use the MACD as confirmation to add to open positions. As long as the MACD lines are moving higher or lower, they indicate the prevailing trend remains in place.

*How to Use It*

Depending on your charting package, the MACD lines will oscillate between upper and lower (+ and −) values, with zero as the median line.

➤ When the lines rise or fall to extremes (this varies from stock to stock), the stock becomes overbought, or oversold.

➤ Buy signal: The MACD line crosses above the signal line.

➤ Sell signal: The MACD line crosses below the signal line. This is known as a crossover.

➤ When the fast MACD line widens its spread between the slower signal line, that means the stock is overextended to the upside or downside, and may soon pull back or rebound.

➤ The MACD does issue bullish and bearish divergences, and you can certainly use these readings. Stochastics and the CCI, however, give faster divergence readings—a trait that traders prefer.

---

**HOT TIP**

On short intraday time frames, a MACD histogram, minus the signal line, displays dependable momentum signals. As always, use these signals in conjunction with candle price action, volume, and moving averages.

This reliable indicator has one drawback. It offers predictive readings for stocks and other trading vehicles that are moving in a trend. If your target stock is doing the side-step across its chart, the MACD loses motivation, moseys along with it, and offers no valuable advice.

Figure 7-20 shows a daily chart of Adobe Systems, Inc. (ADBE), with the MACD plotted in the middle scale.

**FIGURE 7-20** | This daily chart of Adobe Systems, Inc. (ADBE) shows the MACD in the middle scale. The solid line plots the MACD line, and the dotted line plots the signal line. As you can see, the MACD is a gentle, trend-following indicator, although it does signal bullish and bearish divergences. Again, remember to use its signals when a stock is trending, not when it consolidates or moves in a horizontal trend. First, check the two big pops ADBE experienced in December. Now look how the spread widened between the MACD line and its signal line arrows. Those swelling spreads mean the stock may soon contract to earlier levels. Also note that the MACD started heading down in mid-January, unimpressed by lukewarm ADBE's attempt to move higher. The oscillator then continued to slide south. Stocks can make slight rebounds in downtrends, and the MACD will barely look up. The same action is true in uptrends. That's why we use this indicator for long-term signals. Finally, note the MACD buy signal in early April. Combined with other indicators and price action, it signaled to traders holding long positions that ADBE was resuming strength.

At the time this book was published, the NYSE and NASDAQ exchanges, alone, listed more than 8,000 stocks. If the one you're considering doesn't meet the best trading criteria, why play it? There are more than 7,999 others to choose from. As successful traders know, the best profit plays are those where the setup issues corresponding buy-sell signals from price support and resistance, candles, volume, moving averages, and the momentum indicator of your choice.

# QUIZ

||||||||||||||||||

## Questions

1. True or false? A stock in a healthy uptrend displays strong volume on positive days, and lower volume on pullback, or consolidation days.

2. Is strong volume an important ingredient of a successful breakout? Why?

3. A stock breaks out on heavy volume, but the volume continues to increase on the pullback. What does this mean?

4. Is trading a stock (day or swing trade) with average daily volume of fewer than 100,000 shares a good or bad idea? Why?

5. True or false? Moving averages form strong support and resistance areas.

6. A stock you want to day trade is sitting on its 20-period MA on a 5-minute chart. Its 200-period MA slopes overhead, just above the stock's price. Is this a good entry point for a long position? Why or why not?

7. A stock is moving sideways, trading in a range. Its 20 MA is also moving in a lateral direction. Is the MA currently a good storyteller?

8. Why are Stochastics, the CCI, and the MACD effective decision support tools?

## Answers

1. True. A stock in a robust uptrend invites more buyers than sellers. This accounts for high volume on positive days, and decreased volume on pullback, or consolidation days.

2. Yes, strong volume contributes in a big way to a breakout's success. The more buyers (demand + greed) a stock has pushing it up, the more the price will rise.

3. When volume increases on a pullback after a breakout, it means strong selling is taking place. This stock may fall as fast as it rose!

4. Stocks with average daily volume under 100,000 shares make unsatisfactory trading stocks. Low volume means high risk if you have to sell quickly.

5. True. Major moving averages such as the 20-, 50-. 100-, and 200-day moving averages act as strong support and resistance indicators.

6. No, this is not an ideal entry point for entering long or short. Avoid buying stocks trading under their 200 MA, unless you're bottom fishing. As for selling this stock short, because it's riding on top of its 20-period MA that may provide support, at least temporarily. Wait for it to break below the 20 MA, then (if the market and all other signals agree), short it.

7. No. Moving averages make effective indicators in stocks trending up or down. Moving average become ineffectual when moving sideways.

8. These three oscillators give us overbought and oversold readings. They also signal bullish and bearish divergences, which can give us early price reversal warnings.

## CENTER POINT: DETACHMENT—PATHWAY TO FREEDOM

*"Anything you want can be acquired through detachment, because detachment is based on the unquestioning belief in the power of your true Self."*

—Deepak Chopra, *The Seven Spiritual Laws of Success*

It's paradoxical, but true: The best way to acquire goals, circumstances, and material possessions in our lives is to relinquish our need, or our attachment to them.

The opposite of attachment is detachment. Attachment stresses fear and insecurity. Detachment assures freedom and creativity.

The ability to detach ourselves from the need of extravagant belongings assures peace, harmony, and security. Gathering material possessions into our lives, then looking to those objects for security never works. Possessions, though wonderful to enjoy, cannot offer true security. Security doesn't dwell in "things." It dwells within *us*, and in our belief systems.

The ability to detach ourselves from the past sets us free. Surely the most limiting words spoken are, "I can't change. I've always done it that way."

Such attitudes leave no room for improvement or creativity. Along the same lines, when we remain attached to our family history or heritage, and believe past conditions define our future, that belief limits personal growth.

The ability to detach ourselves from our limiting belief systems, and the way things "ought to be," is surely the most difficult detachment to achieve. When we hold our ideas and beliefs about right and wrong in a viselike grip, when we refuse to consider alternative views, we erect walls around ourselves. We allow no room to grow. Loving relationships struggle to survive.

When we establish goals and desires, then attach rigid conditions to their outcomes, it leaves no room for serendipity. On the other hand, working on a goal with a nonjudgmental attitude opens us to new and greater opportunities.

As we free ourselves from the need of material possessions, the need to be right, and the need to control, our spontaneity and creativity attracts exciting new circumstances our way that speed us on the road to success.

# CHAPTER 8

# When the Tough Get Going: Beginning Trader's Boot Camp

If you've already been active in the stock market, you've noticed that stocks, like people, have different personalities. Some you feel comfortable with, some you cross the street to avoid. Some are strong and calm. Others take volatility to extremes, rocketing up one day, crashing down the next. As I've mentioned before, securities on the NYSE and Amex usually act kindlier and gentler than those on the NASDAQ.

I watch a market minder populated with my favorite stocks. These are stocks from current leading and lagging industries that I target for good long and short trades. I know their personalities, which are volatile and which are mild-mannered. When they start misbehaving by acting differently, I "fire" them.

I also know traders who make good livings trading the same one or two stocks—all day, every day—buying dips and selling rallies. This is a valid style. As you learn your tolerance for risk and find your comfort levels, you will establish your own style.

Okay, now comes the fun. For the next two weeks, and the remainder of this chapter, you're going to attend boot camp. If you follow my directions, you'll build a step-by-step foundation constructed of the bricks and mortar of good trading—experience and knowledge.

Important note: From now on, unless otherwise indicated, I will be referring to buying stocks, not shorting stocks. Selling short requires a bit more finesse, and some different rules apply. Chapter 11 explains shorting techniques in detail.

## BEGINNER'S BOOT CAMP: WEEK ONE

If you're a new trader, this "Beginner's Boot Camp" introduces you to the trading environment gradually, without risking your capital.

Before we start, I have a request: During the following two weeks, please don't place a trade. The next ten trading days will acquaint you with the relationships between market and individual stock movements. To learn effectively, it's best to observe without the emotion of having money involved.

Actually, this will be your first boot camp lesson. When you observe the market quietly, without trading, you learn the discipline of sitting on your hands. Believe me, this is a skill! Most traders learn it after they lose money on impulsive trades. You, however, are going to experience it right away. Gaining the discipline to observe and listen without trading will represent one of the most valuable tools in your trading kit.

If possible, start boot camp on a Monday. Then only one weekend will break your momentum. Besides, Mondays usually set the market's tone for the week.

### Monday

Welcome to your first day in Beginner's Boot Camp! Please settle into your home office, community trading center, or wherever you've chosen to trade.

Make sure CNBC, or another financial network is being televised. Though you don't have to see the television screen, it should be loud enough to hear, yet soft enough not to distract you from concentrating. Access to the news is a must.

After a few days, you will learn to listen to CNBC with one ear. Experience will teach you to automatically tune in to information that could affect your trades and filter out what doesn't.

Okay, let's get started. Choose an actively traded target stock from either the NYSE or NASDAQ. Try to choose an industry leader. You can go to my Web site, *www.toniturner.com*, and click on Sectors. If you know which industry groups are hot, check out the stocks under the group headings to find one that's moving higher in an uptrend on its daily chart. Once you choose your target stock, please don't limit your observations to its opening and closing price. Display all the info you can obtain about it, including real-time quotes, a 5- or 15-minute intraday chart, or a Level II screen if it's available to you. Then watch this stock all day.

How does it act at the market's open? How does it react during the 9:45 A.M. to 10:15 A.M. reversal period? How's it acting an hour later? How does it react to overall market action?

Normally, you should leave your computer during lunch to refresh mind and body, and to avoid trading during most of this whippy time period. But boot camp demands are rigorous! So eat a sandwich in front of your screen, and notice how your stock quiets down, or moves erratically, during the noonday doldrums, from 11:30 A.M. to 1:30 P.M. or 2:00 P.M.

At 3:00 P.M. EST, bonds close their trading day. Since bonds and stocks are joined at the hip, that causes a market shift. How does your stock react? How does it react when the traders begin to close out trades at 3:15 P.M.? What about the remainder of the hour, as the big institutions close or reallocate assets? Volatility continues until 4:00 P.M., when the market closes.

If day traders play your target stock heavily—you can recognize this by extreme price movements and 100- to 1,000-share prints (small lots as opposed to block trades of 10,000 shares) going off the majority of the time—look for it to sell off ten minutes or so before the close. Many day traders refuse to hold positions overnight. By the way, specialists and market makers know traders want to go home flat. They may try to wash you out of the stock during this time by dropping the bid.

About five minutes before the close, the "shorts," or short-sellers, buy back their positions to close them, or "cover their shorts." That buying makes stocks spike briefly to the upside.

### Tuesday

Today, pay attention to the way your stock acts in relation to the fluctuations of the Dow Jones Industrial Average and the NASDAQ Composite. Does it mimic them, or wander off on its own like a rebellious teenager? (Most NYSE stocks follow the Dow and S&P 500 Index; NASDAQ stocks reflect the NASDAQ Composite. Naturally, this always happens, except when it doesn't.)

Find another active stock in your target stock's industry group or sector. Pair the two on your screen. Do they move in tandem, or separately?

Bring up five to fifteen minutes of your stock's industry group, either from the symbols listed on my Sectors Web page (best choice), or by an ETF that represents it. If you don't know the industry group, perhaps you can watch the sector. Watch how your stock moves in relation to the index. Does the index move first, and then the stocks follow?

> **HOT TIP**
>
> Boot camp is the time to paper trade, if you want to try it. Keep a record of your trades, and relish every minute of it. It's fun making millions of dollars on paper. Remember, though, paper trading is much different from the real thing. I've met many paper champions. Paper trading is a tool, not a barometer for success.

After the market closes, look at the daily charts of your stocks. Are they in uptrends, downtrends, or trading in a range? Are they in congestion or consolidation patterns? Where are the next support and resistance areas? How did they move today in comparison to Monday's activity? Apply volume, and the 20-, 50-, and 200-day MAs. Plot Stochastics, CCI, MACD, or another oscillator, if you can. Do your stocks obediently ride their 20 MA, rising and falling in gentle curves, or do they hop up and down erratically between the 20 MA and 50 MA?

### Wednesday

By now you may begin to sense, or internalize, the rhythms of the market. Fascinating, isn't it, how events that occur during the day weave the texture of the market? If you don't yet sense the ebb and flow of the market and individual stocks you're watching, don't worry. It will come in time. Experience and knowledge will sharpen your senses into a reliable decision support tool. Spend today in the same manner you spent yesterday, watching the Dow, the S&P 500, the NASDAQ Composite, and your target stocks.

### Thursday

Today, add another stock to you target list. If your current stocks trade on the NYSE, add a NASDAQ stock, or vice-versa. Again, please choose a stock that trades actively to give you a feeling of how stocks move.

Also, before the market opens, examine daily charts of the Dow, S&P 500 Index, and the NASDAQ Composite. If you don't have those indexes available to you, use their tracking stocks, the Dow Diamonds (DIA), the S&P 500 SPDRS (SPY), and the NASDAQ 100 (QQQQ). These ETFs don't track the indexes tick for tick, but they'll give you an accurate idea of where those indexes are trading.

As usual, look for uptrends, downtrends, trading in a range, support, and resistance. Where are they in relation to their 20-day and 50-day MAs? This afternoon, after the market closes, revisit those charts. How did today's closing price affect the overall picture of the markets' direction?

### HOT TIP

Most experienced traders wait until the market has been open for five–ten minutes before they place a trade. When the opening bell rings, specialists and market makers control the stocks and are in hot pursuit of leveling the field from the day before. So remember, when the opening bell rings, early birds who jump into volatile issues don't always get the worm. Sometimes they get shot down.

### Friday

By now, you should be watching three stocks and have developed the skill of watching them, related indices, the Dow Jones, S&P 500, and the NASDAQ Composite, all at one time. Check daily charts of your stocks, sector indices, and the Dow and NASDAQ before you start your weekend, so you have a feeling for what the next week might bring.

Congratulations on completing your first week of Beginner's Boot Camp. I promise your eyes will uncross before the weekend is over.

## BEGINNER'S BOOT CAMP: WEEK TWO

Good morning. It's Monday and I hope you're refreshed and ready to tackle a new week.

Did last week teach you how to watch a zillion numbers blink in front of you like hyperactive neon signs? Good. Now we're going to add three more indicators. Excuse me? Was that you moaning?

Indicators come in two flavors: lagging and leading. Lagging indicators tell you what has already happened. For example, indices like the Dow, the S&P 500, S&P 600 Index (small cap), the NASDAQ 100, and the Russell 2000 Small Cap Index are lagging indicators. So are stock indices, such as the SOX (semiconductors), GSO (software), IIX (Internets), and BIX (banks).

Leading indicators hint at what might happen next; we discussed in Chapter 7 how momentum indicators become leading indicators when they develop bullish and bearish divergences. Three indicators you're going to meet next: the TICK, the TRIN, and the E-mini S&P 500 futures.

These numbers, along with other indicators like the advance-decline line, we label as "market internals." They divulge the true health of the market, and a side of the market most people never see.

Just because the Dow and the NASDAQ 100 show positive numbers to the outside world doesn't mean all is actually rosy. Those two indices represent only 130 stocks out of more than 8,000. Market internals tell the real story. While the Dow smiles or the NASDAQ gets grumpy, internals can fluctuate wildly. We call their actions "whippy," and "choppy," and they lead traders on a merry chase.

On days like this, after the market closes, your friend inevitably strolls up to you and whomps you on the back. "Hey," he says, with a knowing cackle, "you must have made a fortune today. The Dow was up big-time."

You roll your eyes and bite your lip, recalling how you white-knuckled it through every trade you entered. You know only too well how the market can appear sweet and positive on the outside, but act witchy and fickle on the inside!

Nevertheless, internals such as the TICK and TRIN for the NYSE and NASDAQ, and mini stock index futures reveal the true, unvarnished facts. When they point in a certain direction—especially the E-mini S&P 500—traders pay attention. Within seconds, the majority of stocks follow their lead.

Note: While direct-access brokers offer quotes for TICK, TRIN, and mini stock index futures, currently, many online discount brokers do not. You can obtain mini stock index futures quotes on a subscription basis:

Mini-sized Dow futures: Chicago Board of Trade Web site: *www.cbot.com*

E-mini S&P 500 futures, NASDAQ 100 futures: Chicago Mercantile Exchange Web site: *www.cme.com*

If you prefer to trade without these internals, please skip this section and go on to the next. Also, the TICK and TRIN are very short-term indicators, and not vital to swing or position trades.

If you can obtain the TICK and TRIN for the NYSE and/or the NASDAQ Stock Exchange (if you trade only tech stocks) please access these today, and if possible, bring them up on your screen.

Every stock exchange has its own TICK and TRIN. The TICK is a short-term trading indicator. The number it shows represents the number of stocks ticking up minus the number of stocks ticking down on its exchange. Zero is the median.

Even though the actual number of the NYSE TICK measures listed stocks, it acts as a good blanket indicator. Periodically, you can see the NYSE TICK and TRIN during market hours on the CNBC ticker at the bottom of the television screen; they scroll by as part of the CNBC Market Summary.

I keep the NYSE TICK on a ten-minute line chart on one of my screens. When the market acts squirrelly, I check the TICK's support and resistance areas. I also list the number itself in a market minder box right below the Dow, S&P 500, and NASDAQ Composite.

If, for example, the TICK reads +332, that means 332 more stocks on the NYSE are ticking up, than ticking down. Any number over zero means the TICK is positive. If the TICK reads –587, it means 587 more stocks are ticking down than up, and that's a negative signal.

During a morning or afternoon trading session, when the TICK stays consistently in positive territory, stocks acting strong on the day generally keep their upward momentum. But if it screams skyward and soars over 1,000, don't get euphoric—get nervous. At this point, the market is trading in overbought territory and will likely reverse. It's like eating too much chocolate cake. It tastes so good while you're eating it, but afterward, you feel awful.

If you see the TICK climb over +1,100 and you have open day or momentum trades on the long side, lighten up. Chances are the TICK won't stay at such lofty levels for long.

Ditto to the downside. On really negative market days, when your entire screen flashes red (prices ticking down on Level II screens show in red), watch for the TICK to sink to –1,000, or lower. That's a signal Mother Market feels really cranky. The market's oversold, and except in cases of dire news, should reverse within a few minutes.

On a nasty day like this, when the bears rule, and the NYSE TICK plunges hard, many active traders lie in wait for the –1,000 reading and the subsequent reversal that may take place. (The operative word here is *may*.) They look for a pop up and quick profits by buying stocks that follow the TICK.

This tactic is fine for advanced traders, but if you're new at this game, please just observe. The NYSE TICK doesn't always behave as expected. If the market so much as breathes funny, the TICK reverses to the downside. You can be dealt a burning loss before you realize what happened.

My TICK rule: If the TICK falls below zero, I don't enter intraday on the long side. Reasoning: When the TICK reads negative, breakouts to the upside tend to fail. They might poke over resistance, but many times they don't follow through. And even getting out at the entry price turns into a loss because of commissions.

One trader I know, who adopted my TICK rule, conducted an informal study. He told me that when the TICK stayed negative, eight out of ten breakouts failed.

My study, completed earlier in my trading career, became evident one evening when I mulled over the day's losses in my journal. Each of my momentum plays began perfectly, but in the final outcome they mostly failed. A single common denominator stood out. In each case, the TICK was negative.

As you can see, the NYSE TICK is a powerful indicator. Many listed large caps such as GE, American Express, GM, and Wal-Mart follow it closely.

Do any of your target stocks follow the NYSE TICK? To find out, run your stocks' charts and the TICK side-by-side.

The next valuable internal indicator we'll discuss is the TRIN. Richard Arms developed it in 1967, and we owe him a debt of gratitude. An acronym for Trading Index, the TRIN is also called the Arms Index.

The TRIN measures volatility and usually has an inverse relationship to the TICK. A low TRIN means the bulls rule. A rising TRIN tells you the bears are fighting for supremacy.

Just as with the TICK, each exchange has its own TRIN.

You can access the NYSE TRIN, which most traders watch, on your direct-access platform; to date, most online discount brokers do not offer it to their clients. On CNBC, it scrolls on the bottom ticker tape periodically, following the TICK.

Again, I keep a 5-minute chart of the TRIN on my screen, along with the number on my market minder list, right under the TICK. It's advantageous to display the NYSE TICK and NYSE TRIN next to each other since their inverse relationship to one another is key.

If you calculated the TRIN, this is how you'd do it:

$$\frac{\text{Advancing Issues/Declining Issues}}{\text{Advancing Volume/Declining Volume}}$$

Like the TICK, the TRIN is a short-term trading tool. As you can see by the equation, it indicates whether volume is flowing into advancing, or declining, stocks. When advancing stocks dominate volume flow, the number reads under 1.0. When declining stocks command volume flow, the number exceeds 1.0.

A falling TRIN signals a strong market. A rising TRIN foretells a weak market.

> **HOT TIP**
>
> Most traders watch the NYSE TICK and TRIN as overall short-term indicators. If you trade primarily NASDAQ stocks, you may want to add the NASDAQ TICK and TRIN.

I find day trading downright enjoyable when the NYSE TRIN stays below 0.9. If the TRIN edges up into the 1.0 zone, my longs act jittery and start to slip, and for good reason.

When the TRIN hovers in the 1.0 area, it means the bears and bulls are fighting for control. Longs don't break out properly, and shorts don't fall down. At this point, you'll find me with a flat trading account, sitting on the sidelines. I don't take a picnic to the beach during a hurricane. And, I don't jump between angry bulls and bears when they fight for supremacy.

In *Trading for a Living*, Dr. Elder agrees. He writes, "If bulls are much stronger, you should buy and hold. If bears are much stronger, you should sell and sell short. If both camps are about equal in strength, a wise trader stands aside. He lets bullies fight with each other and puts on a trade only when he is reasonably sure who is likely to win."

A guideline to remember: The TRIN always wins.

Say the market feels depressed, with the TICK floundering in the –500 area, and the TRIN at 1.3, or so. Suddenly, the TICK makes a U-turn and leaps into positive territory. But the TRIN maintains its 1.3 to 1.4 level, refusing to sink. You may be witnessing a bull trap, or a sucker rally. Sucker rallies cajole novice traders into buying sprees. You—as a savvy trader—don't buy anything. You merely observe the short-lived pop up as a form of entertainment.

When you see an extreme, like the TRIN wallowing under 0.40, that's usually too good to be true. Watch for the market to sell off. The other extreme takes place when the TRIN climbs over 1.50, and it appears the end of the world draws near. Except in the case of really negative news, bulls should soon start to nibble, and a market rebound should soon appear.

Learn to watch the TICK and TRIN together, noting how they usually move in opposite directions. For the best day trading and scalping setups (on the long side), you want the TICK above zero and the TRIN below 1.0, or the TICK up and the TRIN down. Days when the TICK is negative and the TRIN maintains a level more than 1.0, you either sell short or practice sitting on your hands.

At this point in your studies, you'll want to start formulating some of your own trading rules. My third rule, listed right under protect your principal and trade to trade well, is that I enter a scalp or day trade only when the TICK is over zero, and the TRIN is below 0.9. That rule has saved me a fortune.

The final internal indicator comes to you courtesy of the S&P E-mini futures. You may also want to refer to the NASDAQ 100 E-mini futures, the Russell 2000 E-minis, and the mini-sized Dow. For brief overviews of these contracts and information about obtaining their quotes, please go to my Web site, *www.toni turner.com* and click on Tutorials and FAQ.

In 1982, the Chicago Mercantile Exchange (*www.cme.com*) introduced stock index futures to their growing number of financial futures contracts. Now the Standard & Poor's 500 Index Futures, or the S&P futures, as they are known to traders, are a highly liquid commodity in its own right. More important to us, however, is that the S&P futures reflect public sentiment and the perceived state of the U.S. economy. That gives these futures incredible power in dictating market direction.

Basically, the futures trade closely in alignment with their correlating cash index. When they diverge, the arbitrageurs (arbs) bring them back into position.

The S&P futures trade closely with its underlying index, the Standard & Poor's 500 (cash, or "spot") Index. The S&P 500 Index, also referred to as the S&P cash, is a benchmark index of 500 large-cap stocks from the major exchanges.

As traders, we watch the E-mini version of its underlying "big" S&P contract. Our reasons: The electronic mini contracts have grown in popularity with institutions, and on many days the E-mini S&P trade more volume than the standard contract. The big contract doesn't display volume, while the mini contracts do. Many of us also trade mini stock futures, so it makes sense we'd watch those contracts, rather than the standard versions.

I position a 5-minute chart of the E-mini S&P futures, with a 20-period MA, in the middle of my screen. Momentum traders and scalpers may want to use a three-minute chart. Because the E-mini S&P futures is the primary leading indicator used by traders, trying to day trade, momentum trade, or scalp without this information may be hazardous to your wealth.

Put a 5-minute chart of the E-mini S&P futures on your screen, if available. Now watch line charts (easier to read) of the NYSE TICK and TRIN alongside each other. Interesting, isn't it? On a positive, easygoing day, the NYSE TICK floats happily above zero, and the NYSE TRIN rests in the 0.50 to 0.90 area. The futures draw a nice uptrend, with mild, but expected, pullbacks. On those days, trading can fun and profitable.

On a whippy, choppy day, though, the TICK flies into positive territory one minute, and dives into negative territory the next. The TRIN digs in and stays above 1.0. The E-mini futures have no mercy either, drawing a jagged chart that resembles a kindergartner's first sketch.

After the opening bell rings, if you see the above pattern develop, consider standing aside. There's no way to outguess the market, and your chances of losing money are enormous.

Another alert: On any day, no matter the conditions, if you see the E-mini S&P futures dive very hard and fast, make sure you know where your stops are. Watch any positions you have without blinking. When the futures talk, traders listen.

Now, with the NYSE TICK, NYSE TRIN, and E-mini S&P futures on your screen, you may want to back off to one target stock and its industry index. Watching more than one or two stocks while acclimating yourself to these three indicators will drive you bonkers.

Note: On occasion, the Dow, S&P 500, and NASDAQ indices diverge in direction from one another. That means the Dow may be going up, but the NAS-DAQ is headed down. Or, the S&P 500 is slipping, but the NASDAQ rises higher. Although the E-mini S&P futures mostly lead the other indices, and the NYSE TICK and TRIN are market benchmarks, if your target stock is a tech or biotech, you may prefer to watch the NASDAQ TICK and TRIN and the E-mini NAS-DAQ 100 futures. If your stock is a Dow Industrial component, you can check out the mini-sized Dow quote, along with the NYSE TICK and TRIN.

### Tuesday
Continue to monitor the NYSE TICK and TRIN, and E-mini futures, and your target stock's relationship to them. Is your stock in sync with the indicators? If not, why? One reason might be news, good or bad, that propels the stock into its own trading pattern. Another reason is that some stocks simply rebel against most indicators and do their own thing. When you trip over a stock like that, avoid day trading or momentum trading it until you internalize its behavior.

### Wednesday

Let's add a Level II screen. For those who insist that their vision is already blurred, that they can't add one more thing or their brains will short-circuit, chin up. We're nearing the end of additions to your screen.

Note: If you don't trade with a direct-access broker or online broker who offers Level II screens, you can skip this section and go onto the next.

As mentioned before, since decimalization, Level II screens have lost their status as a primary trading tool. We now use them chiefly as order-entry vehicles. Still, to use them effectively, you need to know how price volatility shows up on the screens.

For our purposes, please choose an active NYSE stock as your target stock to watch. Now bring up your Level II screen, making sure it includes Time & Sales. Position the Level II screen next to your target stock's intraday chart. Next to that, if you have it, add the index chart of the industry or sector your target stock represents. Don't forget your chart of the E-mini S&P futures, in the same time frame that matches your stock's chart. (That is, make them both 5-minute charts, 15-minute, or 60-minute charts—just so they match.) Nearby, keep the NYSE TICK and TRIN. (You can replace the S&P mini futures with the mini-sized Dow, or use E-mini NASDAQ 100 and NASDAQ TICK and TRIN, if you prefer.)

Okay, I'm assuming the market's open. Let's get personal with your Level II screen. As you watch the screen, go over these bulleted points and observe corresponding actions.

➤ Screen action shows momentary supply and demand.

➤ Depth (how many orders are stacked up) of bid or ask shows momentary strength or weakness. Multiple orders at the inside bid and only one or two on the inside ask shows price strength. Multiple orders on the inside ask and only one or two on the inside bid shows price weakness.

➤ Price moves counter-clockwise, from ask to bid: bullish. Price moves clockwise, from bid to ask: bearish. No pattern: no price direction, or chaos.

➤ About the Size column next to the bid and ask column: Supposedly, this column represents how many shares (usually stated in 100s, so 2 translates into 200) the specialist, market maker, or ECN is bidding for or offering out. Don't believe it. Market professionals, and with the right software, individual traders (you included), can hide their true intentions and thus the size of their orders.

➤ Fortunately, the Time & Sales feature on your Level II screen displays facts the way they are. Under the time of day, Time & Sales lists the "prints," or price and lot size for every trade. No amount of fancy maneuvering alters those facts.

➤ Prints accompanied by size (size equals large share lots) gives a reliable indication of current price direction. Pay attention to large size like 5,000, 10,000, and 20,000 prints going off on the Time & Sales screen. Maybe an institution placed a buy or sell order of a half-million shares, and the order is broken up piece-by-piece, then printing. When momentum trading NYSE stocks, it's wise to "trade toward size." After you've satisfied your other criteria for entering the trade, make sure you're headed in the same direction as the big prints. If size tells you you're swimming against the tide, wait on the beach until the tide turns.

➤ On the Time & Sales screen, don't assume the red prints are sell orders and the green prints are buy orders. Although a stream of red usually indicates a selling frenzy and a stream of green tells you people are buying, the colors actually refer to upticks and downticks. A "tick" is the smallest increment—usually a penny—in which the stock trades. So if the last trade went off at $20, and the next trade goes off at $20.01, it will flash green on your Time & Sales screen. If the next trade goes off at $20, it will flash red on your Time & Sales. This $20 trade could be a trader buying at a better price than $20.01. Maybe he or she put in a limit order to buy shares at $20, and the trade was filled.

➤ Next, look at the inside bid and ask prices. When you sell a stock "at the market," you receive the price on the inside bid. Now, though, do the prints tell you traders are "splitting the bid and the ask"? If so, that indicates the specialist may let you sell the stock one or two cents higher than the posted bid price. Or you may be able to buy one or two cents lower than the current ask, or offer.

➤ When you're buying, think of the inside bid and ask as retail prices, and the prices in between as "wholesale" prices. When you split the bid and ask, and buy a fraction lower than the "advertised" price at the offer, it's like buying the stock wholesale instead of retail.

➤ Stocks are not always on sale. When the prints tell you the stock is being bought at the offer price, and not in-between, it's really a positive indicator. The specialist is demanding retail prices for his or her stock and is getting it. Demand equals rising price.

➤ When a NYSE stock I really wants moves up fast, I'll pay retail rather than lose my chance to get in. If, however, the stock's moving slowly and I'm buying it as a swing or core trade, I'll attempt to buy wholesale by slipping a limit order into the middle of the bid and ask. (Limit orders are defined at the end of the chapter.) Sometimes it gets filled, sometimes it doesn't. If I really want the stock, and my order doesn't get filled quickly, I'll cancel it and buy at the offer price.

➤ I do the same when I want to sell. If I want to get out fast, I'll accept the current bid price. If I have time and profits on my side, I'll enter a sell order that splits the bid and ask, and see if the specialist bites. If he or she doesn't, I'll cancel and re-enter the order at the bid price.

➤ You can split the bid and offer with an online broker by issuing a limit order. The drawback: Without Level II access, you can't monitor your order on the screen; therefore, you cannot gauge the odds of it being filled.

For the remainder of the day, watch the prints, and keep close tabs on the other indicators on your screen as well. Notice how the stock price ebbs and flows with the NYSE TICK and TRIN, and E-mini S&P futures, as well as the industry index.

### Thursday

Today, change your target stock to a medium volatile NASDAQ stock that moves at a reasonable pace. If you like, also put up time-correlated screens of the E-mini NASDAQ 100 and the NASDAQ TICK and TRIN. Or, leave those as they were yesterday.

For a quick refresher, let's confirm some points you've learned about the Level II screen. Because you're watching a NASDAQ stock, we'll refer to market makers (from now on referred to as MMs), instead of specialists, although both will be present on the bid and ask on your Level II screen.

Note: The following bullet points are directed to intraday traders, although longer-term traders may benefit from it.

**HOT TIP**

When a stock's moving higher, keep your eye on the bid for true price momentum. If market makers raise the ask price, but leave the bid as is, watch the bid. The price they're willing to buy the stock for (bid price) reveals their true intentions. When they raise the ask, but leave the bid at a lower price, that tells you they're trying to lure unsuspecting traders into thinking the price will jump higher.

➤ The left side, or bid side, of the market maker screen is where MMs wait for you to sell your stock to them. (You sell, they buy.) The right, or offer side, is where MMs offer stock for you to buy from them. (You buy, they sell.)

➤ When you're trading with a Level II order entry system, you get to play MM. You can buy on the bid and sell on the offer. The good news: This saves you the spread, and saves you money. The challenging news: It takes practice and market savvy to capitalize on it. If your stock has a single penny spread, depending on the lot size of your order, it may, or may not, be worth the time spent to save the spread.

➤ Suppose the stock you want to buy has broken over resistance. It's running up fast. Buy it on the offer (but no chasing) and be done with it. Trying to buy on the bid is a waste of time—the stock will run away from you. Why? If you're trying to buy on the bid, along with the other MMs (your order will be posted with the ECN of your choice), somebody has to want to sell their stock to you. When a stock looks as though it's heading for the moon, sellers are few and far between.

➤ However, if your stock's just breaking out, the whole world hasn't noticed, and there's still a little selling pressure, post your buy order at the inside bid price, or a penny higher (this is called "going high bid"). If it's filled, you're ahead. Assuming the stock rises when you take profits, you'll "make the spread" as well. If the stock reverses and heads down, you're in at a lower price than retail, or the offer price, and therefore closer to your stop. That makes for a smaller loss.

➤ Now it's time to sell the position. When your stock is still climbing like a jet bound for heaven, Time & Sales is full of green prints, and you have a tidy profit, that's when you post your sell order at the ask price. Sell into buying pressure. When everybody's still buying, your ask price should be filled in a heartbeat. Be assured the euphoria driving all the green prints skyward can reverse to fear, and falling red prints, in an "ohnosecond." (An ohnosecond arrives at that moment when you realize you've made a mistake, and it's going to cost you.) Wealthy trader saying: "Sell when you can, not when you have to."

➤ If the trade sours, and the stock collapses like a punctured balloon, don't attempt to sell at the offer. To sell at the offer, someone's got to buy that ugly stock from you at a high price. You'd best "hit the bid," or if it's really falling fast, the price level under the inside bid price.

Other factors come into these tactics, and you'll read about them later. For now, though, if your Level II system offers a paper trading mode, during a calm moment, practice buying on the bid and selling on the ask.

**HOT TIP**

If you create charts of the NYSE, *or* NASDAQ TICK and TRIN, try plotting them as line charts. That smooths their volatility and makes their action easier to interpret. I overlay TICK and TRIN on the same chart, in two different colored lines. One glance tells me where they are in relationship to one another.

**Friday**

Today, continue watching the interaction between the TICK and TRIN of your choice (NYSE or NASDAQ, or both, if you prefer), and E-mini S&P futures (and other mini stock index futures of your choice) along with the intraday chart of your target stock and its corresponding Level II screen.

Pull up another chart for your target stock, if possible, and assign it a different time frame. If your original intraday chart is a 5-minute chart, pull up a chart of the same stock, and make it a 15-minute or 60-minute chart. Add the same moving averages, say, the 20 MA and the 200 MA. Then, if you spot a breakout or breakdown taking place on one chart, notice how it appears as a similar pattern on the other chart. Check the volume and moving averages.

**HOT TIP**

If you have access to the Russell 2000 E-mini futures (subscribe at *www.cme.com*), and you have available screen space, keep a quote or 5-minute chart of the index handy. At times, the Russell E-mini will lead the E-mini S&Ps and NASDAQ 100s.

The key to executing highly profitable day trades is to make sure you have the same signal—buy or sell—on three different time frames. For example, your stock is bouncing off support on a daily or hourly chart, then the 5- and 15-minute charts simultaneously show ideal setups and entries.

In addition to the breakout pattern you've already learned, I'll give you more patterns to look at in the following chapters.

At the time you enter the trade, it's best when the stock sits right on top of the moving average on both time frames. If it's riding too many points above the 20 MA, the stock is overextended, and may not rise much farther. Today, watch stocks on intraday charts break out by bouncing off support. Look for support areas formed by price consolidations, price reversals (down to up), and support formed by moving averages.

Watch stocks break out by moving through key, or major, resistance. Observe how volume plays a part. Did volume signal consolidations were ready to breakout? Were the failed breakouts accompanied by weak volume? Or were they caused by deteriorating market conditions? Using what you've learned, analyze why stocks act as they do.

## ORDER TYPES AND DEFINITIONS

Okay, I know your eyes feel bleary and your brain fried, but stay with me. Learning these easy definitions completes Beginning Trader's Boot Camp.

You can buy or sell stocks using the following methods:

**Market Orders:** When you buy or sell a stock "at the market," you're giving the specialist or market maker carte blanche. That person chooses what price you pay or receive for your stock. Also, there may not be shares available at your chosen entry point when your order reaches them. (I've watched market makers, especially on a thinly traded stock, lower the bid when my "sell at the market" order reached them.) If you're trading a high-volume, orderly stock and don't want to chase it, enter a market order. If you must buy or sell in a panic, use a market order. Otherwise, use limit orders. If they don't get filled, don't chase. Other opportunities are out there.

**Limit Order:** When you place a limit order, you give instructions that you wish to buy or sell a specified number of shares of stock when they reach a specified price. You place a limit order to buy at a price lower than the posted inside offer. Or, you place a limit order to sell above the posted inside bid. The specialist or market maker will fill your limit order only when the stock's price reaches your specified price, or better.

You use a limit order to specify a price when you're buying and want to split the bid and ask, or when you're attempting to buy on the bid and sell on the offer. If a stock runs away from you, you can place a limit order to buy a certain number of shares at a certain price, under the current price. Of course, your order may get filled, or it may not. The same procedure takes place with a sell order. If you own a stock and want to sell it at a higher price than it's currently posted, you issue a limit order to sell your shares at a price above the posted price. Again, your order may be filled, but if the stock doesn't reach your specified price, you'll be left dangling. Limit orders can be either "day orders" or GTC, meaning "good till canceled."

**AONs:** AON means "all or nothing." You may also have the choice designated AON. Translation: If the specialist or market maker cannot fill the total number of shares you request, you don't want the order filled at all. That is, if you put in a limit order for 500 shares at a certain price AON, and they can give you only 350 shares at that price, it tells them to ignore the order. I usually leave the AON box unchecked. Sometimes, on fast-moving stock, I get filled for funny, odd lots, like 26 shares at the limit price, out of my requested 1,000. I shrug it off and deal with the odd lots, but you may decide to indicate AON on your orders.

**Buy Stops:** When you place a buy stop, you specify the number of shares you want to buy at a certain price above the stock's posted price. Say Igloo Ice Cream is treading at $20, which is key resistance. If it breaks above $20, that's the perfect entry point. You're well aware, however, that when it moves more than $20, everybody in the entire world will post a buy order for Igloo Ice Cream. How do you get an edge? You place a buy stop order for the number of shares you want, at $20.01, or higher. (I'd set it at $20.05 to give it some room.) Then you sit back and wait. If Igloo doesn't trade over $20, your order will not be filled. A drawback is that buy stops are filled when the stock trades at your specified price, or the next highest price. If you place a buy stop with your online broker for 500 shares of Igloo Ice Cream at $20.01 before the market opens, then the bell rings and Igloo gaps open three points higher, that's where you get filled—at $23.01, or so. Then you have to deal with traders "fading the gap." (To fade a stock means you trade in the opposite direction of the current move. Many traders short stocks that gap open to the upside, called "fading the gap"—as a matter of course.) Stocks that gap open more than a half point higher than their closing price from the day before usually tank—fast. (Gaps down work in the opposite direction.) When the stock opens at $23, and your order is filled, seconds later you could be staring at a posted price of $21. Your lesson? Don't issue buy orders before the market opens. If you're going out for lunch, and there's a slow-moving stock you want to pick up if it breaks out while you're gone, that's good use of a buy stop order.

**Stop-loss Orders:** When you're holding an open long position, you can place a sell stop, or stop loss, under the stock's current posted price. If the stock trades at that price, your stop order reverts into a market order, and your position is liquidated. Or, if you're holding an open short position, you place a buy-to-cover stop for the number of shares you own, at a specified price that's above the current posted price. Again, when the stock trades at that price, the sell stop reverts to a market order, and your position is sold. Because your order reverts to a market order in both of these cases, your position may be liquidated a few cents away from your specified price.

**Stop-loss Limit Orders:** You can enter stop-loss limit orders in the same way you can place stop orders. This tells your broker to sell, or buy-to-cover your specified shares if, and only if, the price touches your stipulated price.

One drawback is that if, for some reason, the price gaps (no shares traded) below or above your indicated price, your order will be left hanging.

➤ Automatic Trailing Stops: Many brokers, both discount and direct access, offer automatic trailing stops. You can set the price amount, such as 10-cents, or 90-cents, or whatever increment you choose, or you can set a percentage amount of the prevailing price. When you send the order, in the case of a long trade, the stop will follow your stock higher, but not lower. If the price tops out and reverses, the automatic trailing stop will stop out the trade when the price falls to the level you set. In the case of a short trade, the reverse is true.

➤ "Fill or Kill" Orders: This indicates you want the trade filled immediately, or cancelled if not filled.

Congratulations. You've completed boot camp. When you start trading you'll be glad you toughed-out the camp, and especially glad you finished it without placing orders. Without stress, you learn more.

In the following chapter, we'll discuss the exact criteria to place trades in each time frame. Then, we'll move into actual trade execution.

This chapter contains a lot of important material, and completing the quiz will crystallize it for you. Consider answering the quiz questions by writing them down. Then refer to your answers during the next few weeks, until the terminology and concepts become second nature.

# QUIZ

IIIIIIIIIIIIIIII

*Questions*

1. Approximately in which time period in the morning does the market generally make its first reversal?

2. True or false? Experienced traders make most of their money on lunchtime trades.

3. Which time of day do bonds close?

4. Stocks played heavily by day traders many times sell off ten to fifteen minutes before the close. Why?

5. True or false? Experienced traders wait at least ten minutes after the opening bell to place their first trade. What reason supports your answer?

6. Indicators generally fall under two headings: _____ and _____ .

7. What's the proper interpretation of the TICK indicator?

8. True or false? When the NYSE TICK shoots over the +1,000 mark, that's a sure sign it's going to rise even higher from there. Smart traders back up the truck and add as many shares as possible to their long positions.

9. What does the TRIN measure?

10. When the NYSE TRIN reads under 1.0, which stocks are the most heavily traded, advancing or declining?

11. When the NYSE TRIN hovers in the _____ area, the bears are fighting the bulls for control.

12. For the best day trading and scalping setups on the long side, you want the TICK _____ and the TRIN _____ .

13. True or false? The S&P 500 futures contract and its E-mini version are one of the most widely used leading indicators in the trading world.

14. On the Time & Sales screen, if a price prints in red, does that indicate those shares were sold? If the answer is "no," why not?

15. If you want to sell a stock fast, do you enter a limit order that splits the bid and ask? Why, or why not?

16. How do traders make the spread?

17. When you're selling a long stock position, is it safest to sell into buying pressure or selling pressure?

18. What is the trick for making the most successful intraday trades?

## Answers

1. Between 9:45 A.M. and 10:10 A.M.

2. Very, very false. Experienced traders rarely trade during the noonday hours.

3. 3:00 P.M. Eastern Standard time

4. Many day traders avoid holding overnight positions; they close all of their positions before the market closes.

5. Experienced traders wait ten minutes, or so, before placing their first trade. Reason: Specialists and market makers control the opening with prices they dictate.

6. lagging, leading

7. The TICK is the number of stocks ticking up (trading at one tick higher than the last trade) versus the number of stocks ticking down (trading at one tick lower than the last trade). Each stock exchange has its own TICK.

8. False. When the NYSE TICK rises over the +1,000 mark, a reversal is in the wind. Smart intraday traders tighten stop-loss points.

9. The TRIN measures market volatility and indicates whether money is flowing into advancing or declining stocks. Each stock exchange has its own TRIN.

10. advancing

11. 1.0

12. above 0, below 1.0

13. True

14. When prices flash green and red on Time & Sales screens, it indicates the trade was executed on an uptick (green) or downtick (red) from the last print. While a red print may be a sale, there's no way of knowing. It merely indicates the stock traded at a lower price than the last trade. Of course, when you see a fast-moving Time & Sales screen with only red prices, you know that the stock's selling off. All green prints show a stock moving higher.

15. No. If you want to sell a stock fast, you don't place your limit order between the bid and ask. In a slow-moving, orderly stock, you can enter a market order or a limit order at the inside bid. If you try to split the bid and offer, you may have to keep canceling and chasing the price down.

16. By buying on the bid and selling at the offer

17. To lock in the safest profits when you're exiting a long intraday trade, sell into buying pressure.

18. To execute the most successful intraday trades, find a stock that's in an uptrend on a daily chart not at former price resistance. You also want it breaking out on two intraday time frames—for example, on both 5-minute and 15-minute charts, with high-probability setups on both charts.

## CENTER POINT: THE POWER OF INTUITION

*"It is only with the heart that one can see rightly; what is essential is invisible to the eye."*

—Saint-Exupery

How do we define *intuition*, our elusive "sixth sense"? Webster's says it's "the power or facility of attaining to direct knowledge or cognition without evident rational thought and inference. Quick and ready insight."

Western civilization teaches and even worships rational, logical thought processes. To depend on a knowingness that exists beyond what we can see, smell, touch, hear, and feel is considered quackery. What a shame! In our strict adherence to judging all situations using only logic and reason, we've ignored a wonderful and intelligent gift inherent in each one of us.

Science now confirms that the human mind operates on two levels: the conscious or rational mind, and the subconscious or intuitive mind. The conscious mind acts like a computer. It processes our experiential data, judges using previous input, and calculates conclusions.

Our intuitive mind, however, has the ability to access a vast storehouse of wisdom and insight beyond our own personal boundaries. It analyzes this information and presents it to us as guidance exactly when we need it. We refer to this insight as intuition, a "gut-feeling."

When we respect and nourish our intuitive sense and allow it to become a guiding force in our lives, our sense of self-trust expands. Feelings of security and empowerment strengthen all areas of our lives.

How do you go about accessing and following your intuition? One way is acknowledging its presence. Another way is by asking questions of this wisest part of you, such as, "What do I need to know, now? What shall I do in this situation?"

A feeling may emerge immediately that you can identify and act upon. If not, trust that the answer to your question will soon appear in an idea, conversation, book, movie, or event. The more you practice, the easier and clearer these communications will be.

Our intuitive power is always available to us. It knows how to overcome challenges and achieve goals. We need only ask, and then trust.

# CHAPTER 9

# Plan Your Trade and Trade Your Plan

Say you're driving to Yuma, Arizona, from Boston, Massachusetts, and you've never been to Yuma before. You wouldn't start driving along the highway without consulting a map, would you?

If your appendix needs to be removed, your surgeon wouldn't (we hope) take scalpel in hand unless he first studied an X-ray, would he? The builder who constructed your home didn't throw pipes and bricks into a pile. He followed the blueprints, right?

Professional athletes don't run onto the ball field without an established game plan.

The legendary UCLA coach John Wooden told his players, "If you fail to plan, you plan to fail." Just as these professionals planned their actions before they executed them, as a successful trader, I'm sure you wouldn't consider placing thousands of dollars on the line without first creating a precise trading plan.

You plan your trade, and trade your plan. Once you've opened a position, the deftness with which you manage the trade determines its success.

First, we'll look at a basic spreadsheet you fill in the minute you buy (or sell short) the stock. We'll discuss top down versus bottom up trading tactics. We'll go on to the simple, but vital, decision support concept called risk-reward analysis. Finally, you'll learn the criteria for entering and exiting long trades in all time frames.

## HOW TO DESIGN YOUR TRADING LOG

Buying a stock is a walk in the park. Consistently exiting trades with a profit, however, involves planning, skill, and discipline. In Chapter 4, we talked about trading with confidence and self-trust. Nothing promotes that terrific feeling like a well-thought-out trading plan.

A simple written plan for each trade is one of the best things you can do for yourself and your account. They stop you from fudging on the stop losses and urge you to take profits realistically.

I keep an informal worksheet when the trade is in progress and complete a trading log when I exit the position. Both are very simple. If you like, combine the two. I don't like too many numbers and columns staring me in the face when the market goes bonkers and I'm searching for stop-loss points.

I trade with a yellow legal pad at my elbow as my worksheet. (Did you know the color yellow promotes better thinking? That's why legal pads are yellow.) My trading log is an Excel spreadsheet.

When I spot a high-probability setup, I calculate the risk-reward ratios on my legal pad, using support and resistance on weekly, daily, and/or intraday time frames, depending on the type of trade (core, swing, or day).

If the setup behaves well and I enter the trade, along with entry price and number of shares, I jot down my initial stop-loss price in the stop column. Then I enter it as a stop-loss order with my broker.

On the rare occasion that I don't enter an automatic stop-loss order, I circle the stop price on my worksheet. (My personal head game to assure I stick to it.)

## HOT TIP

Studies verify that people who mentally store their goals accomplish little. Those who write down their goals accomplish more. The same result occurs when, instead of mentally storing your sell stop, you at least write it down. I realized early in my trading career that when my stock started to drop, I easily justified lowering my mental stop to the next support level. When I wrote that stop down, though, seeing that number on paper supported the discipline to execute it. Of course, your best action is to enter a stop with your broker immediately after entering a trade.

Now that I've taken the trade, even if it's an intraday trade, I record resistance levels on my worksheet displayed on daily, and possibly even weekly, charts. If a stock is overbought, for example, on a daily and weekly chart, it can affect how its price reacts on a daily chart. While buying euphoria and a positive market environment can drive the stock higher in the morning session, profit-taking many times takes over in the afternoon, as traders take their profits and head for the door.

Of course, when my stock nears a potential resistance area that also represents my profit target, I watch it closely. I tighten my stop. I may take partial or all profits.

If the market's strong, though, and my stock shoots through the resistance to a new high, I'll keep the position. Depending on market conditions, I may add to it. Whatever the case, with the resistance number right in front of me, if I'm busy with another trade, I can glance at it and remain aware of the stock's activity.

Figure 9-2 illustrates the columns in a sample spreadsheet.

I allow three spaces on my log to record multiple trade exits. Say you buy 800 shares of Oracle Corp. (ORCL) at $14.29. Then you offer it out in two 300-share lots and a final 200-share lot, taking profits at $14.70, $15.20, and $15.40. It's a good tactic, offers safe profits, and if you design your spreadsheet with multiple exit rows, you have enough room to record each sale separately and the net price, or proceeds.

Of course, if you want to combine your worksheet and trading log, incorporate the column headings in your worksheet into your log. I find that by designating the intended time frame (core, swing, intraday) into my sheet, it keeps me honest. I avoid the urge to ignore mental stops and allow day trades to turn into investments.

**HOT TIP**

The longer the time frame, the stronger the signal. "Buy" signals on weekly charts, for example, are stronger than "sell" signals of the same stock on daily charts. Buy or sell signals on daily charts hold more weight than signals on intraday charts.

| Date | Symbol | Long/short Core, Swing, Day | # shares | Entry Price | Stop | Potential Sup/Res Area (Initial Profit Target) |
|------|--------|------------------------------|----------|-------------|------|------------------------------------------------|
| 5/21 | ORCL | L, Swing | 500 | 14.29 | 13.92 | 15.40 |

**FIGURE 9-1** | Sample of yellow pad worksheet.

| Date | Symbol | Buy/ Short | # shares | Price | Net Cost | Exit Date | # shares | Price | Net Proceeds | Profit/loss |
|------|--------|------------|----------|-------|----------|-----------|----------|-------|--------------|-------------|
| 5/21 | ORCL | B | 800 | 14.29 | 11,442 | 5/23 | 300 | 14.70 | 4,410 | |
| | | | | | | 5/25 | 300 | 15.20 | 4,560 | +608.00 |
| | | | | | | 5/26 | 200 | 15.40 | 3,080 | |

**FIGURE 9-2** | Sample of trading log spreadsheet.

In my book, *Short-Term Trading in the New Stock Market*, you'll find a "trade sheet with a conscience." Besides the basic headings of entry and exit dates, symbol, share size, and profit and loss columns, this sheet lists type of trade (position, swing, intraday), initial stop, profit target, risk-reward ratio, adjusted or trailing stop, and adjusted profit targets. Detailed, yes. But by completing the columns, you learn a lot about risk management techniques and your trading strengths and challenges.

## VIEWPOINT: TOP DOWN VERSUS BOTTOM UP APPROACH

Ask any trader why he or she is a "top down" or a "bottom up" trader, and that person will earnestly try to convince you why he or she is right. Actually, variables in market climate, along with industry group categories, contribute to benefits to both approaches.

### Top Down Traders

Top down traders assess the entire scene before they leap. They're like airline pilots who lift their planes off the ground only when all conditions, including weather and equipment, operate perfectly.

Before placing a trade, a top down trader:

1. Considers overall market trend
2. Checks internal market indicators
3. Inspects a chart of the target stock's industry group
4. Studies the stock's weekly, daily, and intraday charts

If signals align, the trader waits for a precise entry point and enters the trade. If the signals are out of sync or negative, the trader waits for a better opportunity.

### Bottom Up Traders

A bottom up trader looks at the stock's chart at different time frames, and might glance at fundamental information, but ignores market conditions and industry group action.

Sometimes the bottom up approach works well. I've witnessed gut-wrenching days when the Dow tumbled 300 points, and the NASDAQ dove 70, drowning the most stalwart of stocks and making me wonder whether I should give up trading and sell lipstick at Macy's. Even so, when market conditions were at their goriest, a few stocks marched, up two, three, or more points on the ticker tape, blithely ignoring the snarling bears wielding bloody machetes.

### Start Out as a Top Down Trader

Try starting as a top down trader. You want every possible odd in your favor before you risk your money. Three out of five stocks will follow the broader markets higher, especially in a bull market. Four out of five follow the broad indices down in a bear market.

The goal in putting the Dow, NASDAQ, industry indices, and market internals like the TICK, TRIN, and E-mini S&P futures on your screen was to show you how even during the rosiest moments, a strong indicator like the S&P futures can implode suddenly, and drag the majority of stocks with it.

Several trading books show a chart with a candlestick poking through resistance. These books have an an arrow pointing to the breakout candlestick and cheerfully explain, "Buy the breakout." This book gives similar suggestions, but when I write, "buy the breakout," or "sell the breakdown," from this time forward, I'll assume you'll enter that trade from a top down perspective.

Couple the top down trading criteria with common sense. Why enter a position or swing trade (or any trade) on a day when Mother Market is in a rotten mood and odds are good you'll get stopped out? On the other hand, when you already have open core or swing positions, if the E-mini S&P futures undergo a few intraday hiccups, you can ignore them as long as your stop-loss order is in place.

Here is my top down checklist. It applies to all trading time frames except scalping plays. (Scalps are so brief, they need not fill all the criteria, except the market uptrend or downtrend.)

➤ Is the market in an uptrend or downtrend? Remember, the trend is your friend. Trading with the overall market trend increases your odds of success.

➤ Is the FOMC (Federal Open Market Committee), or "the Fed," due to meet in the next day or two, with possible interest rate tightening? (The market dislikes rising ("tightening" of) interest rates. Simply put, it means corporations pay more for their business loans, so their earnings aren't as high.) If so, wait until after the results of the meeting to place longer-term trades.

➤ Is your target company coming out with earnings in the next few days? Please don't risk holding a volatile stock, especially overnight, when its earnings are due to be issued. Companies announce earnings before and after the closing bell. Very few announce during the course of the trading day. If the earnings exceed estimates, the stock may shoot up. But, if earnings are negative, it could gap down the next morning. Now consider the guidance statements issued with earnings. A company might announce good earnings, along with guidance that states the next quarter sales are expected to soften. That can send a stock lower. Also, when giants like Dell or Microsoft announce negative earnings, they take at least their own industry and some-times the entire NASDAQ down with them—otherwise known as a "tech wreck." Stay on top of the dates when giants' earnings announcements are publicized.

➤ If earnings announcements are due and you'd prefer not to exit core positions, check your holdings' Composite Ratings in Investor's Business Daily. Ratings more than 60 or 70 add a comforting, if not foolproof, safety net to the trade.

➤ If you subscribe to a news service that issues pre-earnings estimates by such organizations as Reuters or Zacks, check to see if your holdings' estimates look favorable. They may not be right on the money, but you'll get an idea whether the pros think earnings will be positive or negative.

➤ If your stock is on the NYSE, check the Dow and S&P 500 daily trends; do the same with the NASDAQ Composite if your target stock resides there. Market averages influence stock behavior and direction.

➤ You already know to check the NYSE or NAS-DAQ TICK, TRIN, and E-mini S&P futures to make sure all systems are "going" (TICK posi-tive, TRIN under 1.0, futures in an uptrend).

If this procedure sounds tedious, don't worry. With practice, you'll be able to evaluate this infor-mation in a matter of seconds.

## MARKET SECTORS

There are twelve basic economic sectors in the U.S. stock market. All industry groups, such as banks, biotechs, semiconductors, gold and silver, auto and truck manufacturing, airlines and many more, fall under these headings:

1. Financials
2. Technology
3. Health Care
4. Consumer Cyclicals
5. Consumer Non-cyclicals
6. Industrials
7. Energy
8. Telecommunications
9. Basic Materials
10. Utilities
11. Conglomerates
12. Transportation

## PLAN YOUR TRADE WITH RISK-REWARD ANALYSIS

Risk-reward analysis represents an essential role in pretrade planning. Please enter a trade only if you've conducted your risk-reward analysis.

Here's a basic explanation:

Dicey Delivery presents a good setup and you intend to buy shares of Dicey if it reaches your entry price of $20 per share. You've designated the trade as a swing trade, so your established risk-reward objective should be 1:3. That means one-part risk to three-parts reward.

Next, you decide that if Dicey goes against you, and falls through nearby support at $19, you'll sell. Therefore, $19 represents your initial protective stop and is one point away from your entry price.

Finally, you determine your profit target. You look for resistance, which in this case is the previous high on Dicey's daily chart. Prior resistance is $23. Since your profit goal needs to be at least three points higher than your entry, this price target meets your criteria and adheres to your risk-reward objective. To summarize:

**Entry price:** $20
**Initial protective stop:** $19
**Initial profit target:** $23

You can see how your risk is one point away from your entry price, and your potential profit is three points away from your entry price, yielding a risk-reward ratio of 1:3.

I usually calculate these numbers by establishing my stop-loss point, first. For example, maybe the best entry (break above resistance) is at $30, and my initial stop ("initial" because you'll raise it as your stock moves higher) is at $29.25, a spread of 75 cents.

To achieve a 1:3 risk ratio, I know my profit target has to be at least $2.25 (3 × .75) above $30, or $32.25. That means the prior high, or potential resistance on my target stock's daily chart (swing trade), can be no lower than $32.25. If it is, say, $31, then the potential reward is not large enough to justify the risk.

Can I squeeze the stop-loss price to make it smaller and justify the reward? Sure. However, if you place your stops too close to your entries, you risk getting stopped out a lot. A string of small losses = a big loss.

The longer the time frame of your trade, the larger the reward portion of your ratio should be. Why? Because the longer your capital is at risk, the larger potential reward you should expect.

That's why the recommended risk-reward ratio for swing trades is 1:3, with 1:2 being the minimum. With day trades, a risk-reward ratio of 1:2 is acceptable, but whenever you can find a trade that offers a greater rewards ratio, it's preferable.

Why don't we enter trades with a 1:1 ratio? With slippage and commissions, many times you are starting with a loss when you first enter a trade. The price has to go your way for a percentage of a point just to break even. Over time, a 1:1 ratio delivers a low probability of consistent success.

Certainly, experienced traders take trades with even amounts of risk and reward. Novice traders, however, would do well to keep the odds in their corners until experience sharpens discipline to a razor-like edge.

Calculate your risk-reward ratio before you enter each trade. If it doesn't work out to at least one-part risk to two-part reward—and 1:3 is better—consider avoiding the trade.

## MONEY-MAKING CHART PATTERNS FOR POSITION TRADES

Now let's look at chart patterns and criteria for placing a trade. We'll start with core, or position trades (these are interchangeable terms). In Chapter 10, we'll move into swing and intraday trades.

Study the following patterns carefully. They apply to all time frames.

When you buy a stock for a position trade or short-term investment, plan to hold it for a week, to several weeks, or more. These stocks represent your core holdings. As I mentioned before, they make a nice pillow during times when you feel as though your day trades are using you for a punching bag.

As mentioned in earlier chapters, a position or core trade racks up the highest profits when you locate a stock that's formed a basing pattern for at least two weeks. Longer is better. Why? Price has a better chance of rising when resistance is at a distance. When it breaks out of this base, the sellers are momentarily exhausted. The goal of a core or position trade is to stay in the trade for the breakout and duration of the uptrend on a daily chart.

On core trades, expect multiple points. For these longer-term trades, again, the closer to the leading or initial breakout you enter, the more upside you have ahead of you. In a bull market, high-quality stocks entered at the right time can double in value.

## THE BASICS: CONTINUATION AND REVERSAL PATTERNS

As price cycles move forward in time, these moves create recognizable patterns on charts. As you saw in earlier chapters, the patterns are fueled by human emotions. You could say that you're looking at human behavior on a chart. Because we humans repeat our actions over and over again, they draw similar patterns on charts that hold predictive value to traders.

Technically speaking, these patterns are divided into two basic groups: continuation patterns and trend reversal patterns. A series of horizontal moves create continuation patterns. When uptrends or downtrends become exhausted and reverse, they often form similar, recognizable patterns in the process, known as price reversal patterns.

### Continuation Patterns

Continuation patterns cause pauses, or consolidations, in the stock's prevailing trend. You could say the stock is resting, or taking a break, as swimmers do between laps. After the consolidation, the stock breaks out, and the prior trend resumes (usually). I know we've already covered breakout (and breakdown) patterns, but bear with me. We're going to move in for a closer look.

Remember to differentiate between horizontal moves so you recognize the difference between bona fide consolidations and whippy, choppy, congestion patterns. Stocks in congestion patterns have no clue where they are going.

Also, I've talked about stocks moving sideways, "trading in a range," moving back and forth in two- to three-day or more increments, and moving between a high and low price area. Trading in a range is not consolidation. (If none of this sounds familiar to you, please review Chapter 6.)

As you recall, consolidation means a stock is moving sideways in a tight, orderly fashion. The following interactive demonstration will explain.

Please get up now, and go sit on your bed. Yes, you read correctly. Please go into your bedroom and sit on your bed. Are you sitting? Good. Notice how your weight compresses the bedsprings?

When a stock consolidates, trading in a string of narrow-range days, it has pressure from buyers, or support, pushing it up from below, just as your box spring supports your mattress. The stock also has pressure from sellers, or resistance, who push the price down from above, as the weight of your body applies pressure to your mattress springs.

Now, stand up. When you lift your weight and release the tension by standing, your mattress springs sprang back up, right?

> **HOT TIP**
>
> "Head fakes" are common on daily charts. For example, a stock is moving in an uptrend. Then, it rests in a pennant, or flag. Just when it gives all appearances of moving higher, it laughs and dives down a point, or so. After the rush for the door is done, it climbs higher and goes onto new highs. Moral: Don't load up with more than an initial lot until you have confirmation of a continuation breakout.

The tension builds in a consolidating stock until the sheer volume of either bulls or bears (demand or supply) overpowers the other. At that point, it releases, or even explodes to the upside. You could say the stock's price springs into a breakout; in a downtrend, the stock breaks down (if you refuse to stand up, eventually, the bed sags). As we stated, after a stock consolidates, it usually resumes its prevailing trend.

Common and trader-friendly continuation patterns are called lines, triangles, flags, and pennants. A continuation pattern acts as the "pause that refreshes." It allows the trending stock to rest by moving sideways or pulling back; then the stock continues moving in its current trend. Figure 9-3 shows line consolidations in a breakout (uptrend) and breakdown (downtrend).

The next pattern (Figure 9-4) is a form of consolidation that coils even more spring-like. Depending on the book you're reading, you'll hear it called a *triangle* or *wedge*. You can call it a *turnip*, if you want to, as long as you recognize it when you see it.

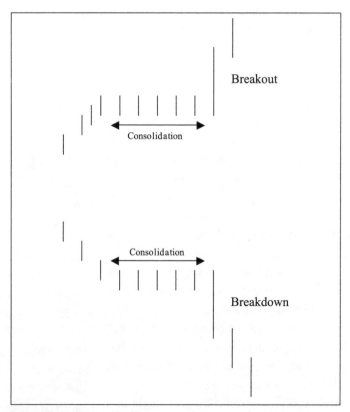

**FIGURE 9-3** | Line consolidation.

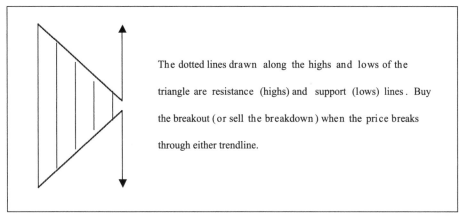

The dotted lines drawn along the highs and lows of the triangle are resistance (highs) and support (lows) lines. Buy the breakout (or sell the breakdown) when the price breaks through either trendline.

**FIGURE 9-4** | Symmetrical triangle. Bulls and bears are evenly balanced.

It consists of a wide range bar, followed by tighter and tighter days. Stay on the lookout for this pattern, and when you see it forming, monitor it for a breakout. It produces dandy trades.

A *pennant* is a small symmetrical triangle, a bit more horizontal in shape (Figure 9-5). At its conclusion, the prevailing trend usually resumes. This is a terrific long-term pattern, and it also forms nicely on intraday charts during the lunchtime period. If it breaks out about 2:30 P.M., with a bullish market environment, you buy the breakout.

A flag develops when prices move sideways in a parallelogram, or rectangular shape; sometimes prices slope against the prevailing trend (Figure 9-6). Think: pullback in uptrend, or rally in downtrend.

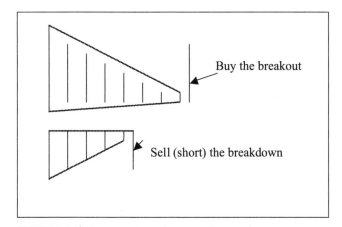

**FIGURE 9-5** | Pennants or descending or ascending triangles.

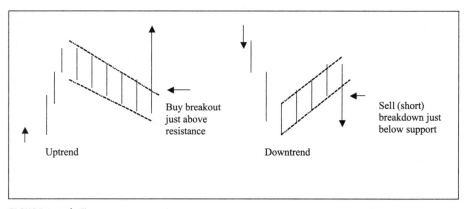

**FIGURE 9-6** | Flag.

As mentioned, patterns are either a continuation or reversal. Reversal, as you know, means a trend changes direction. We'll talk about reversals as we progress. Please keep candlestick patterns in mind. Remember doji, such as evening star doji and morning star doji? How about the hanging man and hammer? When you use these candle patterns in conjunction with the preceding patterns, it increases your odds for success.

### Reversal Patterns

The following trend reversal patterns, detailed in Figures 9-7 through 9-12, are reliable and easy to spot. It's imperative you learn to spot trend reversals on both long-term and short-term time frames. After all, when a stock or an entire market is changing from bullish to bearish, or bearish to bullish, you know to take profits on current positions and prepare to open new ones in the direction of the new trend.

The double-bottom, cup-with-a-handle, and reverse head-and-shoulders are bottom reversal patterns, with continuation patterns tacked on.

You can study additional books on charting and find many more to add to these. When you first start trading, though, you'd be smart to learn two or three patterns and learn them well. Keep it simple. You'll make more money and have more fun.

## DOUBLE-BOTTOM PATTERN

This is one of my favorite bottom reversal patterns. It's one of the most powerful chart patterns for traders and works in various ways for all time frames. If you add two more legs in a V-shape, you get a triple-bottom. Triple-bottoms are rare, but even more powerful than the double-bottom. Add two more legs, and you'll see a quadruple-bottom—even better. Remember, the more times price tests support and doesn't penetrate it, the higher it can move if it breaks to the upside.

**HOT TIP**

Buying a pullback as price moves down, in hopes of catching the bottom of the pullback and the reversal is called "catching a falling knife." To novice traders, the maneuver can result in a sliced and diced account.

A double-bottom formation looks like a W. You'll see the pattern forming on daily charts when the stock is basing, or bottoming. The pattern is only a bona fide double-bottom when it is a complete W shape.

After the double-bottom completes its formation, the stock should pull back slightly, then move in a sideways consolidation pattern for a few days. The longer it consolidates, the more powerful the breakout should be (Figure 9-7).

When and if the stock breaks above the consolidation zone, on strong volume, buy one-half your intended position when the stock trades over resistance.

During the initial pullback, monitor the volume. It should decrease.

On the positive reversal day that ends the pullback—on a daily chart, this would be a clear candlestick with a shaven head—check the stock a few minutes before the market closes. Only if the stock is trading near the high of the day, and the volume is strong, buy the second half of your position. If the stock doesn't close near its high on strong volume, don't buy.

For a safer entry point, wait until the following day, which I call a "nice spring day." When the stock trades a few cents over the reversal day's high, buy.

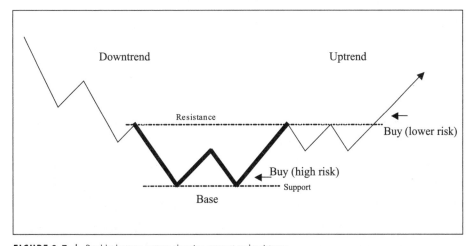

**FIGURE 9-7**  |  Double-bottom pattern showing support and resistance.

Very important: Pullbacks have to halt, reverse, and then break above their own resistance to be playable. Those breakout days I call "nice spring days" are the safe points to enter, once the stock trades a few cents over the reversal day. Buying on the positive reversal day (closing on high with increased volume)—the day prior to the nice spring day—is much higher risk, but as long as your risk-reward analysis is accurate and your stop order is in place, the play can yield nice profits.

Figure 9-8 shows a close-up of the pullback. Figure 9-9 shows how the same pullback pattern appears on a daily chart.

The daily chart of the Lear Corp. (LEA) in Figure 9-10 shows a double-bottom pattern and buying opportunities.

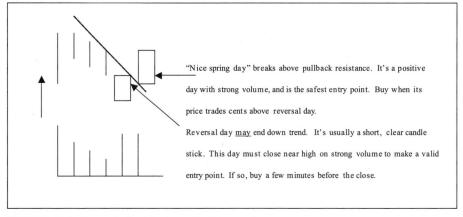

**FIGURE 9-8** | Closeup of pullback breakout with valid entry points.

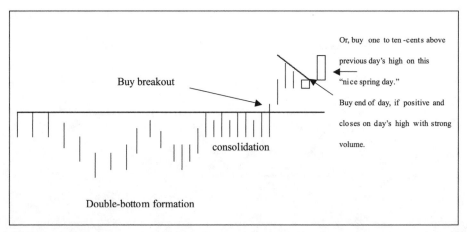

**FIGURE 9-9** | Double-bottom, breakout, and pullback and spring entry points.

One reason the double-bottom creates great buying opportunities is the short squeeze created on the first few reversal days right after the retest holds and starts higher. The traders holding the stock short see that the downtrend may be ending, so they exit their short positions. That creates buying, and with bulls also buying, a stock in this pattern can chew through price levels—fast.

The double-top pattern mirrors the double-bottom, and is shaped like an *M*. As positive as the double-bottom formation is in foretelling a strong uptrend, a double-top is equally negative and warns that a lethal downtrend may be brewing. Short sellers can sell when a weak stock penetrates consolidation

**HOT TIP**

If you're not sure which way a stock will head when it's finished consolidating, check where it closes at the end of each consolidation day. Although there are no guarantees, a stock closing near its high for the day is positive; closing near its daily lows suggests it may break lower. Check your overbought and oversold indicators for divergences.

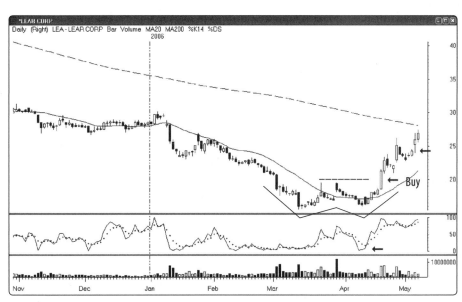

**FIGURE 9-10** | This daily chart of the Lear Corp. (LEA) shows a classic double-bottom and an energetic price upswing from its first pullback in late April. Plotted on the chart is the 20-day MA (solid line) and 200-day MA (dotted line). As you can see, this manufacturer of automotive interiors sold off hard. From January to mid-March, it lost 50% of its equity. LEA retested its March 15.80 low in April and held support. Then it reversed to the upside and quickly completed its double-bottom pattern. By the first part of May, it recovered nearly all of its losses for the calendar year. If you start at the April retest, do you recognize a perfect 1, 2, 3 pattern with an additional upswing? Note the volume on this mini uptrend: high on the upswings and low on the pullbacks—just the way we want it for healthy core and swing trades on the long side. One more signal: Check the bullish divergence on Stochastics just before the retest reversed and headed higher (arrow).

RealTick® graphics used with permission of Townsend Analytics, Ltd. © 1986-2007 Townsend Analytics, Ltd.

support. We'll talk about shorting techniques in Chapter 11 and show examples of double-top patterns.

## CUP-WITH-HANDLE PATTERN

William O'Neil, the founder of Investor's Business Daily, named this pattern. It crops up on all time frames and can deliver nice profits. For core and swing trades, look for this pattern on daily charts when a stock is basing, or bottoming. It resembles a side view of a coffee cup with a rounded bottom and handle, such as the pattern illustrated in Figure 9-11. Figure 9-12 shows a close-up of the pattern with buy signals.

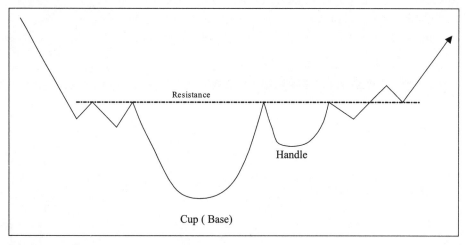

**FIGURE 9-11** | Cup-with-a-handle reversal pattern with breakout into uptrend.

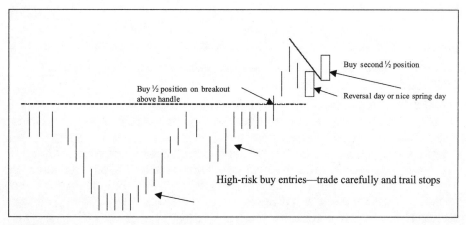

**FIGURE 9-12** | Cup-with-a-handle pattern.

When the cup-with-handle is complete, a period of consolidation will assure the pending breakout rises on a full head of steam. Once the price breaks above resistance formed by the top of the cup, the handle, and consolidation, buy on strong volume. Buy one-half your position when the stock trades above resistance. Buy the second half when the pullback reverses into a nice spring day. For the safest entry, wait for the stock to trade 5 to 10 cents above the high of the nice spring day.

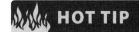

**HOT TIP**

Because we enter position trades with the intent of holding the security for the duration of the uptrend or downtrend, we also refer to these trades as "trend trades."

Figure 9-13 shows a daily chart of Dow component DuPont E I De Nemours & Co. (DD) showing a cup-with-handle, subsequent breakout, and entry points.

**FIGURE 9-13** | This daily chart of DuPont (DD) shows the huge chemical and technology company also selling off in January and into the first days of February. The only moving average on the chart is the 20-day MA. You can clearly see the chart pattern with the sideways view of a cup-with-a-handle. The pattern actually created an island reversal, with a gap down at the beginning and a gap to the upside in the completion. The cup portion also shows a quick double-bottom in January and February. You can buy early in the cup as it reverses to the upside (note Stochastics bullish divergence) and moves above and closes over the 20 MA, but a safer place to buy is the completion of the handle, or after it breaks out of its subsequent consolidation and heads into an uptrend (arrows).

**HOT TIP**

To enter a position trade, I plot Stochastics on the middle scale and use its bullish divergence as one component of my entry strategy. Once I'm in the position trade, I replace Stochastics with the MACD, and watch its signals for a possible sell signal. Remember, with a zippy stock, Stochastics can lose its predictive effectiveness by jumping quickly to its overbought zone and staying there.

Of course, experienced traders will want to enter earlier, as the handle moves up from its higher low.

## REVERSE HEAD-AND-SHOULDERS

In the chapter on shorting, we'll talk about the lethal top reversal pattern known as the "head-and-shoulders." We need to mention the reverse head-and-shoulders at this point, because it's a great bottom reversal pattern. Think of someone standing on his head. Now imagine the outline of his left shoulder, head, and right shoulder.

For some reason, the reverse head-and-shoulders can be a confusing pattern for new traders to spot. My personal learning experience always reminds me of a coloring book my mother gave me when I was a youngster.

She pointed to a page drawn with nothing but large jungle leaves. "Can you find twelve monkeys in that jungle?" she asked. I remember staring at the page intently. Finally, one by one, the leaf formations revealed monkeys staring

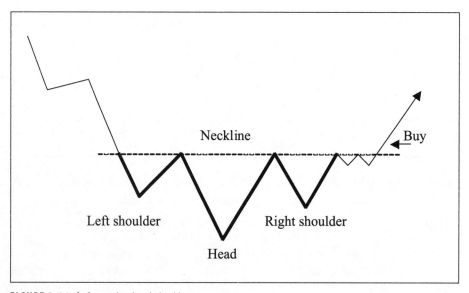

**FIGURE 9-14** | Reverse head-and-shoulders.

out at me. After a few minutes of concentration, I proudly pointed to all twelve monkeys.

After you stare at charts long enough, reverse head-and-shoulders will start appearing here and there. With experience, you'll spot them as they are forming. They are potent patterns and offer excellent setup opportunities.

Figure 9-14 illustrates the outline of a reverse head-and-shoulders. The "neckline" refers to the resistance that lines up across the pivot points of the dips that form the shoulders and head. A price break and close above the neckline is generally the safest entry point for a long position trade.

Figure 9-15 displays a daily chart of the Chevron Corp. (CVX) and a reverse head-and-shoulders pattern that led to a profit-making move.

**FIGURE 9-15** | This daily chart of the Chevron Corp. (CVX) shows the global energy company selling off at the end of January. Although it didn't break down to much lower levels, it did move through a reverse head-and-shoulders pattern before rising higher and overcoming prior resistance. The optimum entry for this pattern arrives when the price breaks above the neckline, although experienced players may have taken initial shares when CVX held the lows of the right shoulder and began to push higher. In this case, the neckline break experienced choppiness, and players might have gotten stopped out before CVX pulled back and started higher.

Once again, note the bullish divergence on Stochastics that signaled a buy before CVX began its reversal. Please remember, leading indicators may display bullish or bearish divergences, but they do not offer price or time projections that tell us how much, or for how long, the price reversal will last.

## PLAIN VANILLA BREAKOUT

As you know, every stock has a different personality. When a stock wanders sideways in a basing formation, it may not develop a cup-with-handle, or a double-bottom. It may just consolidate until good news, earnings, or accumulation propel it higher. It's still very playable—in fact I like these patterns better, as entry points are easy to determine.

 **HOT TIP**

Sometimes bases form in shallow, rounded bottoms. We also call these patterns "saucers."

**FIGURE 9-16** | This plain vanilla, easy-to-spot base etched by United Technologies Corp. (UTX) on its daily chart created an equally easy-to-enter setup. We drew a horizontal line over the tops of the base's highs, and once the services and technology conglomerate shot through the resistance, we bought UTX at 52.30 for a position trade. Because the angle of the uptrend proved so steep, and as we know, steep uptrends can result in steep pullbacks, we decided to use the initial trendline, stretched along the continuing price move, as our stop-loss objective. You could think of the line as a "deadline." Once UTX crosses below the line, we exit the trade. You could have also used the 20-day MA, which paralleled our trendline, moving just beneath it. Note the sell signal issued by the MACD plotted in the middle scale (arrow), a couple of days before UTX rolled over. Another signal that the trend was losing strength: The sell month was December. Many traders, investors, and fund managers who thought the stock was overbought decided to take their profits before the end of the year. Of course, serious traders who noticed the shooting star that gapped above the price pattern and the subsequent exhaustion gap back down probably grabbed their profits one point higher, at 58, rather than wait for UTX to hit the trendline or 20 MA. Nice trade!

The tighter and more orderly the consolidation pattern, the lower the risk. As long as it fits your top down criteria and pushes above the highs of the base resistance price zone, you can play it for intraday, swing, or position trades.

Figure 9-16 shows United Technologies Corp. (UTX) breaking out of a clear-cut base and shooting into an easily defined uptrend. Traders profited five solid points in this trade, offered by a steady, but steep rise higher.

**HOT TIP**

Many fund managers track stocks bouncing off their 50-day MAs and their 200-day MAs on daily charts. If you find a stock springing off its rising 50 MA at the same time the market's breaking out, it could prove to be a terrific entry for a profitable intraday and/or swing trade.

## KNOW YOUR STOP BEFORE YOU SHOP

In a class I was teaching a few years ago, I talked to a young man whom I knew had steadily lost money. Still, he hung on. He showed me a day trade he was playing. It looked risky to me, and out of habit, I asked, "Where's your stop?"

He blushed and shrugged. As much as I liked him, I knew from experience that trading without stops would whittle his account down to bedrock as surely as the Colorado River etched out the Grand Canyon. Unfortunately, I was right. This young man blew his entire account and had to go back to his original day job. Since then, I've seen this happen over and over again, to traders who ignore risk management.

As I stressed before, the trick with stops, no matter what time frame you're trading, is to write them down before you enter the trade. (Your best bet is to enter an automatic stop order with your broker immediately after taking a trade.)

When the stock you're playing hits your stop, that's where the rubber meets the road! That's when you arrive face-to-face with the emotions we discussed in Chapter 4. Fear: *Is this the right thing to do?* Need to be right: *I don't have to sell now. This is a good company.* Greed: *If I sell now, I'll take a loss. I'll wait until it bounces.* Hope: *In just a minute, the futures will hit support. If I get lucky, they'll bounce, and this stock will recover with the futures.*

Please shut your ears to these voices, no matter how insistent and tantalizing they are. When your stock hits its stop, execute your sell order swiftly,

**HOT TIP**

If you see volume coming into an orderly base and the stock doesn't move lower, and your top down criteria is in agreement, buy an initial lot to get an early start on the potential breakout. Enter an automatic stop with your broker just under base support lows.

robot-like, with no emotion. The trader saying, "Your first loss is your smallest loss," is mighty accurate.

First and foremost, if you instituted the risk management strategy listed in Chapter 3 that stated you would risk no more than 2% of your account equity on a single trade, adjust your shares for each trade to conform to that strategy.

For position and swing trades, place your initial stop-loss order 10 cents to 70 cents below the entry day's low, or 25 cents below intraday support (adjusted for stock's volatility) on a 60-minute chart.

Please use common sense. If you are trading a $50 stock with an average price range of $1.50 per day, you have to give it a wider stop—say, 50 to 75 cents under support—to allow for volatility, than you do a quiet $10 stock. The $10 stock may move in an average price range of 50 cents per day, so a 20-cent stop below the support level would work well.

As your stock moves up, establish a trailing stop: Whenever the stock progresses through a continuation pattern, and then moves higher, pull your trailing stop up and place it 25 to 50 cents under the continuation pattern's lows (support zone). That way, you won't give back your profits if the stock decides to make an unexpected dive. Of course, you can trail your stop under a trendline or 20-day MA, if you wish.

Here's an alternative stop method for position trades: Adhere to the stop-loss method just discussed until your stock's uptrend makes at least two pullbacks and two prominent highs. Then, draw a trendline connecting the lows of the pullbacks, as we discussed in Chapter 5. Next draw a channel line connecting the highs as shown in Figure 9-16.

Just as the bottom trendline acts as support, when you connect two or more highs with the top channel line, it defines the resistance area where the new highs of the uptrend will likely reverse. The next time your stock (daily chart) approaches this upper channel line, yet fails to touch it, consider taking a portion of your profits. If the right conditions prevail, you can buy the shares back when or if it bounces off the lower trendline. This way, though, you've locked in gains, and the rest is gravy.

If you want to take profits early on, wait until you make one or two points, then sell half or two-thirds of your position. If the stock continues to defy gravity, replace those shares at the pullback bounce.

**HOT TIP**

Ultra-strong stocks experiencing a mega-steep breakout may rise three days in a row. When swing trading: At the end of the third day, the stock is considered overbought. By the fourth day, expect it to retrace, or pull back. Depending on market conditions and trading time frames, traders should consider taking half or all of their profits at the end of the third day.

Another profit point, particularly for swing trades: If your stock goes ballistic and gaps open to the upside two days in a row, grab your profits at the end of the second gap day (third day up). On the second gap open, shorts and sellers wait right around the corner, drooling and sharpening their claws. Few things are more irritating than riding a stock up to sky-high profits, then holding on while it drops back to your entry price, or worse, to your old stop.

> **HOT TIP**
>
> When you establish your stop-loss price before you enter, you may realize the spread between your entry price and stop price exceeds your risk-reward level. If it does, you'll be glad you looked before you leapt.

Time stop: Say you take a trade and after two to four days (sooner, if you prefer) the stock hasn't moved in the direction you predicted. Although it hasn't touched your stop-loss point, perhaps it's acting listless or drifting lower. If you also see a negative market environment, you may want to lighten up on your lot size.

Final stop-loss point and exit: If your long position trade makes a lower low, that's the absolute deadline for you to exit the trade. Remember, the definition of an uptrend is a stock climbing in higher highs and higher lows. If a stock makes a lower low than the previous pivot low, the uptrend is broken.

These stop-loss points and exit strategies come with a caveat. If CNBC suddenly announces a highly negative global event or the Fed chief appears on the screen and utters the words "inflation" or "tighten interest rates," tighten your stops or exit. Don't wait for your stocks to crash and burn. Take profits fast. Then you can cluck sympathetically and hold the door open for the squealing slowpokes.

Here's a checklist to guide you through position and swing trade entries. You may want to keep it next to your computer. Remember, before you run through the checklist and place your order, your top down criteria should be satisfied.

### Buy Checklist: Position Trades

1. Either stock is in an uptrend (higher highs and higher lows) or it shows strong evidence of breaking out and initiating an uptrend on daily chart.
2. Stock is trading over its rising 50- and 200-day MAs (optimum: bouncing off of 20-day MA). If you are bottom fishing, the stock should be trading above its 20-day MA.
3. MAs are layered in proper order (20-day MA above 50-day MA, and 50-day MA above 200-day MA), not inverted, except in cases bottom fishing. Then, buy only when it has closed above its 20-day MA.
4. Entry day shows strong volume.

5. Stochastics, CCI, or MACD displays oversold reading and hooks up in a bullish divergence, or is trending higher.

6. Perform your risk-reward analysis. Use entry, stop, and profit target prices. The stock's initial move should offer a 1:3 risk-reward ratio.

7. If all conditions read "go," when stock trades one to 10 cents above initial breakout resistance, buy one-half of your intended position.

8. Buy the second half of position on pullback reversal day only if your stock is closing near day's high on strong volume.

9. Or buy the second half of position when nice spring day trades above pullback reversal day's high.

10. Adjust stop-loss between 25 cents and 70 cents (not more than $1.50) under nearby support.

11. When the second pivot low from the bottom is established, draw a trendline under the lows. Establish your risk strategy: stop-loss under each succeeding consolidation support, or under initial trendline, or under 20-day MA (or 30-day MA, if a wider stop is preferred). Close position if the stock closes below the trendline or MA on its daily chart.

From now on, you'll see the entry price stated as "buy when the stock trades one to 10 cents above resistance . . ." Again, and always, please use common sense. The entry just above resistance simply assures that other traders are willing to buy at a higher price than nearby resistance highs. With some volatile stocks, no matter how fast you enter your order, the price may jump missile-like. It may take 10 cents above the breakout price to have your order filled. I specified 10 cents as a limit to remind you not to chase the price higher and higher. You will miss entries. It's part of trading. Let the price run without you and wait for another opportunity there, or elsewhere.

In Chapter 10, we'll look at additional chart patterns and buy criteria that apply to both swing trades and day trades.

# QUIZ
||||||||||||||||||

## Questions

1. Briefly describe the "top down" criteria.
2. True or false? The best way to assure a successful trading career is to jump headfirst into momentum plays on your first trading day.
3. Basically, price draws two types of patterns on a chart: _____ and _____.
4. A double-bottom pattern on a stock chart resembles a big _____.
5. True or false? When the stock reaches the top of the last leg of the W, and breaks through resistance, it's a buy signal.
6. Every breakout, no matter the time frame, needs one common ingredient to assure its success. What is that ingredient?
7. How does a "trailing stop" work?
8. Describe a stop-loss strategy for position trades.
9. When you're ready to buy a stock, in which order, from the top down, is the optimum moving averages line up?

   **A:** 200, 50, 20.
   **B:** 50, 20, 200.
   **C:** 20, 50, 200.
10. True or false? A wise trader buys half of his or her position at the breakout and the other half at the next pullback reversal or breakout.

## Answers

1. Before entering a trade, the "top down" trader considers overall market trend; checks market internals; rates the stock's industry group; knows of no earnings or economic reports that would sour the trade; and studies the stock's weekly, daily, and intraday charts.
2. False. Not a good idea.
3. continuation, reversal
4. W
5. False. Always wait until the stock finishes the W pattern, then pulls back and experiences multiday consolidation before buying the breakout.
6. Strong volume
7. Each time the stock creates a resting stop or continuation pattern on its daily chart, the trailing stop is adjusted to 25 cents to 75 cents under support lows.
8. A risk management plan for position trades is to exit the trade if or when the stock breaks the initial trendline and closes below it.
9. C: 20, 50, 200.
10. True

## CENTER POINT: PRACTICE HEALTHY SELFISHNESS

*"Do you want to be a power in the world? Then be yourself. Be true to the highest within your soul and then allow yourself to be governed by no customs or conventionalities or arbitrary artificial rules that are not founded on principle."*

—Ralph Waldo Emerson

The quest for self-understanding takes time and effort. Those who believe time spent dwelling on inner growth is selfish may want to reconsider that supposition.

To achieve balance and true power, we must travel the inner and outer path. Either one by itself will not take us where we need to go. The inner path is the most difficult—it's the path of self-knowledge and of consciousness development.

We've explored and transformed the frontiers of the outer world magnificently in the last two centuries. We've dissected the atom and delved into its secrets. We've invented wonderful gadgets, machines, and computer networks to modernize our lives. We've landed on the moon and sent cameras and telescopes to explore distant planets. The Hubbell telescope revealed that the universe is bigger and older than we thought it was. Indeed, we humans find it quite acceptable to spend time investigating our outer world.

Yet, we've scarcely inquired into the other frontier—ourselves, and our unique inner space.

Those who take time to reflect and study their own emotions, beliefs, and personal goals may appear selfish to those around them. Yet, is it truly selfish to spend time exploring your own potential? Is it selfish to learn your own power and discover your highest possibilities? Is it selfish to live fully, with a deep inner sense of meaning and satisfaction gained from self-knowledge? Is it virtuous to remain unaware of our deepest belief systems? Is it healthy to live in inner darkness, instead of inner light?

It's impossible to give to others what we, ourselves, don't have. We only forgive fully, once we've forgiven ourselves. We only love truly, when we love ourselves. We give authentic support, peace, and joy only when we bring them up from our own internal well of strength, serenity, and happiness.

We can share more good and enrich the lives of others if we spend time knowing, forgiving, and loving ourselves. Healthy selfishness not only improves our own experience, but it improves the world around us.

# CHAPTER 10

# The Swinging Day Trader

We owe a debt of gratitude to a twelfth-century Italian mathematician who wrote several highly regarded texts named Leonardo Pisano, and nicknamed "Fibonacci."

In one of his books, *Liber Abaci* (*Book of Calculation*), he posed the problem: If a pair of rabbits is enclosed for one month, how many pairs of rabbits can be produced from that pair in one year if every month each pair begets a new pair? Believe it or not, in his studies with rabbits, he discovered the unique relationship among a series of numbers that are now referred to as Fibonacci numbers.

## FIBONACCI NUMBERS

The Fibonacci number sequence develops by starting at 1, and adding the previous number. The sum is the new number, for example: 0 + 1 = 1, 1 + 1 = 2, 2 + 1 = 3, 3 + 2 = 5, 5 + 3 = 8, and 8 + 5 = 13. Therefore, Fibonacci numbers are 1, 2, 3, 5, 8, 13, 21, 34, 55, 89, 144, 233, and so on.

A Fibonacci number equals 1.618 times the preceding Fibonacci number. In turn, a Fibonacci number equals 0.618 times the following Fibonacci number.

Analysts anticipate changes in trends by using four popular Fibonacci studies: arcs, fans, time zones, and the most popular, retracements. On a Fibonacci scale of 0–100%, the retracement levels within that scale are 38.5%, 50%, and 61.8%. It's amazing how many creatures in nature, human beings included, are proportioned exactly to those ratios.

Those familiar with Elliott Wave Theory know wave counts adhere to the Fibonacci numbering sequence. Many trading software platforms offer Fibonacci studies as part of their charting features. Later, I will recommend you apply the retracements to your E-mini S&P futures chart.

"How fascinating," you mutter, scratching your head. "But what's this got to do with me making big bucks in the market?"

Plenty. Especially when it comes to the numbers 2, 3, and 5. From now on, we're going to keep the numbers 2, 3, and 5 in the forefront of our minds. These numbers crop up repeatedly on charts, and we use them to help predict price movement. We'll also talk more about Fibonacci levels in later chapters.

Stocks in strong uptrends tend to move up three days, then down (pull back) for two. Or they move up for five days, then retrace for three days. In a downtrend, reverse those numbers. A probable pattern is three days down, followed by two rally days; or five days down, and three days up.

If a stock moves down for four days, you can bet it will continue into negative territory into the fifth day. (This always happens, except when it doesn't.)

In *Pit Bull*, renowned trader Martin Schwartz cites his Three Day Rule:

> Whenever a stock like a Microsoft or Intel has had a large three-day move in one direction, you do not want to be buying on the third day, or selling [short] on the third day of a down move. That's a sucker play. Usually stocks will have big moves in three days. The first day the smart people are moving, the second day the semi-smart people are moving, and by the third day, the dunces have finally figured it out. This is an important rule. If the stock has bad news and it sells down, by the third day you may want to start looking to buy it because the bad news probably has been fully discounted.

## MONEY-MAKING SETUPS FOR SWING TRADES AND DAY TRADES

Picture a basketball thrown with strong momentum, bouncing up a flight of stairs.

Some of the most successful swing and day trades you can enter entail catching stocks in powerful uptrends that are climbing their rising 20 MAs, or 50 MAs (the stairs) using the same motion as the basketball. They rise for two to five days (three is average), then pull back or consolidate for one to five days (two is common). As a savvy trader, you'll choose patterns that display orderly moves and appear reasonably predictable.

If top down criteria is bullish, swing and day traders watch the pullback or consolidation for a nice spring day bounce off the MA to enter. (Reverse this method to sell short.) The nice spring day is confirmation that bulls are back in charge of the uptrend.

For swing trades, it's extremely profitable to target the initial breakout and enter as price trades above pullback resistance, especially when price begins to bounce from the 20 or 50 MA. As long as the uptrend or downtrend stays intact, you can enter and exit at key support and resistance points. Just remain aware that extremely "toppy," "frothy" stocks sell off fast.

Once in the swing trade, if all goes well, you'll enjoy the ride for two to three days. With luck and good risk management, you can earn a multiple-point profit.

When you're trading strictly intraday, you can use the same setup from the daily chart. That's where the potential momentum's going to be. With intraday trades, though, we jump in as soon as possible. As the stock bounces off the 20- or 50-day MA, you drill down to your five- and/or 15-minute charts, and buy as price rises above consolidation or pullback resistance on a daily chart. Plan to sell before the market closes.

**HOT TIP**

The CCI can give valuable feedback in the form of a bearish divergence on an intraday chart that signals it is profit-taking time. I like its sell signals intraday, better than its buy signals. Opening gaps or volatile opening price action skews the CCI's signals for a few bars.

When you're monitoring stocks with these criteria, keep the consolidation patterns and flag pattern in mind from Chapter 9. (The patterns work in *all* time frames.) Then scan your daily charts for stocks that:

➤ Are moving in an uptrend
➤ Are presently climbing up their 20 or 50 MA in an orderly stepping pattern
➤ Have pulled back or consolidated for one or two days, and are nearing the supporting MA
➤ Have overbought/oversold indicators that signal a bullish divergence, or are trending higher
➤ Show strong volume on the prior breakout, then decreased volume during pullback or consolidation

Don't forget to incorporate candlestick reversal patterns, such as doji, morning star doji, hammers, and bullish piercing patterns, shown in Chapter 5. They may form as pullback reversal days at the conclusion of a consolidation or pullback, and predict that a nice spring day will develop next.

For a quick review, these two "close-ups" in Figure 10-1 show money-making setups you're looking for to enter a swing or day trade on the long side.

Learn to spot these two setups on daily charts. Apply the top down criteria to them, and enter at the proper points. Once in, adhere to your stops, and take safe profits. Utilizing these two setups, along with Marine-like discipline and common-sense money management tactics, you can add substantially to your bottom line.

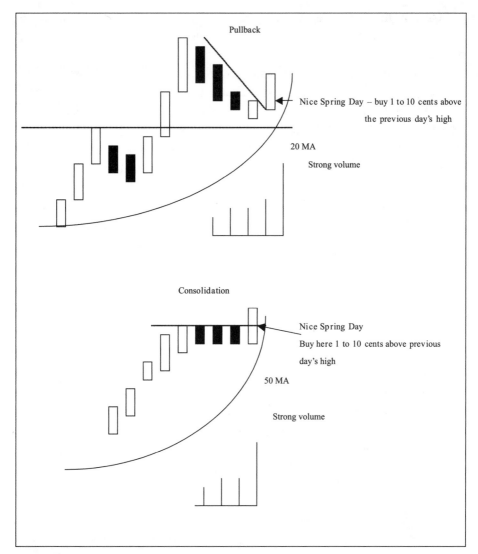

**FIGURE 10-1** | Pullback and consolidation entries.

Figures 10-2, 10-3, and 10-4 show setups for swing trades and day trades using stocks in an uptrend, 20- and 50-day MAs as support, and entries on "nice spring days."

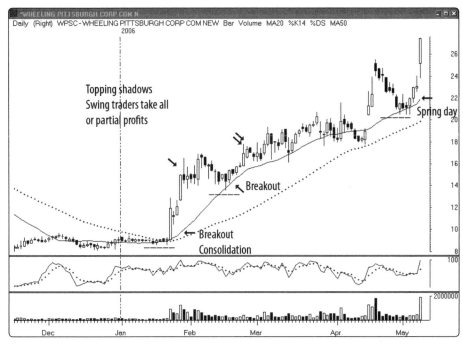

**FIGURE 10-2** | On this daily chart of the Wheeling Pittsburg Corp. (WPSC), you can see a great entry for a position trade using the initial breakout. Note how Stochastics created a bullish divergence back in late December. The obvious breakout arrived on January 24. This breakout of nearly three points on the first day presents a great incentive to create a watch list of basing stocks. You would have entered at 9.54, just as the steel producer shot over the consolidation highs. In this case, most swing traders would have held the stock on the strength of its momentum, for the four-day run-up.

I didn't point out the breakout in late April that delivered that big gap up because the nice spring day (sitting on the 50-day MA dotted line) closed under the 20 MA. My personal rule dictates that I don't buy stocks trading under their 20 MAs. Early in May, WPSC offered another pullback and nice spring day. Clue: Three candles in a row with lower shadows indicate buyers are present. An entry at 22.39 carried traders to at least the current high of 27.50. An automatic trailing stop on this one will help lock in profits.

RealTick® graphics used with permission of Townsend Analytics, Ltd. © 1986-2007 Townsend Analytics, Ltd.

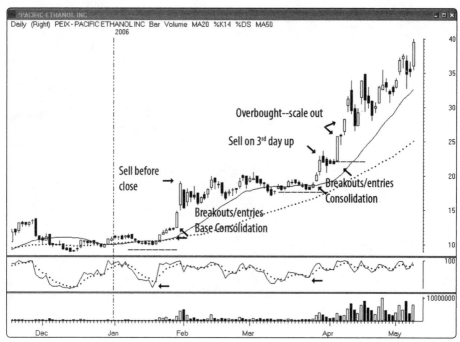

**FIGURE 10-3** | This daily chart of Pacific Ethanol, Inc. (PEIX) shows three orderly setups and entries that turned into great swing and intraday trades. Let's start with the breakout in January. The ethanol producer consolidated through the first weeks of January, carving a tight base. Then, when ethanol came into the spotlight as a gasoline additive that could cut fuel costs, PEIX's volume increased. Note the dramatic bullish divergence signaled by Stochastics, coupled with the moving average crossover (20 MA rises over 50 MA). Experienced traders could have entered as PEIX pushed through January resistance ($11.54). Others might have waited until the stock rose above November highs ($13.78), or added to their positions. Why sell just before the close on January 31? The stock closed at $18.83. That's a huge profit, percentage-wise. The April breakouts formed a perfect 1, 2, 3, pattern, although traders holding through the pullback might have gotten stopped out. Now, here's a great example of a stock going from orderly to disorderly behavior. After PEIX shot through $25, it began to gap and pull back dramatically. Not only is it overbought, the company is still raising money to open plants. It has no earnings related to ethanol production as of this time. The volatility increase (note volume as well as price) is due to traders speculating like crazy, and selling as fast as they buy.

RealTick® graphics used with permission of Townsend Analytics, Ltd. © 1986-2007 Townsend Analytics, Ltd.

**FIGURE 10-4** | This daily chart of the Boeing Company (BA) shows three dandy swing trade entries that used the 20-day MA for support. The first developed in May, as the giant aerospace stock pulled back and consolidated from its February rise. Savvy traders bought as BA popped off its 20 MA, then added to the position when the price jumped through resistance. The next entry unfolded in April, as BA consolidated nicely into its 20-day MA once again, and then flew higher. Although you could have bought the mid-April pullback, I prefer setups where price retraces to the MA. The final pullback and breakout took place the end of April. A small initial lot could have been purchased when BA closed in a near-doji perched atop the 20 MA. More shares would be added on the nice spring day that followed. Note that in both setups, Stochastics signaled early bullish divergences. Also note that this price move didn't have to be traded . . . a position trade with a trailing stop would have delivered great profits, with very little work. That's a perk for trading orderly stocks.

RealTick® graphics used with permission of Townsend Analytics, Ltd. © 1986-2007 Townsend Analytics, Ltd.

## GAP OPENINGS: HOW TO MANAGE THEM

Stocks gap open when they open higher or lower than the previous day's close. We say they "gap up," or "gap down."

In candlestick technology, a gap is called a "window." The Japanese believe that at some-time, all windows will close.

Stocks gap up or down at the open because of economic reports, earnings announcements, industry news, upgrades and downgrades, and news that targets that particular stock.

Say Terrific Truck Lines closed Friday evening at $52.25. It opens Monday morning at $53. The ¾ point difference in price comes from an imbalance of orders on Monday morning. More buy orders than sell orders caused the specialist or market maker to open it at a higher price on Monday morning.

This gap up can be either a blessing or a curse. Those who owned Terrific Truck Lines at the close Friday evening woke up ¾ point, or 75 cents per share, richer Monday morning. If you didn't own Terrific, but had been waiting for days for the perfect setup to enter long, the gap up negates your entry at the open Monday morning.

A common practice in the trading community is to "fade the gap." That means whatever direction the gap is headed, we take the other side. To "fade" a market, take a trade in the opposite direction of the prevailing trend.

Volume is key in gap trading. A stock that gaps up at the open on heavy volume will likely have enough demand to overcome shorts and selling pressure. It may go higher. The reverse is true with gaps down.

On the other hand, stocks that gap up at the open on light volume attract short sellers like white on rice. The light volume indicates low commitment, so shorting the gap can offer a great momentum trade opportunity. The reverse is true with gaps down on light volume.

When a stock gaps open more than 35 cents from its prior close, for swing trades, it's best to wait for it to pull back, and then reverse higher. For the safest entry, wait until it trades over the initial intraday high, then buy.

When a stock gaps up, trades above its opening price all day, then closes near the daily high, odds suggest that stock will move even higher. These odds improve if the stock closes over the previous day's high.

Use common sense with gap openings. If a $5 stock gaps open 35 cents, that gap represents a large percentage of price. Wait to see how the stock handles the opening minutes before trading. If an $80 stock gaps open 35 cents, it's not as significant. It's the stock's behavior after the gap that should receive your attention.

If you're momentum or day trading, watch the stock for the first 15 minutes to see if it fills half of, or all of, its opening gap. Strong stocks typically fill less of their gap than weak stocks. Again, keep an eye on volume.

Here's another example: Terrific Truck Lines closed at $52.25 Friday evening. It opened at $53 on Monday morning. It might shoot up from $53 to $53.50 in the opening minutes, then—typical of most stocks that gap open, especially if it's on low volume—drop like a stone during the next ten minutes to about $52.25. It waffles around through the 9:45 to 10:15 A.M. reversal period. At 10:15 A.M., Terrific starts showing life again. When it breaks above $53.50 (it formed resistance there, at the day's high), then buy and place a stop under this support zone. The

> **HOT TIP**
>
> If you have Fibonacci retracement lines available to you and you know how to plot them, you can do so from the gap's low price (prior day's close) to the opening price and measure how much of the gap it fills. Or, stretch the lines from the bottom to the top of the entire swing move on a 15-minute or hourly chart, to locate support or resistance areas in the gap.

price pattern indicates it's strong, and has a good chance of continuing to rise up as long as the market stays in positive territory.

On the flip side, some stocks gap open, use all of their energy during that first price spike, then tank and stay down for the day. That's another reason you avoid buying stocks that gap open.

The reverse happens when stocks gap down at the open. Scenes like this one cause sweaty palms for those holding long overnight positions. Terrific Truck Lines closes at $52.25 Friday evening, then opens Monday morning at $51.75. Typically, it slides down a bit more, maybe to previous support at $51.50. Then the buyers and traders fading (in this case, buying) the gap arrive. *Maybe.*

If bulls do arrive, within minutes Terrific will recover some territory. Just how much territory depends on market conditions, and the reason Terrific slid in the first place. Trader terminology for stocks that gap down, then recover lost ground is "gap and snap."

When you're waiting to short a weak stock, and it gaps down on low volume, wait until the gap fill takes place, resistance re-exerts pressure, and the stock begins to tumble, again. Hanging men, doji, and dark cloud cover candle patterns are extremely useful to indicate the gap fill is complete.

If the price remains above the opening gap for the first hour of trading, it's a bullish sign.

> **HOT TIP**
>
> Stocks that gap open on big volume tend to continue their momentum higher, intraday. Stocks that gap open on low volume are inclined to close the gap quickly.

## TO HOLD OVERNIGHT, OR NOT TO HOLD OVERNIGHT

Swing trades necessitate holding positions overnight. The preceding explanation of gaps explains why holding stocks overnight can make you yell with happiness, or pass out cold.

It all depends on your personal risk tolerance levels. One camp of day traders would sooner stop breathing than hold a position overnight. Other traders make fine profits on overnight plays. I belong to the latter camp. I've made money buying a stock five minutes before the market closes, and selling it the next morning, just seconds after it opens.

Dissenters argue that holding a stock overnight exposes you to risk. Occasionally, Mr. Big Shot Analyst from Mega Brokerage has to earn his pay by downgrading industries and/or stocks. Of course, if Mr. Shot downgrades a stock you're holding after the market closes for the day, the stock will likely open much lower the following morning. If you own a large position in that downgrade, the loss can dent your account.

One of my friends, bless him, has an unfortunate flair for buying stocks that get downgraded overnight. I somehow escape with profits that far outweigh my occasional calamities.

Here's how I do it: I hold (long) stocks overnight:

➤ That reside in an industry group engaged in a healthy uptrend.
➤ That represent the leaders of their industry group.
➤ When the overall market is bullish.
➤ When the stock is in a strong uptrend (optimally closing at, or near, its high for the day).
➤ When it's the stock's first or second day (not the third day) up from a breakout,.
➤ I take home small positions. If any of these so much as breathes funny before the close, I close the trade or reduce my share size.
➤ If the stock gaps open the next morning, I sell at least half my position.

---

### 🔥 HOT TIP

These days, some moon-shot stocks gap open multiple points. To enter these high-risk stocks after the gap, please protect your principal by waiting out the gap fill. It takes a lot of buying energy for a stock to open halfway to the moon. Many times stocks gap open, fly even higher, then fall like bricks, erasing half—or all—of their opening gains. If the stock continues higher, shrug it off. Trading smart means you wait until the stocks stabilize. And remember an earlier lesson: Things that go straight up tend to come straight down.

If you cultivate the knack of holding overnight and making money consistently, go for it. If you attract downgrades like ugly on an ape, leave overnights alone.

## NITTY-GRITTY STUFF ABOUT DAY TRADING

Early on, I suggested opening two trading accounts, one for position and swing trades, the other for momentum and day trades. I also stressed that if you did decide to manage dual accounts, it's very important to keep the two separate.

Goals and risk-reward ratios differ between position and swing trades, day trades, momentum trades, and scalping plays. Time frames dictate those ratios. Position and swing trades lean a little more toward investment objectives. Particularly with position trades, you focus mostly on the individual stock's progress. If Mother Market slips into a rotten mood for a morning or afternoon, as long as your stop loss isn't violated, the trade remains in tact.

Intraday trades, however, involve abbreviated time frames. Traders superimpose every nuance of market mood onto open positions. When Mother Market frowns for even ten minutes, she causes many stocks to join her bad mood. As the saying goes, "when Mama ain't happy, ain't nobody happy."

In a swing trade, a 65-cent drop may not cause concern. In a day trade, it could easily stop you out. In a swing or position trade, your stop might be at as far as $1.50 points away from your entry point. In a day trade, depending on the stock's volatility, your initial stop price will reside less than a point from your entry price.

As mentioned before, potential rewards should outweigh risks. In position and swing trades, you look for multiple-point profits. In day trades, you may offer out (sell) at a point, or even a half-point profit. Momentum and scalping plays grab fractions of points.

Day trading demands keen concentration. You focus intensely on chart patterns while monitoring market internals.

The heightened pace of day trading encourages many new traders to "overtrade." They jump at any stock with a decent setup and end up stockpiling stocks into their account. Suddenly, they find themselves in Panic City.

I've been there. When I started trading, I crammed ten or twenty positions into my account at one time. Trouble was, I couldn't keep track of all of them. Instead of trading to trade well, I became a troubleshooter. And I shot big holes in my bottom line at the same time.

Overtrading leads novice traders to forget their goal: to protect their principal and cherry pick the best trades. Instead, they jump in and out of positions

**HOT TIP**

Remember, when stocks gap open higher than they closed the prior evening, specialists and market makers have to take the other side of the trade. They must short those rocketing stocks. How do you think they cover those short positions with a profit? By waiting until the steam escapes from the initial run up, then bringing the stocks down—hard.

far more than necessary, stacking up losses, slippage, and commissions. The losses goad them into over-trading even more, which attracts more losses . . . you get the picture.

Experienced traders take their time. They pluck out the best trades and ignore the others. They also stop trading when odds go against them.

## DOES YOUR STOCK WALTZ OR JITTERBUG?

When you start day trading, a good prevention against ulcers is to learn your target stock's *modus operandi*. That way, when it pulls back an entire point, you won't faint at your desk.

Just as they do on daily and longer-term charts, stocks draw trends, continuation patterns and pull-backs, or retracement patterns on intraday charts. The price range of the pullbacks depends on the stock's daily price range and intraday volatility. This is illustrated in Figure 10-5. Remember, pullbacks on intraday charts represent profit taking, just as they do on daily charts.

Remember that each stock has its own personality. Medium to mild-mannered stocks average 25-, 50-, to 75-cent intraday pullbacks on average. More volatile issues fall back a point, even more.

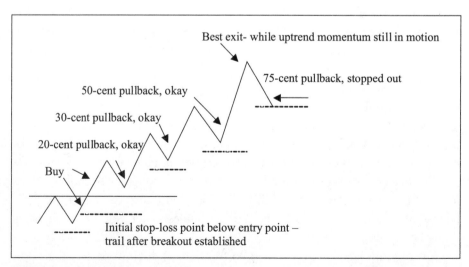

**FIGURE 10-5** | Example of intraday uptrend and pullbacks.

When you target a day trading stock, survey its intraday price action for the previous three days. Calculate the average pullback. Knowing what to expect helps you from exiting positions too soon. It also tells you how much room to give your trailing stop.

### WHERE TO PLACE YOUR STOP-LOSS ORDERS

Stop placement can make for heated discussions. There is no one stop fits all answer. As an old trading coach of mine used to say, "Where you put your stops depends on your tolerance for pain."

It's true. Those who have a high tolerance for risk will place their stops farther away from the trading action. They don't get stopped out as often as their risk-averse buddies, and their rewards can be large. Still, when they do get stopped out, the losses are acute.

> **HOT TIP**
>
> If your trading software includes the ATR, or Average True Range indicator, you can determine what the average price range of your stock is per day, over the default period (usually 14 days). If your target stock's ATR is 88 cents, and by the afternoon session it's risen on the day by 80 cents, there's not much room for additional upside action.

Traders with low risk tolerance will keep their stops tighter to lessen the Maalox moments. They experience their own variety of pain, however, because stops set too tight to price result in trades stopped out too soon. The constant re-entries and attempts to make back the string of small losses can cause overtrading.

An overall guideline: Set your stop orders far enough away from your entry price to give the trade time and space to evolve, and close enough to prevent damaging drawdowns.

After entering a trade, place your initial stop-loss 10 to 50 cents below the day's low, or if that's too far away, put it 10 to 30 cents below support on a 15-minute chart (10 to 50 cents above if you're shorting). Again, use common sense. If you're trading a stock priced at $115 per share, with an average daily range of $4, you'll have to give the stop more room. A $20 stock with a one-point average price range will probably be all right with a 30-cent stop. Of course, you'll

> **HOT TIP**
>
> Your broker, whether an online discount broker or direct-access, should offer automatic trailing stop orders. This makes the stop process easy. Measure your stock's average pullback range on your intraday time frame, during the last three days. Then enter your trailing stop order to fit that range, and add on a few extra cents so you don't get whipsawed. Good idea: As the stock moves higher toward your profit target, tighten the trailing stop amount so you reap the most profits, if possible.

check support and resistance to make your final decision. Once the stock makes a new high, adjust your stop loss up to the current price, minus the pullback average range.

Here is an example of moving your stop up with the price move to preserve your profits. Suppose your entry point on Simple Software is $20.25. You place your initial stop loss at $19.70. You've designated Simple's pullback range to be 40 cents. When and if Simple climbs to $20.90 (or thereabouts), you move your stop to $20.50, or 40 cents below the current price. Each time the stock makes a new high on the day, adjust your trailing stop order to 40 cents beneath the high price. Now, if you see Simple closing in on resistance, depending on the overall strength of the market, time of day, and whether or not your stock is losing steam, you may want to take partial or all profits instead of waiting to be taken out by your stop order.

Remember, once you establish your stop point, you may move it up, but never down.

## DAY TRADING SETUPS: WHAT YOU'RE LOOKING FOR

Earlier in the chapter, you noted the illustrations and learned the two classic setups for entering swing trades and day trades: breakouts from consolidations and breakouts from pullbacks. As I mentioned then, if you trade only these two setups, while combining signals from candles, volume, moving averages, a momentum indicator, and top down criteria, you can develop a successful trading career.

For those who want more adventure, we'll look at additional setups and fine-tune the entries. Start by doing your homework. Analyze the previous day's (yesterday's) price movement; it tells you where and when you can or should not enter (in the case of a gap opening) today.

A given for the following plays: Moving averages play a role in day trading as well as longer-term plays. I use the 20-period MA and 200 MA on all intraday charts because they're powerful support and resistance. (For scalping the mega-quick plays, I use one-minute charts and add the 10 MA.) As you develop your own trading style, you may add a 100 MA and/or 50 MA, or change your MAs to exponential (if your trading software offers that option). Please remember that you'll have better odds with your intraday long plays if the stock's current price rides above the 20-day MA on a daily chart, and the 20-period MA on the intraday time frame you've targeted.

The 200 MA is particularly powerful on 15-minute charts. If it's above your stock's current price and ready to bop it on the head, it exerts pressure as the stock tries to rise.

Imagine you're in a swimming pool treading water. A bully standing next to you keeps dunking you. Every time you come up to gasp for air, he puts his beefy hand on your head and pushes you back underwater. The 200 MA resembles the bully. Yes, of course, the stock can rise through the 200 MA and keep climbing. It's just that playing stocks with the 200 MA overhead (other MAs overhead can also push a stock under water) reduces your odds of winning.

### Buy Setup 1: Figure 10.6

Find a target stock that's breaking out of a base or already trading in an uptrend on its daily chart. For the last two to three days, it's pulling back. Yesterday (assuming you'll enter the trade "today"), the stock closed in a narrow range doji, with the low resting on the rising 20-day MA. Today, it opens at, or near (within 35 cents) yesterday's close. If it gaps open slightly, it fills the gap quickly. It reverses and moves back up, breaking the morning's high. Buy at the break above the daily chart's doji high price. If conditions say "go," take an early initial lot on the entry day, and then add to it over the doji day high. This trade works best when captured in the morning session.

Alternative: If the market environment suggests the stock can move higher in the afternoon session, and risk-reward analysis is favorable, take half of your profits near the end of the trading day and hold the second portion as a swing trade.

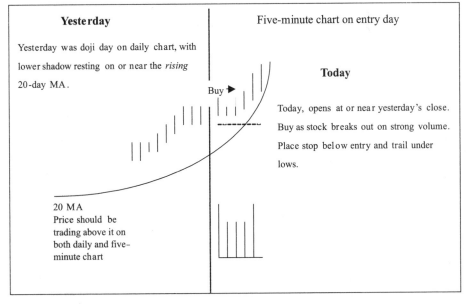

**FIGURE 10-6** | Buy setup 1.

**HOT TIP**

Look for stocks that close at the high of the day on strong volume. These make the strongest setups for a potential entry the following day.

Figure 10-7 shows a daily chart of Consolidated Edison (ED) pulling back in an early uptrend (making higher lows). In two instances, the pullback days resulted in narrow range doji, meaning the day opened and closed at nearly the same price, and the range between the intraday highs and lows remained relatively small. These doji days act as "pressure cookers." When the next day is positive, it often offers good long intraday trade opportunities.

The 5-minute chart of ED shown in Figure 10-8 shows Buy Setup 1 in action.

By the way, May 10 was Fed day and the FOMC announcement. You can see how even a calm stock like ED dropped hard on the news of an interest rate hike, even if only for a few minutes. If you were day trading on this day, you knew to exit your positions before 2:15 P.M. EST, or at least to have good stop orders established.

**FIGURE 10-7** | This daily chart of Consolidated Edison shows (ED) the energy and utilities company reversing from its downtrend to stages in an early uptrend. On both May 4 and May 9, ED pulled back to its rising 20-day MA, and closed above it on doji days. The doji highs give us an entry point for intraday and swing trade entries on the following days.

RealTick® graphics used with permission of Townsend Analytics, Ltd. © 1986-2007 Townsend Analytics, Ltd.

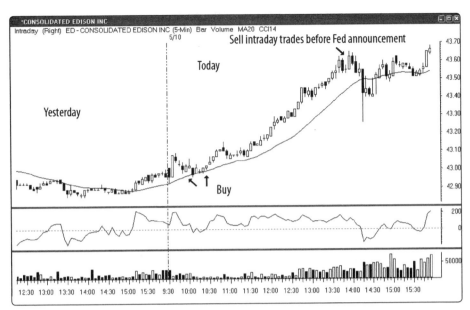

**FIGURE 10-8** | This 5-minute chart of Consolidated Edison (ED) shows a good example of Setup 1. Climbing in an early uptrend on its daily chart, yesterday it closed in a doji that rested on the rising 20-day MA. Today, May 10, ED opened even with yesterday's close. You could have bought on the first bar up (second candle from open), or you could have waited for the reversal period and the bounce off the 20-period MA. To answer the question you are thinking—which is "Isn't volume low?"—it's not so much that ED's volume is low during the first part of the day; it's rather that the second half, as ED climbs, is unnaturally high. You would have seen that if we could have stretched the chart back a few days. Day traders would have made a nice profit of about 70 cents on this trade, and could have held half of the position overnight, as the stock closed on the high of the day on very high volume and continued higher the next day. Note how the stock rolled over on the FOMC announcement. If you were day trading this (or any other) stock, you wisely took half or all of your profits before the announcement.

RealTick® graphics used with permission of Townsend Analytics, Ltd. © 1986-2007 Townsend Analytics, Ltd.

### Buy Setup 2: Figure 10-9

Once again, find a target stock in an uptrend. Yesterday was positive, and the stock closed near its high on its daily chart. A consolidation pattern into the close is preferable.

Today, on a 5-minute chart the stock opened at or near yesterday's close. It may move slightly to the upside. But then, perhaps during the 9:45 A.M. to 10:15 A.M. reversal period, it drops to a low-on-low volume and holds on previously established support (drop should be no more than 1.5% of stock price). A narrow-range bar, called a "bottoming bar," shows the mini-downtrend may reverse. Next, a reversal candle confirms the reversal. Buy when the reversal candle trades 1 to 10 cents above the bottoming bar (don't chase). Place your

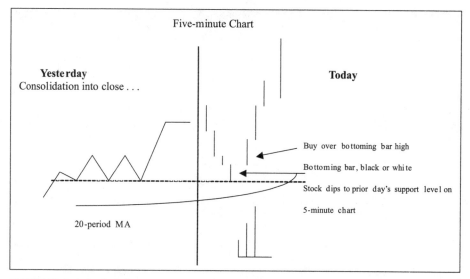

**FIGURE 10-9** | Buy Setup 2.

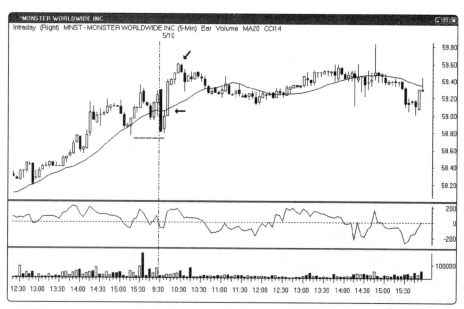

**FIGURE 10-10** | This 5-minute chart of Monster Worldwide, Inc. (MNST) shows the online recruiter rising in an uptrend during the prior trading day. (The stock is trading in a strong uptrend on its daily chart.) May 10, it opens even with the prior day's close, then drops about 50 cents to the prior day's nearby support area, and on low volume. MNST held that support (dotted line) and created a reversal candle. This entry would be just as price trades over the high of the bottom reversal candle, which is also just above the 20-period MA, at 59.06. Place initial stop under support, and adjust when stock breaks above the intraday high (or place trailing stop order with broker). The narrowing range white candles appearing above the wide range breakout candle tells you MNST buyers are tiring. If you haven't exited into one of these, then definitely take profits when the dark cloud cover appears at 59.60.    RealTick® graphics used with permission of Townsend Analytics, Ltd. © 1986-2007 Townsend Analytics, Ltd.

stop 10 to 40 cents (adjust to suit) under entry point. When the price reaches the high set earlier in the morning, raise your stop.

The 5-minute chart of Monster Worldwide, Inc. (MNST) in Figure 10-10 displays Buy Setup 2 in action. Since this is a medium-risk setup, I take all profits on this momentum trade once it shows signs of buying exhaustion.

Remember, in all of these entries, the top down criteria is a given.

### Buy Setup 3: Figure 10.11

This setup is easy to spot, trader-friendly, and reliable as long as Mother Market is in a cheerful mood in the afternoon session. Target a stock in a long-range uptrend. Yesterday isn't that important, but today is. Today the stock must be positive and moving up, with plenty of upside potential available and no nearby resistance present on a daily chart. On a 5-minute chart, it reaches a high in the morning session, then pulls back in an orderly fashion into the lunchtime period, preferably more than 50 cents, or 1.5% of its price.

The stock "straight lines" through lunch, or forms an orderly consolidation pattern just above or below its 20-period MA.

After 1:30 P.M., you may notice many candlesticks are positive, closing on their highs. Soon after, with all systems at a "go," the stock breaks out and climbs into an afternoon rally.

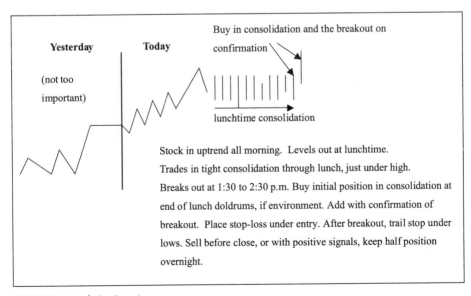

**FIGURE 10-11** | Buy Setup 3.

## HOT TIP

On muscular days when the market trends up, and your already uptrending stock goes along for the ride, some traders buy when the stock rises above the 20-period MA on a 5- or 15-minute chart, and sell if a 5- or 15-minute candle closes below that MA.

When you see volume coming into the consolidation, buy an initial, small position while the stock is still trading sideways and place your stop a few cents under consolidation lows. If your stock is trading under its 20-period MA on a 5-minute chart, you may want to wait until it closes a 5-minute candle above it. If the breakout follows through, add to your position. Take profits before the close. This one usually delivers nice take-home pay.

Figure 10-12 shows Buy Setup 4 in action on a 5-minute chart of Phelps Dodge (PD).

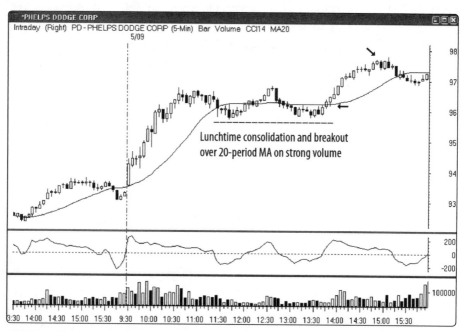

**FIGURE 10-12** | This 5-minute chart of Phelps Dodge Corp. (PD) shows the copper manufacturing giant popping into a nice morning rally (very tradable). Then PD slows down for the lunchtime period. While PD doesn't consolidate in a flat line, its volume tapers considerably and it sidesteps in relative quiet. Yes, there's a little rally, but not sustainable during this period. At 2:00 P.M., PD wakes up to increasing volume and jumps over its 20-period line. The CCI shoots through its zero line, and we buy this breakout at $96.20. We watch for signs of weakening at the noontime high, but none occur. PD continues to climb until about 3:00 P.M. The CCI is weakening, traders are exiting for the day, and we join them. We close our trade at $97.45, with a tidy point-and-a-quarter profit.

## QUICK LEVEL II REVIEW AND INTRADAY TRADING TACTICS

You can make money on position and swing trades using only an online broker. To profit safely and consistently on intraday trades and scalping plays, however, it's advantageous to have access to a Level II order entry system.

Since you've graduated from Boot Camp, you already have a good idea of how Level II works. Let's brush up a bit.

When you've targeted a stock to trade, first check your Level II screen for the spread between the inside bid and ask. As a rule, trade stocks with a spread of 3 cents, or less.

Why do you trade only stocks with a 3-cent spread, or less? To narrow your risk. Say the stock is trading at the offer, and not between the bid and offer. That means buyers will pay the inside offer, or market price for the stock. You'll see that on your Time & Sales screen.

Before you buy, think: *Because I have to pay full price for the stock, if it turns against me the second I enter, where can I get out?* Your answer is the inside bid. The most desirable spread is a penny. But if the spread widens to 5 cents or more, your risk increases. That means if the stock turns against you as soon as you buy the stock—and it happens—you'll have to sell at the market, or the bid (if you're lucky). Your immediate loss on a 1,000-share lot, including commissions, could total $100 in a hurry. Do that five times a day, and you've got a $500 loss you have to make up. If you do the math for a weekly run . . . you get the point.

Next, with listed stocks, if you see block trades going off (10,000 shares), trade toward size. Watch your Time & Sales screen. Are the biggest lot sizes traded on upticks or downticks? Please go with the trend here. If institutions or big investors are buying, that's what you do also. If they're shorting, and your setup agrees with that, go for it.

 **HOT TIP**

NASDAQ stocks rarely show accurate size; most players conceal their true intentions. Trading toward size on NASDAQ stocks is not as common a tactic.

Once again, if the stock is trending up quietly, and the spread is 3 cents, you can attempt to split the bid and ask by placing a limit order for the price between. Example: Igloo Ice Cream is trading $27 × $27.03. Issue your limit buy order at $27.02.

You can sell the same way as long as the stock is trading quietly, and you are not rushing to get out.

Use the Time & Sales screen as a storytelling device. Say you enter a stock on an early morning breakout. It consolidates into the 9:45 A.M. reversal. At 10:20 A.M., it shoots through resistance again. If Time & Sales shows strong volume streaming into the buy side, and your chart agrees, you can add to your position.

Conversely, say you're in a profitable trade, and the price is nearing resistance. The market is overbought, and you see size selling off on the Time & Sales screen. Consider taking profits.

Remember that the trades in this discussion are short, intraday trades. Level II screens for volatile stocks change in nanoseconds. Once you're in an intraday trade, refer only to the chart. If you sit and watch the Level II screen, intraday gyrations play games with your head and cause "Level II fakeout." You'll jump out of your trade long before your profit objective.

More and more stocks have widening spreads between the inside bid and ask. You must be extremely careful when you trade these stocks on an intraday basis. What happens if the market turns against you before your stock has a chance to rise? Ouch!

Say you lift (buy) the offer at $20.10. The bid is $20. If the stock suddenly heads south, the market makers will drop the bid even lower. Prices get trampled as traders rush for the door, and you may suffer acute pain trying to get out of your position. Wise traders avoid these stocks.

Okay, back to the good stuff. Say the perfect setup for your target stock presents itself. If the stock moves slowly enough, you can buy on the bid. Post a limit buy order for the inside bid price.

Before you place any order, though, please become proficient with your order entry system. When I started, systems sprang from their incubators directly into the hands of the guinea pigs who ordered them. We downloaded the software, and that was it. Limited (read: none) training and support was available.

My total training (this was ten years ago) on my Level II order entry system consisted of a man's voice on the other end of the telephone. He said, "Okay, honey. Got the program downloaded? Good girl. See that buy button? When you want buy something, click on it. Bye."

To this day, I can only whisper how much money I lost learning how to trade by the trial-and-error method. Please learn from my mistakes. Study your order entry system and do plenty of dry runs before you trade with real money.

**HOT TIP**

With some muscle stocks, the spread between the bid and ask fluctuates wildly. One second it's 5 cents, the next it widens to 30 cents or more. Please don't jump into these stocks unless you're well aware of the acute risks involved. Getting in is always easier than getting out.

## PREMARKET AND AFTER-HOURS TRADING SCENE

Many brokers offer premarket and after-hours trading. The premarket opens at 8:00 A.M. up to the market open. Some brokers allow after-hours trading up to 8:00 P.M.

If you're a new trader, I suggest you avoid the pre- and post-market sessions. If you must take a pre- or post-market trade, please be aware of the following:

➤ During extended hours trading, the bid and ask are represented by ECNs. Specialists and market makers do not participate. The spread between the bid and ask can resemble the Grand Canyon.

➤ Seasoned professionals reign over pre- and post-market sessions. They may have access to prices available in other markets. That puts individual traders at a disadvantage.

➤ Pre- and post-market sessions tend to be illiquid. Breaking news, earnings announcements, and chat room sessions can add to extended market volatility in the targeted stocks.

➤ Low liquidity + high volatility = high risk.

➤ Just because a stock trades higher in the after-hours session, it does not mean it will open at that price the next morning. Exaggerated price movements during these sessions may not sustain momentum.

➤ You must place limit orders in these sessions. No market orders are taken. Your order may, or may not, be filled.

Keeping all the above points in mind, I have bought limited positions in post-market sessions that looked attractive to me in after-hours research. I trade with caution, however, and remain aware of trade limitations.

## THE ULTIMATE DAY TRADING SCENE

If you've toughed out the journey thus far, you're on your way to a successful trading career.

As a day trader, you're similar to the ringleader in a three-ring circus. You outthink tigers and lions (specialists and market makers), shoo the clowns from the tent when they act too rambunctious (exit stocks that misbehave), hold the net for trapeze artists (adhering to stops under open positions), and at the same time, direct the remainder of the cast (monitor market internals and industry indices). This is a big role to fill.

One effective way to set up your screen—two monitors hooked to the same computer is better—is to position your 5-minute, 15-minute, 60-minute, and daily charts. (Most intraday traders rely on the 5-minute chart as a staple, then add another intraday chart of their choice as they develop their own style.) Next to the charts, add a Level II screen(s). (Cover the Level II with a chart if the flashing colors distract you.) Then add the NYSE and/or NASDAQ TICK (TRIN if available), the E-mini S&P futures (and other mini stock index futures, if available), and the major market averages. Finish it off with industry indices you're targeting, a watch list of stocks, and perhaps a ticker with those stocks on it. If you have a news service, keep that in a corner of your page. You'll also want a window that opens easily to market research.

Your goal is to locate stocks in which top down criteria and charts and time of day agree.

Let's say that this is a fantastic Tuesday morning, just after 10:00 A.M. Market internals glow with positive numbers. Yesterday, your target stock consolidated into the close near its high. It opened this morning and danced a half-point higher, then consolidated into the 9:45 A.M. reversal period. Now, it's making a nice, tight edge across your 5-minute chart. The 200 MA rides way below the current price, and the 20 MA sits just under it. The same setup is developing on the 15-minute chart.

Suddenly, you notice buy orders heating up on your Time & Sales screen. Buy orders eat through the offer like a hot knife through butter. A quick check of your charts shows the current volume spike rising. This stock's going to break out any second.

You double-check resistance on the 15-minute chart—none to worry about. (On the daily chart, you noted earlier that major resistance was more than four points away, and that was two months ago.)

You pounce onto the offer. Got it. Buy recorded. Stop order entered. The stock noses over resistance. One more click adds to the position. See the stock rising. See the trader smile!

Do you understand what I mean about everything coordinating? Yes, that was the perfect scenario. Trader heaven. I've been there, and you will be, too. Only experience will teach you how to glance at each reading and weave them all together into a single decision—to enter or not to enter.

Please err on the side of caution and avoid trades you're not sure about. If you buy—and in the next ohnosecond wish you hadn't—sell immediately. When in doubt, get out.

In the next chapter, we'll fine-tune day trading into scalping plays. Then we'll learn why your shorts fall down.

# QUIZ
||||||||||||||||

*Questions*

1. What are the first four Fibonacci numbers?
2. Give one reason traders look to these numbers for guidance.
3. Strong stocks in an uptrend tend to bounce off their _____ or _____ moving averages.
4. Define a "gap opening."
5. When your target stock meets your entry criteria, but gaps open, how do you play it?
6. Why do you study your stock's previous intraday pullback range?
7. When you day trade, what is the maximum loss you accept?
8. True or false? If your stock acts irritated, you're justified in moving your stop order down to a safer place.
9. True or false? Odds of morning day trades increase (on the long side) when the target stock consolidates into the prior day's close and closes near the day's high.
10. What's the best overall guideline for setting stops?
11. Before you enter a trade, what do you check first on your stock's Level II screen?
12. What is the ideal spread between the bid and ask ? Why?
13. With listed stocks, if possible, trade toward _____.
14. At the end of this chapter, we pictured a Tuesday-morning scene. Please imagine the same scene again. This time, however, a total of three negative conditions suddenly crop up. Using everything you have learned so far, what might they be? Hint: Any one of the three causes you to reconsider the trade. All three together cause you to sit on your hands.

*Answers*

1. 1, 2, 3, 5

2. Because stocks tend to move in increments of these numbers. For instance, a stock may move up five days and down three, or up three days and down one or two.

3. 20, 50

4. A gap opening occurs when a stock opens higher or lower than the previous day's closing price.

5. Play a gap opening by waiting until the stock fills all or part of it, then reverses back to the opening direction and confirms that reversal with price. If the stock doesn't fill the gap within the first hour of trading, odds increase that it will continue in the direction of the gap.

6. We study the amplitude of our stock's pullbacks over the days prior to the entry day to aid our stop-order placement.

7. An acceptable loss for a day trade is 40 to 50 cents (per share) unless it's a highly volatile, high-priced stock; then the acceptable loss may jump to 80 to 90 cents.

8. False

9. True

10. Set your stop orders far enough away from your entry price to give the trade time and space to evolve, and close enough to prevent damaging drawdowns.

11. The width of the spread between the inside bid and ask.

12. The ideal spread between the bid and ask is three cents or less. The narrower the spread, the quicker you can exit the trade if it goes against you the minute you enter.

13. size

14. Any one of the following conditions should make you reconsider placing a (long) trade. More than one warns of low probability of success.

    1. Low volume on the breakout
    2. You see the 200 MA sloping above the stock's current price.
    3. The TICK takes a sudden dive.
    4. The TRIN rockets through 1.0, and keeps going.
    5. The E-mini S&P futures drop like a rock.
    6. The stock approaches strong resistance from higher time frames.

# CENTER POINT: RELEASE THE PAST

*"People are always blaming circumstances for what they are. I do not believe in circumstances. The people who get on in this world are the people who get up and look for the circumstances they want, and if they cannot find them, make them."*

—George Bernard Shaw

Do you know anyone who has fully left the past behind him or her? Few of us achieve that freedom. For all of us, at some level, the past is not really the past. Even when painful circumstances occurred weeks, months, or years ago, at a deep emotional level we still hold onto them.

We attempt to bury them, but they still affect our lives. The energy we use in regret and resentments burns at an unconscious level, so we don't realize why we are nagged by feelings of negativity or unhappiness. Yet, unless we somehow release that negative energy, the past affects our present-day experience and shapes our future.

We cannot hold onto negative energy from the past in the form of grudges, resentments, and fears, and at the same time move toward our highest potential. Why? Because negative feelings block the flow of positive energy into our lives.

The best way to release the past is to forgive . . . forgive ourselves and those people and situations that hurt us. Just as our bodies heal physical bruises, our inner self wants to heal emotional injuries. We heal by releasing those injuries. We release by forgiving.

To forgive, we face the matter and own it. We acknowledge that the negative energy we've been carrying around no longer serves us. We choose to leave the situation behind and in doing so, we forgive.

Forgiveness is a gift to ourselves. It releases us from the past, fills our lives with positive emotions, and frees us to shape abundant, successful tomorrows.

# CHAPTER 11

# Scalps and Shorts, or the Quick and the Dead

One successful scalper says, "Scalping is the closest you'll get to being a fighter pilot and flying into battle. Your rivals are professionals who capitalize on your errors if you interpret their actions incorrectly.

You must lock onto your opponents' movements and accurately assess their intentions. Are they playing head games or, is what you see real? Once you decide, you either engage or stand on the sidelines and live to fight another day. If you choose erroneously, your best move is to retreat to safety and re-strategize for the next battle."

His analogy is highly accurate. When you scalp, you go head-to-head with market professionals who are as unforgiving as any opponent you will ever encounter.

## WHAT IS SCALPING?

As mentioned before, the trading style known as scalping—taking a trade with the profit objective of grabbing a fraction of a point within seconds to minutes—has greatly diminished in popularity since decimalization replaced fractions in the market quote system. A few scalpers remain, though, and if you want to try this type of trading, you must be:

➤ Able to focus with razor-sharp intensity for long periods of time
➤ Able to execute orders rapidly
➤ Able to maintain a nimble mindset at all times

Successful scalpers have zero tolerance for ignoring stops or hoping for a stock's recovery. Reality check: When you play this game, many of your foes are institutional traders who likely have more experience, more money, and more quote information than you do.

If you decide to scalp, these are overall tactics: Trade large share size, at least 500 to 1,000 shares per trade; make multiple trades per day; and your risk-reward is 1:2. (Scalpers aren't known for their long sentences, or their patience. You rarely see them studying charts in time frames larger than five minutes.)

If you don't trade large share size, profits will be too meager, and commissions will soak up any gains. Making less than a dozen or so trades a day won't net you enough gains to make it worth your while. Remember, many of your trades may be losers. The risk-reward ratio assumes more than 50% of your trades are winners, so you'll have to generate a high percentage of winners to stay afloat.

My strategy is to use 2- to 5-minute charts to target scalping setups, then execute our orders on a Level II order entry system.

I do not recommend scalping with an online discount broker. It can take too many clicks to enter an order. Once the order is entered, you have little control over it. When you scalp, speed is your primary weapon. The Level II order entry screens furnished by direct-access brokers offer price transparency, quick execution, and act as an additional guide to managing the trade.

## BASIC SCALPING TACTICS

When you're scalping, mental discipline dictates whether you make or lose money. As just mentioned, greed, fear, hope, or the need to be right have no room in a scalper's cool, calculating mindset.

Greed, especially, tempts traders to stay in scalping plays too long. Then greed laughs and slaps traders with a loss. How do I know?

When I first started trading, this was one of my biggest challenges. Once in a scalp, I clung to the trade like white on rice. Call it greed, or dignify it by calling it optimism. Whatever the name, I learned that holding onto the trade for an extra 5-cent profit nearly always boomeranged into a smaller profit, or a loss.

In other words, if you're in the midst of a successful scalp and hear yourself making oinking noises, it's time to cash in your profits.

When you scalp, time and risk-reward ratios compress. Since your profit objective is small, you keep your risk even smaller. Scalping plays usually last from seconds to minutes. Profit objective: 15 to 75 cents (per share).

To make money scalping, you need a high percentage of winning trades. When you're swing trading or even day trading, one multipoint gain can erase two or three losing trades. Not so with scalping. You make 25 cents. You lose 12 cents. You lose another 13 cents. Uh, oh. You're not even, you're down on the day. Remember, commissions add up when you're only clearing 15 to 25 cents.

## PRICE BEHAVIOR AT WHOLE AND HALF NUMBERS

Certain numbers create natural support and resistance—such as whole and half numbers. Stocks moving up tend to stall at whole numbers, or they creep a few cents over, then slice back through them.

Example: Let's agree that Igloo Ice Cream represents typical intraday stock movement. It shoots to $25.98, then hesitates just below the whole number. If it's having an extremely strong day, it will rise through $26 to $26.05, then dive, maybe to $25.90. That's why you consider taking profits—part or all—just below or on the whole number, or on it.

Whole numbers also act as support (unless the price just jettisoned through it, as in the example described). When Igloo pulls back, it will slow or halt at $25. If it slips below $25 to $24.90, on a puny day it may slide lower—fast. Investors and traders know that stocks tend to bounce off whole numbers. Therefore, a multitude of stop orders perch just below whole numbers. When a stock slips through a whole number and hits the .90 or .75 mark, the triggered stop orders increase supply. Supply drives prices lower.

Half points don't deliver quite as much support and resistance, but they can slow movement. If Simple Software rises to $25.47, watch for a stall and pull back at $25.50. When it rises to $25.85, or $25.95, and then pulls back, it will probably stall at $25.55 or just above the half mark.

## SCALPING TECHNIQUE: EARLY ENTRIES

Today's scalper can't wait for breakouts. The brevity of the trade dictates early bird action. Capitalizing on initial momentum, scalpers take initial positions while the price still sidesteps in consolidation zones. More shares may be added when breakouts or breakdowns solidify. Or, traders may peel off half of the position trade when the breakout or breakdown follows through, again capitalizing on momentum. The process depends on the individual trader. Whatever the style, the objective is to seize a quick profit and leave.

Receivers on professional football teams must have good hands. As a scalper, you need fast hands. If you can (on the long side), buy on the bid, then offer out on the ask, while the stock is still running.

## LEVEL II REVIEW AND SCALPING STRATEGIES

Here are Level II strategies to add to your scalping skill set. These tactics may help you scalp and trade intraday with more precision.

Scalp stocks with a 1- to 2-penny spread. This is a must. When you scalp, you risk no more than 5 to 10 cents loss. Therefore, if you have to buy on the offer, you want no more than a two-cent spread between you and a possible instant loss. The tighter the spread, the smaller the risk.

After you note the spread between the inside bid and ask, note your stock's Level II screen for the depth of participants. How many specialists, market makers, and ECNs line up at the inside bid to buy your stock if you want to sell in a hurry? The longer the line of participants at the bid price (sell side for specialists, MMs, or ECNs), the more depth it has. (Do the same procedure in reverse—participants at the ask—if you're selling short.)

When a breakdown occurs in an active stock, thousands of traders hit the bid, simultaneously. For example, say Igloo Ice Cream starts melting. You and I, along with thousands of other traders, issue sell orders. Those orders eat through bids in nanoseconds. Specialists or market makers on the level below the inside bid will likely evaporate. Orders posted by ECNs will have left long before. That leaves the level below that, which will also dissolve. *Gulp.*

Market maker strategy is to let a falling stock drop like a stone. They wait until you're sweating and will take a rock-bottom price just to get rid of it. Then, when the selling pressure lifts, MMs will dole it out to new buyers at a much higher price.

Enter only with good depth on the bid when you're scalping long, and good depth at the ask when your selling short. A good rule: Only enter scalps on the long side where specialists or market makers on the inside bid number four or more. Stocks showing one or two market makers on the inside bid or ask are too thin. When you're scalping, thin price levels equal fat losses if the trade goes against you.

**HOT TIP**

More than any other trading style, scalping encourages overtrading. Please remember to choose your entries carefully, and cherry pick only the best. If market internals reverse and confirm the direction, either reverse direction with them, or watch from the sidelines.

Figure 11-1 shows a Level II screen of the volatile Research in Motion, Ltd. (RIMM). Although depth of bid and offer on roller coaster stocks like RIMM are short-lived, for rapid-fire scalps and momentum plays, they offer added information.

If your stock is climbing a little faster—but not too fast—and if there's enough room in the spread, you can go high bid. That means if the spread allows, you split the bid and ask by entering a limit buy order a penny higher than the current inside bid.

In a fast market, when your target stock is trading on the offer—and running up too fast to hit the bid—you lift the offer.

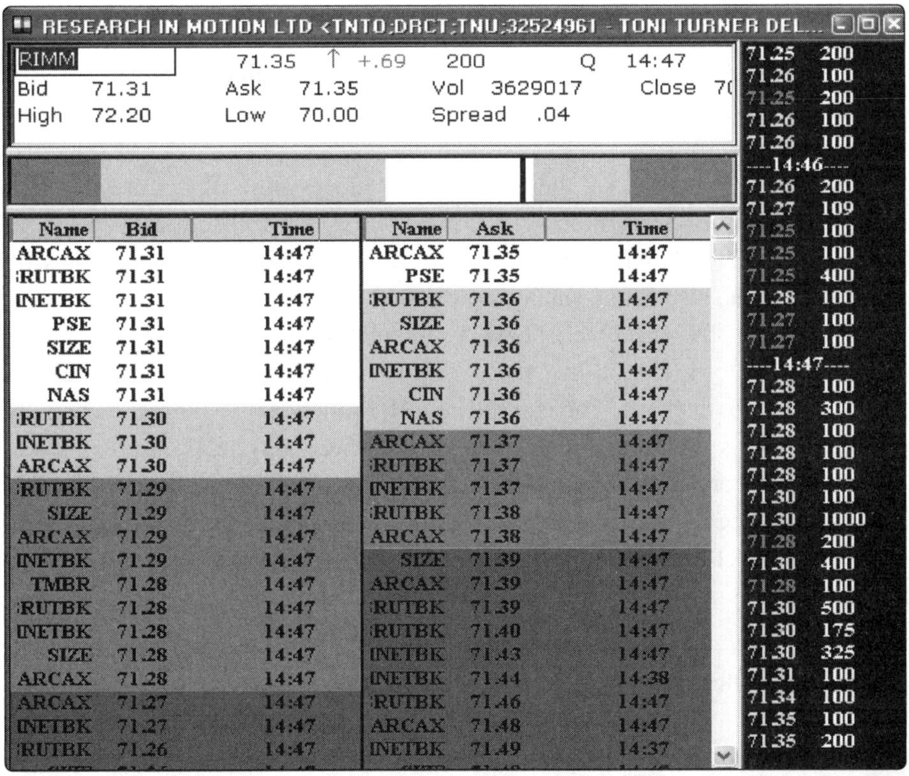

**FIGURE 11-1** | This Level II screen of Research in Motion, Ltd. (RIMM) shows the manufacturer of wireless communications devices with plenty of depth on the bid and less on the ask. This translates into more buyers than sellers, at least for the moment. If you look down to the last price trades, you'll see traders are lifting the offer at $71.35. If you're planning to buy RIMM right now, you'll have to pay the inside ask ($71.35). As well, the ask column shows only two participants at that price level, ARCAX and PSE. Shares may be lifted so fast that you'll have to pay the next level up, $71.36.

RealTick® graphics used with permission of Townsend Analytics, Ltd. © 1986-2007 Townsend Analytics, Ltd.

Once in, assuming momentum propels the stock higher, you offer out quickly, grabbing as much of a point as you can before the sellers take over and the pullback begins.

Before you buy, check out your target stock's personality, just as you do for day trades. What is its average pullback range? What is its average run-up range? Measure recent upswings. That helps you anticipate how far it might run once you're in.

Although 500 to 1,000 shares are the minimum size you'll want to scalp when you're learning, practice with small lot sizes. A neophyte pilot who's used to flying a Cessna asks for trouble if he climbs into the cockpit of an F-16. Similarly, a novice trader used to trading small lots in extended time frames who suddenly pumps up his share size to 2,000 may end up as the scalpee, instead of the scalper. Please go slowly and hone your skills carefully.

## ADDITIONS TO YOUR INTRADAY TOOLBOX

Although we are discussing scalping techniques, you'll find the information in this section and those that follow will provide you with additional tools for all of your intraday trades.

Depending on the stock they are trading, successful scalpers use the mini-sized Dow, E-mini S&P futures, or E-mini NASDAQ 100 futures as a trigger. Of course, the NYSE and/or NASDAQ TICK and TRIN, interpreted along with the mini futures, also act as valuable indicators.

Figures 11-2A and 11-2B show 5-minute charts of the ES (E-mini S&P 500) and The Home Depot, Inc. (HD). The 10- and 20-period moving averages are plotted on both charts. You can see how HD followed the general movement of the ES (ES is the root symbol of the E-mini S&P 500 index futures). (Note how volume decreased for both the ES and HD during the lunchtime doldrums.) Unless stock-specific news is in play, the ES will influence the general direction of large-cap S&P stocks like HD.

Both charts in Figures 11-2A and 11-2B have the 10- and 20-period MAs plotted on them. The 10 MA moves closest to the price pattern. As long as both MAs are running under the price pattern, the 10/20 MA crossover (up for longs,

**FIGURE 11-2A** | 5-minute chart of the E-mini S&P 500 futures with 10-period and 20-period moving averages.

RealTick® graphics used with permission of Townsend Analytics, Ltd. © 1986-2007 Townsend Analytics, Ltd.

**FIGURE 11-2B** | 5-minute chart of The Home Depot Inc. (HD) with 10-period and 20-period moving averages.

RealTick® graphics used with permission of Townsend Analytics, Ltd. © 1986-2007 Townsend Analytics, Ltd.

down for sells, or short plays) can act as a signal line to enter and exit intraday trades. Note: If you use these signals during the lunchtime doldrums, you're liable to get whipsawed.

If you have Fibonacci retracements available, apply them to your 2- or 5-minute mini futures charts. They give you high-probability support and resistance levels for the futures. Fibonacci retracements are illustrated in Figure 11-3, on the same ES chart as that displayed in Figure 11-2A. I stretched the Fib lines from the initial pivot low (0%) to the initial intraday high that created a pivot high at 10:40 A.M. You can see how the ES spent the remainder of the trading day fluctuating between the Fib levels.

If your software offers "daily" pivot levels (this means the pivot levels are calculated from daily high, low, and closing prices), you can plot them on the mini futures to indicate support and resistance levels. I find that in most instances, the daily pivot levels provided on RealTick work well on 5-minute charts.

**FIGURE 11-3 |** Many intraday and mini futures traders plot Fibonacci retracement lines on mini index futures and stock charts. On this 5-minute chart of the E-mini S&P 500 futures contract, I stretched Fibonacci retracements from the first low of the trading day (0%) at 1289.50, to the intraday high (100%) at 1299. As you can see, for the remainder of the market's trading day, the ES fluctuated among these retracement levels. Naturally, if the ES or any other trading instrument closes above its intraday 100% level, or below its 0% level, that move is considered to be significant.

RealTick® graphics used with permission of Townsend Analytics, Ltd. © 1986–2007 Townsend Analytics, Ltd.

**HOT TIP**

A "pivot high" is a new high created on a chart of any time frame, in which the highs immediately prior and immediately after rest at lower price points. A "pivot low" is defined as a new low, in which the low immediately before it and after are above the pivot.

Pivots are support and resistance levels calculated by a simple formula. They were originally created by floor traders. Because floor traders can't refer to charts, they refer to certain support and resistance price levels (pivots) to trade successfully.

You can calculate pivot levels yourself, but naturally, it's helpful if you have software that does it for you.

Traders plot pivot levels from monthly, weekly, and daily charts. The daily pivot levels are the most popular. To plot these, you need the high, low, and close from the prior trading session (be it month, week, or day). With the basic pivot formula R = resistance and S = support:

**R2:** Pivot + (High – Low)
**R1:** 2 × Pivot – Low
**Pivot:** High + Low + Close / 3
**S1:** 2 × Pivot – High
**S2:** Pivot – (High – Low)

For most basic scalping and intraday trading techniques, daily pivot levels work fine. Advanced traders many times add weekly and monthly pivot levels to their charts. Figure 11-4 exhibits daily pivot levels on a 5-minute chart of the E-mini S&P 500.

The main Pivot (median line) represents the strongest line. If the futures trade below this line, they are regarded as weak on the day. If they dive below S1 (Support 1), they are weaker, yet. Of course, if they dive below S2 (Support

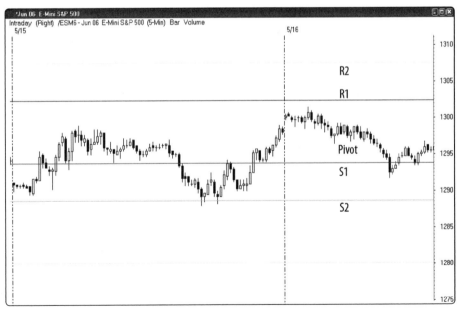

**FIGURE 11-4** | On this day and a half, 5-minute chart of the E-mini S&P 500 stock index futures, you can see how the contract used its daily pivot lines as intraday support and resistance. On 5/15, the contract danced above and below its daily pivot line all day, using its S1 line for support. On 5/16, the contract moved up and nearly touched its R1 line, but could not rise above it (mild negative). When you use Fib lines and pivot lines as support and resistance indicators, use two closes of 5-minute candles for signals. This reduces the chance of getting whipsawed.

**FIGURE 11-5** | This 5-minute chart of Inco Ltd. (N), a global mining and metals company specializing in nickel, shows the stock using its daily pivot plus and R1 and R2 lines for support and resistance. S1 and S2 are not shown, as on this day, N did not approach them. N is in a strong uptrend on its daily chart. This morning at the open, it bounced off its pivot, and rose to R1. Scalpers who took advantage of this move reaped a nice profit. The volatile metal company sold off as quickly as it rose, and soon fell below its daily pivot level. It held the session low, however, and reversed at noon, making its way back to R1. Low volume stops it from shooting through R1 until about 2:30 P.M. The break above R1 at $65, which is also the earlier intraday high, gave traders a good reason to enter long momentum and scalping plays. Scalpers should take profits when the stock trades just below R2, and while buying momentum is still in force. Swing traders would hold this position overnight. Note, two scalps are indicated by the arrows. Lunch period scalps are not included. Although they would have been profitable, my discipline states I don't scalp during the doldrums due to low volume.

2), the bears are very much in control. (On RealTick R2 is yellow, R1 is blue, the Pivot is red, S1 is green, and S2 is yellow.)

On the flip side, when the futures climb above the main pivot line, that's positive. If they shoot through R1 (Resistance 1), that's additionally bullish, and if they rise through R2 (Resistance 2), close above it, and continue to move higher, that's mega-bullish on a short-term basis.

I've found that pivots also hold dandy predictive value with various stock charts on 5-minute to 60-minute time frames. To find out, apply the pivots to your target stock's intraday chart, and note whether or not it uses the lines for support and resistance levels.

Figure 11-5 illustrates a 5-minute chart of mining stock Inco Ltd. (N). You could have scalped this stock both long and short using the daily pivot levels plotted on the chart.

Basic strategy: Buy after one or two closes just over the pivots and sell just under them. If you jump into a long trade every time a 5-minute candle shoots over R1 or R2, for example, you'll end up with a string of losses. Wait until one or two 5-minute candles (or 15-minute candles, if that's the time frame you're trading) close above or below resistance or support lines. You may also want to experiment with 50% levels between the pivot levels. Just don't add so many lines to your chart that you come unglued at every possible support and resistance price level.

## TICK CHARTS

Let's talk briefly about tick charts. A tick chart is different than an intraday chart dictated by time. Whereas a 5-minute chart displays one candle for each 5-minute increment, a tick chart forms candles when a designated number of trades take place. For example, a 50-tick chart is made of candles that are formed of 50 ticks, or trades, each. The actual contract, or share size of the trade doesn't matter, as long as the trade takes place.

Scalpers use tick charts because momentum can be more apparent. When trading is slow, the candles slow formation. When the action heats up, the ticks print fast and furiously and momentum is apparent.

When scalping, many traders use tick charts to replace or accompany time charts. Figure 11-6 displays the same chart of the E-mini S&P (morning session only) as represented in Figure 11-2A. This time, however, the ES is illustrated in a 233-tick chart. Note the difference in configuration.

Although many traders use 50- or 100-tick charts for scalping, I usually configure my tick charts in Fibonacci numbers, such as 144 or 233. Trader and

**FIGURE 11-6** | This 233-tick chart is the morning session of the same E-mini S&P 500 futures chart shown in Figure 11-2A. The candles are not formed in the context of time, such as 2 minutes, or 5 minutes, but rather from a set amount of ticks, or trades (not contracts, but actual trades). With tick charts, when an index or stock slows its trading momentum, the chart slows, too. Increased momentum, especially to higher or lower prices, rapidly becomes apparent with an increased tick pace. I chose 233 ticks per bar, because that is a Fibonacci number and it seems to work well with the ES contract. Some fast-moving stocks draw good 144-tick charts, and others do well with 233-tick increments (or 89 ticks—they're all Fib numbers). It depends on your personal preference.

author John Carter, who wrote the foreword to this book, also utilizes Fib numbers to plot his tick charts. In his excellent book, *Mastering the Trade,* John writes, "The Fibonacci numbers are clean, useful and make sense, and that's why I use them."

If you plan to use tick charts for scalping stocks, I advise targeting stocks that trade an average daily volume of more than one million shares a day. High-volume stocks with broad daily trading ranges carve clean, useful tick charts, while illiquid, mild-mannered stocks may only form a few tick bars for the entire day.

Figure 11-7 displays a 233-tick chart of Titanium Metals Corp. (TIE) and two killer trades scalpers could have executed with the added signals of Fib lines.

**FIGURE 11-7** | This 233-tick chart of the Titanium Metals Corp. (TIE) shows the stock rallying from the open, then chopping sideways until approximately 10:50 A.M. At that time, the titanium products manufacturer rolled over and in a steep decline, tumbled three points. Scalpers and momentum players could have shorted TIE when it traded below the current session low, at 37 (dotted line and arrow). Once the capitulation low was established at 11:45 A.M., and a reversal began, I stretched Fibonacci lines from the high of the move to the low. TIE's price shot straight up to the 61.8% line, and prior price resistance. Wise momentum players and scalpers took profits there (and surely pocketed a portion of the profits earlier). Price then pulled back to the 50% line, before reversing and driving higher once again.

RealTick® graphics used with permission of Townsend Analytics, Ltd. © 1986-2007 Townsend Analytics, Ltd.

## SCALPING SETUPS

One excellent aspect of trading is that every chart pattern applies to every trading time frame. I've noted different patterns for position, swing, day, and momentum trades, and now scalping plays, because certain setups and patterns appear with more regularity in different time frames.

When you narrow your trading time frame down to minutes and seconds, you'll end up scalping the most basic of patterns—consolidations breakouts and breakdowns, and reversals from pullbacks or rallies. It's still important that you recognize the bigger patterns, though, as optimum scalps are born of larger pattern momentum.

From my own experience, I find the best scalping plays setup by forming tight consolidation patterns in the context of established trends. Those patterns move sideways in a tight price range, for at least fifteen to thirty minutes. The longer the better. Optimum scalping setups:

➤ Form on sturdy trend days, during the morning or afternoon session (not during the choppy lunchtime session)
➤ Move sideways in a tight, orderly fashion for fifteen minutes or more
➤ 10- and 20-period MAs ride just below price pattern for support (longs).
➤ As the steam builds, several candlesticks close on their highs.
➤ Volume provides strong momentum.

Early morning plays don't always have the luxury to consolidate for a long period of time. Many times the best morning scalps are reversals off of long-term (daily chart) support levels. As the day continues—and especially through the midday doldrums—the flat lines, shelves, or ledges they draw can fuel breakouts that deliver sweet scalping profits at the beginning of the afternoon session.

You can buy before the breakout while the stock's still consolidating, as long as you use precise timing and have performed your risk-reward analysis. The narrow-range candlesticks forming the consolidation should start closing on their highs. Next, judge by volume, activity on your Level II screen, Time & Sales, E-mini S&P futures, and perhaps TICK and TRIN, that a breakout is imminent.

When you jump in early, you chance the stock reversing, falling through support, and diving fast. (When it falls below support, the short-sellers grab it and force it lower.) Good strategy: Buy half your anticipated position size before the breakout and the remaining half as the breakout is confirmed. You can sell the first half when you make a 25-cent profit, and let the second half rise a level or two higher, depending on the play and the stock's strength.

**HOT TIP**

When you scalp to the long side, don't wait for the stock to show weakness to take profits. Sell while buying momentum is carrying the stock higher. Don't worry about leaving money on the table. This style of trading capitalizes on exploding price momentum and the quick profits it brings.

When I buy reversals, I generally buy the entire position in one lot, then scale out one-half portion at a time.

The setups shown in Figures 11-8 and 11-9 apply to intraday charts. Depending on how fast the stock is moving, I use 2- or 5-minute charts. One-minute charts have too much "noise" (unnecessary movement) for me, but that's personal preference.

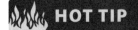

**HOT TIP**

When a stock consolidates, look for a bullish divergence on your Stochastics or CCI indicator. That can indicate the stock is getting ready to break out.

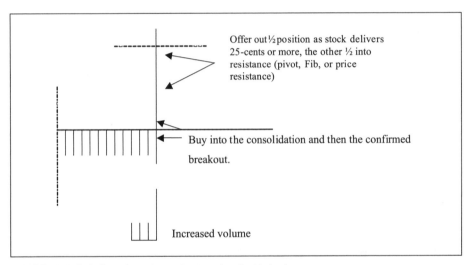

Offer out ½ position as stock delivers 25-cents or more, the other ½ into resistance (pivot, Fib, or price resistance)

Buy into the consolidation and then the confirmed breakout.

Increased volume

**FIGURE 11-8** | Scalping play on two- to 5-minute chart (or tick chart).

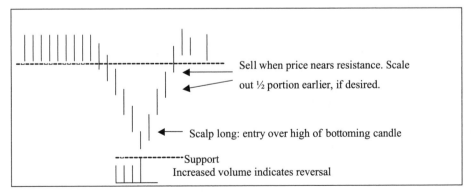

Sell when price nears resistance. Scale out ½ portion earlier, if desired.

Scalp long: entry over high of bottoming candle

Support
Increased volume indicates reversal

**FIGURE 11-9** | Long scalping reversal play on intraday or tick chart.

The intraday charts shown in Figures 11-10 through 11-12 display actual scalping plays on 5-minute charts. After you study them, pinpoint similar setups and entry patterns during market hours. Paper trade until you feel comfortable with the process and the rapidity of the plays.

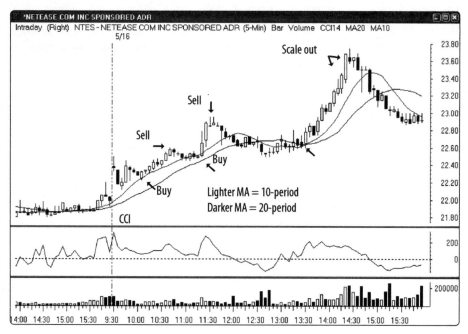

**FIGURE 11-10** | On this 5-minute chart of Netease.com Inc. (NTES), the stock gapped open, then filled about 50% of the gap in the first three candles. Traders let the gap fill take place, then they buy as the Chinese Internet and wireless communications provider dipped to the 10-period MA. A rise off that MA and reversal candle on increased volume triggered the first scalp. A fast breakout out of the subsequent consolidation activated the second scalp and the gravestone doji gave final warning to exit. The breakout out of the lunchtime consolidation generated the final scalp to the upside. More than a point could have been pocketed with that afternoon session play. The volume spike, bearish divergence on CCI, and overbought condition all warned intraday players on the long side to take profits (two arrows indicate a scale-out tactic).

RealTick® graphics used with permission of Townsend Analytics, Ltd. © 1986-2007 Townsend Analytics, Ltd.

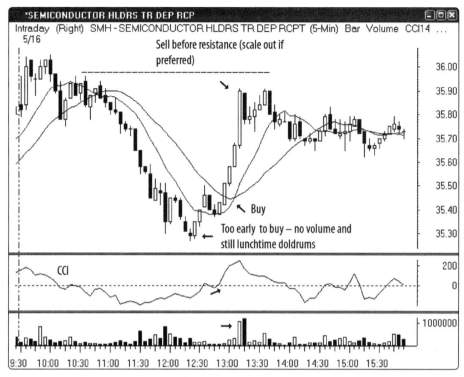

**FIGURE 11-11** | This 5-minute chart of the Semiconductor HOLDRS ETF (SMH) shows the semiconductor exchange traded fund chopping out of the open, then dipping lower and breaking down. (Short scalpers could have sold short when the SMH broke the session low at about 35.75.) The stock tumbled into the lunchtime doldrums, then formed a tiny reverse head-and-shoulders reversal pattern. At a few minutes past 1:00 P.M., volume came back into the SMH and it reversed in a missile-like uptrend. Scalpers who entered would also be watching the E-mini futures (S&P or NASDAQ) for a similar move, and perhaps the SOX, the semi-conductor index.

RealTick® graphics used with permission of Townsend Analytics, Ltd. © 1986-2007 Townsend Analytics, Ltd.

**FIGURE 11-12** | This 5-minute chart of Schnitzer Steel Industries (SCHN) shows the stock rising out of the open in the first 5-minute bar. (All fast scalp opportunities you see are not detailed here because of high risk.) The metal recycling and mini-mill steel manufacturing stock quickly hit its first session high at $38.60, then tumbled fast and furiously to near the $37 line—which was also the prior day's low. At that point, I stretched Fib lines from the high down to the low, because they could help predict price levels for the rest of the trading day. When SCHN reversed on increasing volume and shot over its doji bottoming bar, we entered over the high of that doji. Our stop was just beneath it. SCHN quickly rose to $37.40, at which point some scalpers would scale out a portion of their position. Another portion could be offered out right before the $38.2 Fib resistance line, although SCHN zoomed right through it. By the time the stock reached resistance and the 61.8 Fib line (price resistance + Fib resistance is a strong signal) at $38, it was time to take remaining profits.

## BOOST YOUR SCALPING PROFIT POTENTIAL

Target one or two scalping setups that fit your personality, and work exclusively with them. Gradually, you can add variety to your setup arsenal.

Do your risk-reward analysis before you enter a scalp. Check your target stock's prior resistance level on its daily chart, and 5- to 15-minute charts. If resistance lies less than 75 cents away, find another scalp to target. The best high-probability scalping setups provide lots of headroom.

Remember to check intraday charts for nearby resistance and especially check the 200-period MA on the 5- and 15-minute charts. If it slopes down ready to dunk your target stock, look for another play. More than 8,000 stocks make up the major markets. Why choose a low-probability play when a high-odds setup waits just around the corner?

What if, mid-scalp, the S&P futures suddenly make a U-turn, and your stock follows? Issue a market order, fast. Or, issue a limit order one or two levels under the inside bid (above the offer for shorts). Why do you place your order under the current bid price? As I've mentioned before, it gets crowded when everyone's heading for the door at once. First come, first serve. Give yourself a price cushion.

Otherwise, you'll find yourself in the gut-wrenching position of chasing the stock down. If no buyers want your stock, it could take one or two points, or more, before you finally sell. I've seen that happen a zillion times, and experienced it plenty when I was a novice. That's why you don't get greedy and wait for the extra dime. That's why you get out while momentum is still positive. That's why you get out when you can, not when you're forced to. Finally, that's why you need fast hands and cast-iron nerves to play this game.

Remember, on days market internals tell you a strong uptrend or downtrend rules, you can day trade and let your profits run. But on choppy, whippy days, scalping—or better yet, washing your car—makes for the smartest strategy. When in doubt, stay out.

## SCALPING CHECKLIST

Scalping guidelines are listed below. Consider making copies and keeping them handy until these steps become second nature to you. If more points occur to you, add them to this list.

*Scalping Checklist*
1. Top down criteria is in place. (Overall market, NYSE or NASDAQ, your stock's industry, TICK, TRIN, S&P E-mini futures, and/or E-mini NASDAQ 100 futures in an uptrend; you'll want these market internals negative for shorts.)
2. Resistance on daily chart and intraday chart (moving averages or overhead price congestion) will not hinder immediate price movement.
3. Intraday chart forms tight, orderly consolidation pattern, with majority of candlesticks closing on their highs.

4. Strong volume coming into stock; increased volume spike forming on breakout.
5. Level II screen: Spread between inside bid and offer is three cents, or narrower.
6. Good depth on inside bid—four or more specialists, market makers, or more.
7. Buy orders are eating through levels on the ask.

## SELLING SHORT: DON'T SELL IT SHORT!

Rarely will you find a stockbroker or investor who likes to short stocks. Traders short more often, and a few traders shun the technique. Why?

Number one excuse: The market has an upside bias.

Reply: Sure it does, but it's a long-term bias. Traders profit from the short term. Plus, the market falls one-third of the time. Every stock moves through cycles; corrections and downtrends are inevitable. When they do fall, they fall faster than they rise because panic (the ultimate fear) drives stock prices down faster than euphoria raises them.

As I write, the Dow ended the week down 300 points. Many stocks are groveling near or under their 50 MAs. Savvy traders somewhere are much richer from shorting that drop.

Number two excuse: We Americans take pride in our optimism. We like our glasses half full and our endings happy.

Number three excuse: It's not nice to kick someone who's down. We defend the underdog and shy away from capitalizing on another's downfall. And that's exactly what selling short boils down to—capitalizing on an underdog.

Retort to the last two excuses: Short sellers eventually cover. That adds liquidity to the stock, and actually bolsters the price.

Number four excuse: There's an unlimited potential for loss. After all, if you buy a $20 stock, it can't fall below zero. What if you sell short a stock at $20, and it makes a U-turn and rockets to $100? When you cover, you lose a gazillion dollars.

In practice, this is absolutely true. If you're silly enough to let any position go that far against you, all the rest of us can do is roll our eyes, cluck sympathetically, and pray you go back to your day job. (You won't have a choice.)

To limit your losses on shorts, place automatic buy-to-cover stops. Adjust them down according to good risk management procedures. End of problem.

And, end of excuses. Let's learn how to make money shorting stocks.

## THE SHORTING PROCESS: HOW IT WORKS

When you buy a stock, we say you are "long" that position, or you own it. You buy it with the intention of selling it later, at a higher price. You profit from the difference.

When you "short" a stock, you sell the stock with the intention of buying it back later, at a lower price. Again, you profit from the entry and exit spread.

Let's say Cranky Computers barks it way into an ugly downtrend. It's a real dog. You, as a wise trader, notice the breakdown, and feel sure Cranky will fall to its next support area at about $50. You sell short, or "short," 100 shares of Cranky, valued at $60 per share. Total cost, $6,000, plus commission.

**HOT TIP**

The biggest professional traders would rather sell short than buy long positions. They make fatter profits faster on a falling stock than a rising stock. Why? Momentum to the downside fueled by panic and fear delivers bigger gains than upside momentum propelled by greed.

Your broker removes $6,000+ from your account and tucks it away as a security deposit, so you can return the stock if need be. Then he or she borrows that stock from another client's account. In its place, an IOU guarantees the stock returned on demand. Next, the broker sells the borrowed 100 shares of Cranky for $60 per share. He puts the $6,000 away for safekeeping.

As you suspected, during the next week, Cranky falls to support at $50. You quickly issue an order to buy it back, known as "covering your short." Your broker takes $5,000 out of the safekeeping account, goes to the market, and buys 100 shares of Cranky at $50 per share, the current price. He returns those shares to the account of the other customer he originally borrowed it from and cancels your IOU.

Now your broker returns to you the $6,000 security deposit he took from your account, plus the $1,000 leftover when he bought the stock back, minus a commission. Your original $6,000 investment yields a $1,000 profit, minus commissions. Nice trade!

The final quirky aspect of selling short: With the exception of ETFs, you cannot short most stocks on a downtick. You can only short a stock on an uptick, or zero-plus tick. (A zero-plus tick means a stock trades on an uptick, then the following trade goes off at the same price level.)

**HOT TIP**

All stocks are not available for shorting at all times. The larger your brokerage firm, the larger the list of shorting candidates it has on hand.

The uptick rule, developed by the exchanges, is meant to prevent violent market selloffs. It also softens the blows to a tanking stock—a variation of "don't hit him while he's down." Specialists and market makers are exempt from the uptick rule.

When the market environment invites selling short, the following objectives work well for locating high-probability entries for position, swing, and intraday day trades:

➤ Top reversal patterns
➤ Continuation patterns breaking into legs of downtrends
➤ Moving average crossovers just above the price pattern and heading to the downside
➤ Stocks trading just below their 20-day MA on a daily chart (preferably under the 50-day MA and 200-day MA)
➤ Momentum indicators show bearish signals
➤ 1:2 or 1:3 risk-reward ratios

## CHART PATTERNS FOR SELLING SHORT: WHAT TO LOOK FOR

My two favorite top reversal patterns for shorting in longer-term trades are the double top and the head and shoulders. Position and swing traders will spot these two patterns on daily charts, and day traders will recognize them on intraday charts. These patterns can spell "doom" for bulls.

As mentioned in a previous chapter, the double top, which is illustrated in Figure 11-13, resembles an *M*. It forms a reverse image of the double bottom. Just as the double bottom can forecast a powerful uptrend, the double top presages a lethal downtrend.

The double top begins to form as an overbought stock in an uptrend, making new highs. Then, it encounters buying exhaustion. It makes a new high, sells off, then shoots up to another high, or the retest. The second high cannot break through the price resistance formed by the previous high. Buyers refuse to pay up, and those holding smell trouble and begin to sell.

Now the stock falls to prior support (middle pivot of the *M*). It may rebound slightly, but weak volume can't propel it higher. Fear takes over, stop orders are hit, and short sellers arrive with their claws fully extended. Now, the unhappy stock tumbles into free fall.

When you see a complete double top form on a daily chart, monitor it for a possible setup and entry below support to sell short. Your time frame could be position, swing, or intraday.

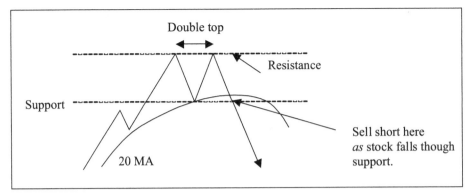

**FIGURE 11-13** | Double top—all time frames.

Remember to check moving averages. Make sure the stock has dropped below its 20-day MA, and preferably its 50-day MA, on a daily chart. The entry point is the same as for going long—just reversed.

I already hear your next questions, "Why can't I sell short early? What's wrong with shorting the breakdown of the second top (retest) on a daily chart—as it occurs?"

Answer: You can. But how do you know it's "the top"? Until the prior low is broken, you are shorting a stock that's still in an uptrend. Lots of folks who buy stocks can't read charts. When a popular stock pulls back from its highs, people tend to buy. Unless the market environment is strongly bearish when your stock tops out, a rush of late buyers could cause a quick price spike that stops out your short position. Newcomers to shorting will find easier profits in stocks that are trading in early or established downtrends.

Figure 11-14 shows a weekly chart of Mittal Steel, Inc. (MT) and its disastrous double top formation. As you can imagine, when a complete double top forms on a weekly chart, it means a meltdown may soon take place. If you're long a stock and haven't exited it by the time it falls to the midpoint of a steep *M*, sell fast. The next step down can be a long one.

Figure 11-15 shows a daily chart of MDC Holdings, Inc. (MDC), the homebuilder who constructs Richmond Homes. Note how MDC topped out in July at about $88, and then pulled back. It retested that high about a week later, then rolled back over and dove below its prior low. Now, the double top formation came to completion.

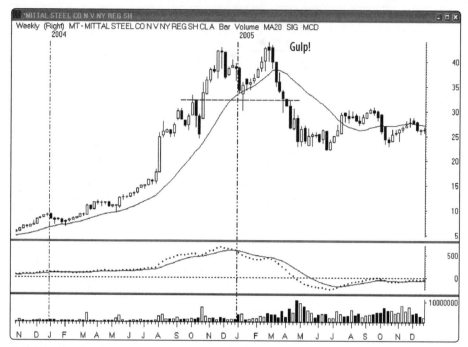

**FIGURE 11-14** | This weekly chart of the Mittal Steel Co. (MT) shows a perfect (if lethal) double-top formation. Since you know that the longer the time frame, the stronger the signal, when SCHN reached 44 for the retest and couldn't climb above it, the failure indicated that the steel maker would fall lower. Of course, it did so in tandem with other components of the basic materials sector. By the time it reached 25, it had lost nearly 50% of its value. Note how both highs involved a doji or spinning top candle. These candle patterns hold great predictive value as top reversal candles, or bars.

RealTick® graphics used with permission of Townsend Analytics, Ltd. © 1986-2007 Townsend Analytics, Ltd.

On the MDC chart, check the failure of the second top (also called the retest) and note these important reversal signals:

➤ Price quickly sliced through the 20-day MA
➤ Volume decreased
➤ Stochastics had already carved a bearish reversal

Short sellers grabbed positions at $83, as MDC showed signs of weakening. Although MDC crashed through its first support level at $78, it managed to hold for the mid-August consolidation at $75.

During the two days after the subsequent gap down (the gap usually occurs when a double top completes its formation), short sellers who held overnight bagged several points.

**FIGURE 11-15** | This daily chart of MDC Holdings, Inc. (MDC) offered short sellers two profitable double top formations from which to profit. Remember the simple psychology inherent in this pattern: When bulls refuse to pay higher prices the second time a stock approaches new highs (whatever the time frame), supply will send the stock lower—at least on a temporary basis. Note the candle patterns on each of the four tops. Spinning tops, dark cloud covers, shooting stars, and doji all warn that a price reversal could take place.

RealTick® graphics used with permission of Townsend Analytics, Ltd. © 1986-2007 Townsend Analytics, Ltd.

As a bonus play for short sellers, MDC created another double top in September and October. I've noticed that a second double top often takes place after a particularly steep initial double top meltdown on daily charts.

The double top shown on the 15-minute chart of Netease.com, Inc. (NTES) in Figure 11-16 shows a brief retest in the form of a failed breakout that falls below its daily pivot and 20-period MA, all at the same time. This convergence of signals tells intraday traders that the Chinese Internet stock offers a good intraday shorting opportunity.

The second reversal pattern we'll look at that creates high-probability setups for short position, swing, and intraday trades is the head-and-shoulders pattern illustrated in Figure 11-17. This pattern resembles a human silhouette. The stock rises at the conclusion of uptrend and pulls back, forming the left shoulder. It rises again, making a higher high, and forms the head. Again, it pulls back to

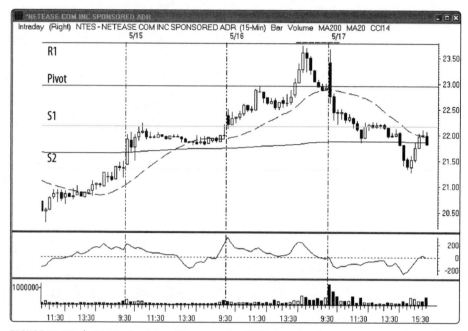

**FIGURE 11-16** | This 15-minute chart of Netease.com Inc. (NTES) shows intraday long opportunities, then results in a quick but deadly double top. Interestingly enough, daily pivot lines tell you that R1 couldn't be broached on 5/16—so when the price gapped open and failed again (long black candle) on 5/17, intraday panic selling set in. A good short entry came when NTES fell below the prior day's close and the daily pivot +20-period MA at 23. Shorts made a quick point, and if they held on as NTES waffled around its S1 line, then profited an extra 60 cents per share.

RealTick® graphics used with permission of Townsend Analytics, Ltd. © 1986-2007 Townsend Analytics, Ltd.

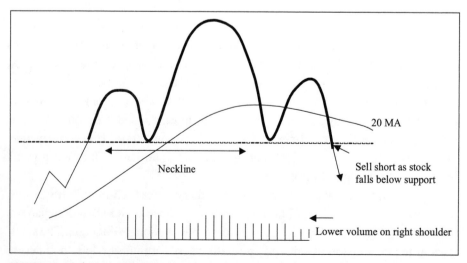

**FIGURE 11-17** | Head and shoulders shorting pattern.

---

**🔥 HOT TIP**

In most instances, when you see a double top or head-and-shoulders complete its formation on daily charts and plummet through support, the following morning the stock will gap down at the open. Besides panic selling and short selling, here's a third final reason: Truckloads of traders and investors have entered automatic stop orders for their long positions directly under the obvious support zone. When price slides below support, it fires off scores of sell stops, creating much more supply than low demand can absorb. Another reason: panic selling.

---

previous support. This support line is called the "neckline." The last gasp is an upturn to form the right shoulder, then a rollover and retracement to the neckline support.

If price slips below the neckline, you can bet a downtrend follows. Sell short as the stock breaks down. Set your buy-to-cover stop 10 to 70 cents above the entry day's high.

In the case of the head and shoulders, for an optimum trade, check the volume as follows: higher volume on the left shoulder and possibly the head, and less volume on the right shoulder. If heavy volume comes into the right shoulder, beware. In this case, the stock could be preparing to start another uptrend. Hold off on your early short entry until the breakdown is confirmed with a daily close below support. By waiting, you might miss out on profits—or, you might miss out on a nasty short squeeze. When price forms a head-and-shoulders, and then decides to ignore it and scoot higher after all, the resulting vertical price pop causes short sellers' ulcers to pop as well.

Figure 11-18 shows a head-and-shoulders formation on a daily chart of the Lennar Corp. (LEN). While head-and-shoulders do form on intraday charts, they are more obvious on daily and weekly charts, where the price has time to draw defined silhouettes.

Two additional shorting tips for shorting completed top reversal patterns:

➤ Choose stocks with moon-shot tops. The steeper the top, the steeper the drop.
➤ The less support available at the breakdown point, the sooner the stock stumbles and heads south.

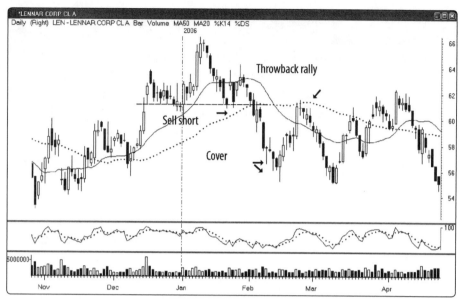

**FIGURE 11-18** | This daily chart of the Lennar Corp. (LEN) shows the homebuilder forming a clear head-and-shoulders top. Note the doji at the top of LEN's head. After that LEN got a haircut! On the right shoulder, you can see the 20-day MA (solid line) quickly flattened out, and the long, upper shadows of two of the candles warned that sellers lurked overhead. LEN didn't give up easily, and rallied for one day after it broke the neckline support and fell through the 50-day MA at the same time. Still, that weak white candle didn't scare the sellers away, nor did it take out many short stops. LEN fell steeply after that, padding short seller's pockets. Another great short entry appeared at the retest of neckline resistance in the form of a "throwback rally," in which LEN rallied back to neckline resistance, then rolled over and slid south again. In fact, several more opportunities for shorts presented themselves in the months to follow.

RealTick® graphics used with permission of Townsend Analytics, Ltd. © 1986-2007 Townsend Analytics, Ltd.

An additional indicator that's useful for selling short comes to us courtesy of John Bollinger (*www.bollingerbands.com*). Bollinger Bands resemble moving average envelopes. The duel lines ride above and below the stock's price pattern on the chart, with the price moving between them.

Standard Bollinger Bands are twenty-period exponential bands with two standard deviations. (Standard deviations measure volatility.) Most charting packages offer Bollinger Bands as a basic feature.

The primary characteristic of Bollinger Bands: When price touches the top of its upper Bollinger Band, it has a good likelihood of traveling down to its bottom band.

To learn how the bands react and if they agree with your trading style, apply them to your target shorting stocks and monitor them. If your stock is at the top of its Bollinger Band and can't rise above it, chances are good it will fall. (I still won't short it unless it falls under its 20-day MA; that's a standard component of my short criteria.)

Figure 11-19 shows a daily chart of Dell Inc. (DELL) with Bollinger Bands applied.

**FIGURE 11-19** | This daily chart of Dell Inc. (DELL) shows the computer manufacturer in a steep downtrend. We plotted Bollinger Bands over the price pattern along with the 20-day MA (dotted MA line) that's customarily used with the bands. The computer manufacturer showed signs of weakness in February, when it could not sustain its breakout. The best short signal arrived in April. The Bollinger Bands came together in a "squeeze" pattern that indicated, in this case, a breakdown. DELL fell under its 20-day MA and could not push its upper Bollinger Band higher. Soon it walked down the line, broke support, and was unable to push toward the upper line at all—all signs of decided weakness. Short sellers profited nicely in this downturn. At 26, DELL rallied, and touched its upper band, but the quick failure to continue to the upside gave yet another short signal.

RealTick® graphics used with permission of Townsend Analytics, Ltd. © 1986-2007 Townsend Analytics, Ltd.

## BOTTOM LINE SHORTING STRATEGIES

Just as you buy position and swing trades when a stock in an uptrend rises through resistance highs, you sell short when a stock in a downtrend penetrates support and trades one to 10 cents below support lows.

Always perform risk-reward analysis before entering short positions. Use the same ratios, 1:2 or 1:3, that we talked about in the earlier discussion. This time, look for nearby resistance and calculate that as your risk (buy-to-cover stop) price. Previous support on a daily chart will serve as your profit target. Note: It's best to estimate your profit target 50 cents or so above the actual support price to avoid getting caught in a short squeeze.

For momentum and day trades, adjust your risk-reward parameters to fit intraday objectives. Make sure your stop (above nearby resistance) sits close enough to your entry price to protect your principal, and your profit target (nearby support) provides the trade enough room to unwind and pay rewards.

When shorting a rapidly falling stock, place a limit order two to 3 cents below the inside bid. If the stock is still in rally mode, enter your limit order at the ask price.

Place a buy-to-cover stop 10 to 70 cents above the entry day's high. If that's too far away, find a resistance area on the one-hour intraday chart, and place your buy-to-cover stop 10 to 70 cents above that. As always, the 10 to 70 cents depends on your stock's price and volatility range. Don't even consider moving your stop higher. No reason is good enough. If the stock hits your stop, cover your position.

For swing and position trades, as the stock moves down, establish a trailing buy-to-cover stop 10 to 70 cents above each new rally high or consolidation on its daily chart. Cover half your position after you make a point or so. Cover the other half of your position either when you get stopped out, when the trend weakens, or at your profit target.

For the safest short entries, look for a stock in a solid downtrend. You can short any valid breakdown as it stair-steps its way down through lower lows and lower highs, with the 20-day and/or 50-day MAs acting as a resistant "ceiling" overhead. Wait for the stock to rally, and sell short when it weakens. Remember the nice spring day? Flip that pattern upside down and sell short on a "dark fall day."

This is an excellent time to brush up on candlestick patterns in Chapter 5, such as bearish engulfing patterns, the hanging man, and evening stars. As you recall, these patterns warn of impending doom.

You may also want to review the section on breakdowns in Chapter 6. Setups evolve from the same continuation patterns you learned for buying stocks—again, just turn them upside down.

On intraday charts on crumbling stocks, look for continuations consolidations and rallies ripe for reversals. Look for stocks on the 5- and 15-minute charts trading under their 20-period MAs. The more MAs they're trading below, the better.

Check out support levels on an intraday chart of the prior trading day, as well as the present day levels. Where could a price reversal to the upside take place? It should be at least one to two points away. The closer it is, the higher the risk.

Figure 11-20 shows a daily chart of Nike Inc. (NKE) with a short entry that works for swing and intraday trades. Figure 11-21 displays an hourly chart

**FIGURE 11-20** | This daily chart of Nike Inc. (NKE) shows the popular athletic sportswear manufacturer falling into a downtrend. Short sellers sharpened their claws when NKE's 20-, 50-, and 200-day MAs converged in April. Note how the 20-day MA slid down, cutting through the 50- and 200-day MAs. That's a potent negative crossover combination, and a great shorting signal. Stochastics headed south, too; volume stayed relatively quiet during the drops. Swing traders could sell short the fall through support at about $84, in early April, placing buy-to-cover stops no higher than $85 (just above the 200-day MA). The first cover signal came at $82, just before prior support at $81. A spinning top also warned of a possible rally. The next good short entry for swing trades showed up in May, three days after NKE rallied into prior resistance at about $83.50, and then reversed again. The break below short-term support at about $81 delivered gains current levels at $78. Intraday traders could use the swing trade entries to execute short momentum and day trades.

of NKE with more detailed short views, and Figure 11-22 zooms in with a 15-minute chart.

These three charts show multiple time frames that give the same short signals. This technique is optimum for swing and intraday entries and risk management.

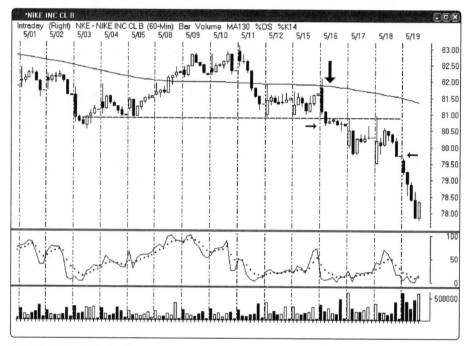

**FIGURE 11-21** | This hourly chart shows a close-up of the daily chart of Nike Inc. (NKE) in Figure 11-20, from May 1 through May 19. The 130-period MA on this chart closely correlates to the position of the 20-day MA on the daily chart. Note the four most recent days on the daily chart, with the 20-day MA coming down over NKE's price pattern on May 16. Now, we zoom in on a 60-minute chart and see the same MA action (block arrow). Gap up to the MA resistance, failure, and subsequent break of initial support offered a swing and intraday short entry. The stop can be placed just above the resistance line, at $81.50. On May 17 and 18, it attempted three times to move above $81, but no dice. (The S&P Index was negative, as well.) The final rally attempt on May 18 proved the last gasp. On May 19, NKE gapped slightly to the downside, then tanked. The final white candle on that day shows possible short covering before the weekend. Besides the profitable swing trade, several intraday candles furnished money-making short trades.

RealTick® graphics used with permission of Townsend Analytics, Ltd. © 1986-2007 Townsend Analytics, Ltd.

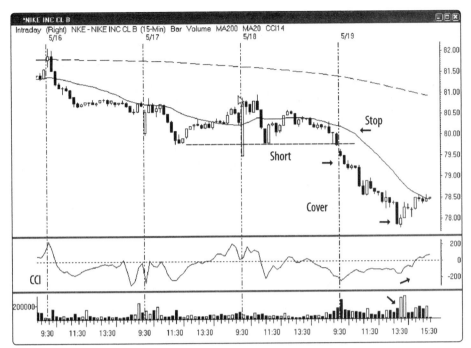

**FIGURE 11-22** | This 15-minute chart zooms in on the final action of the daily and hourly charts of Nike Inc. (NKE) shown in Figure 11-20 and Figure 11-21. Now you can see the price action of May 19 in detail. You can also see a great entry for a day trade. NKE gaps down slightly at the open, but cannot muster enough energy to fill it. That signals short sellers to jump in. With a trailing stop, the trade could be held until 1:30 P.M., where the two huge volume spikes (one's enough for me) warned short sellers that a reversal was imminent. Traders would cover at about $78, pocketing more than one point profit.

RealTick® graphics used with permission of Townsend Analytics, Ltd. © 1986-2007 Townsend Analytics, Ltd.

When you're shorting, remember to use the top down criteria in reverse. Look for a weak overall market, or at least a weak NYSE or NASDAQ, depending on which exchange your stock resides. For good measure, the stock's sector should be downtrodden as well. The TICK should be negative and the TRIN positive (above 1.0, or higher.) Naturally, the E-mini S&P and/or the E-mini NASDAQ 100 futures should be trading in negative territory. If you're using Stochastics or the CCI, look for a bearish divergence or a downtrend.

*Shorting Don'ts*

**Don't** enter a short trade and then go to the beach for the day, unless your position is covered by an automatic buy-to-cover stop. Besides, once in a while, it's fun to watch your shorts fall. Making money on a crumbling stock is like watching the opposing team's quarterback get sacked. We're finally getting revenge for all the times we entered long positions and got creamed. Now, we're the creamors.

**Don't** short a stock in an uptrend on its daily chart. Short stocks in downtrends or stocks creating reversal patterns. Also, for position trades, check your target stock's Composite Rating in *Investors Business Daily*. Make sure the stock has a Composite Ranking of 50 or less.

**Don't** short a stock because, in your opinion, it's flown way too high. I remember when Yahoo! (YHOO) was one of the first Internet stocks to soar into space. In March 1998, YHOO rocketed to the $100 mark, making multiple-point leaps per day. Back then, we weren't used to that kind of volatility. I remember a gang of deep-pocket traders who shorted the stock when it hit $99. They bet the ranch, shorting thousands upon thousands of shares. YHOO rocketed over the $100 mark, while laughing derisively. The traders gritted their teeth and held on—rock-jawed in their stubborn belief—this stock could not defy gravity much longer. Still, YHOO galloped higher. In fact, the stock didn't look back for a long time to come. The move wiped out most of those traders—for good.

You would have known better. After studying this book, you would have looked at the strong volume on the continuing breakouts and decided the stock could easily climb even higher. You would have been right.

**Don't** attempt to scalp stocks on the short side if you are a novice trader. Get some experience under your belt before you dive in. Unless you're shorting ETFs or mini stock index futures, the uptick rule often makes entry difficult, time consuming, and imprecise. It's not worth it for a possible 25-cent gain.

**Don't** short a thinly traded stock, that is, a stock that trades fewer than 300,000+ shares per day. That proposition is unwise on either the long or short side.

# QUIZ
|||||||||||||||||||

*Questions*

1. In relation to scalping, what's the trading style, share size, and risk-reward ratio?

2. Certain types of numbers play a role in support and resistance. What are they?

3. When you scalp, what is the ideal spread between the inside bid and ask?

4. Name three ideal scalping setup components.

5. When you're scalping to the long side, which is better? Good depth on the bid or ask?

6. True or false? When you want to chase a running stock, just place a market order, and be done with it.

7. Scene: You're in the midst of a successful scalp. Suddenly, the E-mini futures tank, the TICK drops below zero, and the market makers evaporate from your stock's bid. How do you get out?

8. Define the "uptick rule."

9. If you see a stock touches its upper Bollinger Band, but can't close above it, and on the next candle falls lower, where will it probably move next?

10. True or false? To find shorting candidates for swing trades, use daily charts and look for stocks in a downtrend, trading below their 20-day MA, and better yet, below their 50- and 200-day MAs.

11. Is increased volume necessary for a stock to plunge into a downtrend?

12. True or false? When you're in a short position and the dopey stock starts rising, it's best to move your original buy-to-cover stop at least one or two points higher.

13. On a head-and-shoulders pattern that sets up for a good shorting opportunity, look for lower volume on the _____ shoulder.

14. True or false? Thinly traded stocks are good short candidates.

*Answers*

1.  The scalping style includes multiple trades, with share size of 500 to 1,000 shares, and a risk-reward ratio of 1:2.

2.  Whole numbers, and to a lesser degree half numbers, play a role in support and resistance.

3.  Scalp stocks with a one- to two-penny spread between the inside bid and ask.

4.  (1) Stock is consolidating in the context of an intraday trend. (2) It moves sideways in a tight, orderly fashion for twenty minutes, preferably longer. (3) Most of the candlesticks are closing on their highs.

5.  When you're entering a long scalp, enter with good depth on the bid.

6.  False. That tactic is only for people who want to explain to their spouses how they lost so much money trading.

7.  When good scalps suddenly go sour, issue a sell limit order one or two levels under the inside bid.

8.  Stocks can be sold short only on an uptick. The trade can take place only if the stock trades above the last tick, or on a zero-plus tick, meaning the same price as the last uptick.

9.  It will probably head lower, and possibly to its lower Bollinger Band.

10. True

11. No

12. False. Very bad idea.

13. right

14. True, for people who enjoy thrill-seeking adventures and have disposable trading accounts.

## CENTER POINT: CREATE A PROSPERITY MINDSET

*"But know that you can achieve the total freedom of financial independence if you choose, and it will work to uplift your consciousness to accommodate that level of completeness."*

—John Randolph Price, *The Abundance Book*

Each and every one of us is entitled to prosperity and abundance. In order to attract it, however, we must take charge of our beliefs and our thoughts. We must focus not only on what we do, but how we label the world around us.

Our prosperity, or lack of it, reflects to a great degree on our level of thinking. For example, as individuals, we may not have a direct impact on global economic conditions, but when we complain about these circumstances on a consistent basis, we align ourselves with negativity. That negativity exerts a powerful influence on our lives, and the lives of those around us.

Do you hold onto the old belief that righteousness resides in poverty? Do you pepper your thoughts and conversations with phrases such as, "I can't," "I'm afraid," "I don't know how," and "There's not enough"? Consider replacing those feelings with thoughts and resultant feelings of prosperity, sufficiency, and self-worth.

Know that you are a very special person. A unique awareness dwells within you and flows through you. Life is biased on the side of healing, triumph, and success.

Assume that inner and outer prosperity is your right. Center your thoughts on your blessings rather than on what you perceive as lack or limitation. Stretch the boundaries of faith in yourself and faith in life. Create conditions within your mind that support positive results and attract them into your experience.

# CHAPTER 12

# Love Your Losses: They're a Trader's Best Friend

You probably read the title to this chapter and made immediate plans to have me carted off to Pecan Manor. But before you send me to the nut house, hear me out.

The success or failure of your trading career does not depend on your gains. It depends on your losses—how you manage them, and what you learn from them.

Socrates wrote that an unexamined life wasn't worth living. Guess what? Unexamined trading losses will send you to the soup line. Trust me. I've approached the end of that line, spoon in hand, more than once.

The single most important thing you can do while you learn how to trade: Keep a journal of your wins and losses. This is not a self-flagellation diary. In fact, call it your Success Journal—because if tended to properly, that's exactly where this exercise leads.

Either purchase a notebook with a green cover (the color of money), or create a new file folder on your computer. When the market closes each day, record your entries. Write down the stock symbol, entry price, and exit price. Start the first sentence, "I entered this trade because . . . ," then finish the sentence with your reasoning.

Maybe you entered for terrific reasons: orderly chart pattern, high-probability setup, 1:3 risk-reward ratio, perfect entry point, and good top down criteria. Still, the trade turned sour. Begin the next sentence with, "I lost money on this trade because. . . ." Without criticizing yourself, list the reasons your trade went against you. No words like "stupid," or "dummy" allowed. Just the facts. Now study those facts and own the choices you made.

Once you understand what happened, think forward. Get on the other side of the loss.

Last, write, "When this situation arises again, I will. . . ." Finish this sentence with the steps you'll take the next time you encounter similar circumstances.

The next time, how can you better protect your principal? What would you do to make sure you're trading to trade well?

When you execute a particularly awesome trade, include that in your journal too. Study how the trade evolved, so you learn to repeat your successes.

The following trading morning, review your last Success Journal entries. If you have time, review others you have entered.

As I've mentioned before, people who write down their goals prove to be far more successful than those who simply store them in memory. This premise holds true for traders and their journals. The wealthiest traders I know completed this process early in their trading careers. It absolutely, always delivers valuable results.

## SEVEN "SUICIDE SCENES": HOW TO AVOID THEM, PROTECT YOUR PRINCIPAL, AND LIVE TO TRADE ANOTHER DAY

Let's haul some typical losses into the light of day, so we can inspect them. Because I've experienced every one of these losses, you don't have to.

## SCENE ONE: STUFF HAPPENS

You buy a strong stock, in a strong market, at the right entry point. A few minutes later, though, negative economic news interrupts the routine commentary on CNBC. The market screeches to a halt and does a U-turn. Your stock joins the stampede to the south and hits your stop. You sell and are out with a small loss.

Loss avoidance tactic: There isn't one. You entered a strong stock, in a strong market, at the appropriate time. Unexpected news happens. When you exited at the proper stop point, your loss represented a calculated risk of the business.

Compressed into cold, hard reality, the scene boils down to good trade, unexpected event, stock dives, proper exit action, and small loss incurred. Study and reflect upon the sequence. Look simple to duplicate? It isn't. (You guessed it. The "proper exit action" usually gets in our way.)

This type of loss is the only justifiable loss you'll ever take. If you exited at your stop or sooner, you took the correct action. Losses like these are not the ones that hurt you. Those that follow are.

## SCENE TWO: THE GOOD NEWS, BAD NEWS ROLLER-COASTER RIDE

Soon after the market opens, you buy a strong stock at the right entry point. You've designated it a day trade. By 11:30 A.M., your stock rises to the next resistance area, two points away. Instead of exiting at this predetermined profit objective with $2 earnings, you hold on. You think: Surely after the market's midday blues, the stock will conquer the next resistance area, and earn another point or two.

Fast-forward to 2:30 P.M., same day. Your stock and the market grind through the next hour, apathetically. Could it be the unemployment numbers due out tomorrow? Finally, your stock drifts down to your entry point, sinks beneath it, and hits your stop. You sigh and exit the trade.

I can't count the times early in my trading career that I've ridden a good stock to fine profits, refused to sell, and ridden it all the way back down to my stop—for a loss. Yes, it happens to everyone. No, that doesn't make it feel any better.

*Lethargy* and *optimism* (greed?) are the operative words here. You get caught up in the euphoria of what may happen, instead of looking at what is.

Loss avoidance tactic: First, in a day trade, when a stock makes two points, then nears resistance, take your money and run. I don't care if the thing points to Mars. Do it anyway. Nine times out of ten, you'll congratulate yourself later.

Second, a stock that smacks up against resistance at 11:30 A.M. will likely pull back. The midday doldrums will push it down, if nothing else.

Third, stay abreast of major economic reports, such as unemployment reports, the CPI (Consumer Price Index), ISM (Institute of Supply Management), and PPI (Produce Price Index). These reports come out monthly, and are usually announced at 8:30 A.M. or 10:00 A.M., EST. Financial network commentators discussing bond futures' reactions will tell you whether or not the market liked the news.

For explanations of reports and their schedules, go to my Web site, and click on Tutorials, and Economic Calendar.

The day prior to a highly anticipated economic report, the market typically quiets in the afternoon. Many professional traders, including floor traders in the exchanges, go home for the remainder of the day. Pros refuse to commit to a position when economic news threatens to yank it from underneath. Join them. Exit some or all of your positions before lunch. If the market decides to rally, you can always jump back in.

Fourth, the market has become so volatile, you might consider the morning and afternoon sessions as two different days. Many times, in the afternoon, the market reverses its morning action. So don't assume that because your stock is strong in the morning, it will continue its rise later in the day. Maybe, maybe not. Closing out a winning trade or two before lunch promotes healthy digestion. Remember the smart trader saying, "You'll never go broke by taking a profit."

## SCENE THREE: DROP THE STOP GAME

You're scalping. Your target stock consolidated nicely, and showed signs of breaking out. You bought a small position then, and added to it as it broke out on strong volume—perfect entry points. Suddenly, the tide turns, really fast, and the stock drops like a stone—right through your stop loss. You chase it down. Instead of issuing a sell order a few cents below the bid, or even a market order, you stubbornly shoot orders at the current bid. It dissolves and gives way to the next level down. You cancel and shoot again. Oops. Bid gone. "Doesn't anybody want to buy this stock?" you wail. *No.*

Within minutes, your stock grovels two points down from your original stop. Then a light bulb flashes in your mind. You'll switch this from a scalp to a day trade. No problem. You check the day's initial low for a new stop point. Uh, oh. Stock's already crashed through that. What about yesterday's low? Gulp. That was a half point ago. Worse, you're down almost three points. AAACK!

But, wait, your frantic mind flashes another light bulb. This isn't a day trade. Doesn't have to be. As of right now, it's a swing trade. Swing trades have much wider stop parameters than day trades. Sure. That'll work.

With stomach churning and palms sweating, you pull up a daily chart and search for yet another support zone, anywhere that the stock might find buyers. Glumly, you find it—four points below the current price.

Get the picture?

Loss avoidance tactic: When you enter a trade, designate the time frame, figure your risk-reward analysis, plan your trade, and stick to it no matter what obstacles jump into your path. All scalping entries do not a swing trade make. Or a day trade for that matter.

Please raise your right hand and repeat after me:

"I swear on my mouse that from this day forward, for as long as I trade, I will never, ever, ignore my stop parameters."

## SCENE FOUR: HOW NOT TO CATCH A FALLING KNIFE

It's a grim day at the ranch. Mother Market heard a Fed watcher mutter the words *rising inflation* on CNBC, and she's fallen into a sullen mood. The TICK wallows in the −500 area, the TRIN is climbing over 1.2. Unhappiness prevails. You're flat, thank goodness, and you see nothing you want to sell short, but your trigger finger itches.

Hmm. There's a stock, a leader in the pharmaceutical industry that's plummeted for a week. It's got a bad case of the uglies. Makes sense because that industry is ailing as well. Betcha' that stock will reverse when it lands on its 50-day MA on a daily chart. That should be today. You pull up the chart.

Oops . . . it just did. It just hit the 50 MA, and it popped 50 cents. Sweet. Just like the stockbrokers say, you'll buy low, sell high. You buy.

After a brief rally, the market resumes its downward plunge. Your immediate profits get wiped out, and the stock drops through your stop and slices down through its 50-day MA on the daily chart. You stare at your screen, paralyzed. It slides another point, then another. You let it drop, unwilling to gag on such a large loss. By the end of the day, you are down four points. Numbly, still holding the position, you hear the closing bell.

Loss avoidance tactic: A wise trader saying goes, "Never try to catch a falling knife."

First, if the market trends in a negative direction and you feel signs of boredom—leave. If you're not in front of your computer, you can't commit one of the foremost novice trader mistakes—overtrading, or trading for no reason.

What if the market reverses while you're gone and you miss a couple of opportunities? That's part of this game. Shrug it off.

Second, no matter which way the market trends, "the trend is your friend." Most stocks follow the market's direction. Swim with the current.

Third, when stocks drop, they drop for a reason. More sellers than buyers. Nobody wants them. Traders call stocks like these "falling knives." Please don't try to catch one. The results can hurt.

"Buy low, sell high" works well in real estate. It doesn't always work as well in the stock market, especially in short-term trades. Remember, when you choose a stock to buy, it's like choosing players for your ball team. You don't choose the guy with a broken arm, or the girl who's clumsy. You choose the strongest people available to make a winning team. When you're trading, you choose the strongest stocks to make winning profits.

## SCENE FIVE: HEY, WAIT FOR ME!

It's 8:30 A.M. on a weekday, and you're watching CNBC. The stock index futures are up nicely. The Dow flew into record territory yesterday, and things look rosy.

You're sipping your coffee, anticipating the money you'll make today. Your favorite brokerage stock listed on the NYSE reported earnings last night after the bell—and they were golden. Beat the Street by 10 cents. By 9:31 A.M., CNBC says the stock isn't open yet, but when it does, it will open higher. It dawns on you that you could get your order in ahead of the opening crowd.

You turn to your computer and enter your order. You've designated this a swing trade; you place a buy order for 500 shares, at the market.

When the stock finally opens at 9:35 A.M., it gaps open to the upside—two points. You get filled a point higher. No problem. You know once it starts running it'll never look back.

Five minutes later—and you're right. It's up another point. Fantastic! Heck of a trade.

You take a short break for a phone call and invite some friends out for dinner to a fancy restaurant—your treat—then return to your computer. Market's still going strong. Indexes, TICK, TRIN, futures, all fine. Your gaze moves to your stock. Huh? Good grief. *It's fallen two points.* Worse, it looks like it's in free fall. The bid's dropping like a brick. When it tumbles through the session's low, you jump out with a loss. What happened?

Loss avoidance tactics: First, never place a market order to buy before a stock opens for the day. A market order placed before the opening bell, or before the stock opens, will get filled at the absolute top price possible. A subsequent gap-and-crap (opening price gap that fills quickly) scenario can deliver an instant and devastating loss.

Second, monitor a stock with a good earnings announcement. Don't buy until you're sure of the direction it takes. This might take two or three days. Heard the old trader saying, "Buy the rumor, sell the news"? It's true. If the stock ran up big time before its earnings announcement on rumor of those good earnings, that run-up absorbed the pending news and resultant gains. What's going to happen when the news is announced? Profit-taking. Fast and furious.

"But," you reply, "the stock ran up after it opened. Somebody bought it. Who made it do that?"

You. You and Joe Public who acted on logic. You thought good earnings equal rising stock price for the rest of the trading day.

Sometimes. Not always.

Third, when the stock ran up in the days before the announcement, the specialists (in this case) had to sell their own shares. (Market makers are forced to take the same stance.) Remember, when buyers outnumber sellers, specialists and market makers have to short the stock. Do you really think they'll let it run to infinity without slapping it back down again so they can cover their shorts? Not hardly. Specialists and market makers aren't known for their charity work.

They fill orders at the open, then drop the bid as soon as they can to make their own profits. After you panic and sell it to them at bargain prices, they raise the bid—and sell it to someone else at higher prices.

Conclusion: Don't jump into a good-earnings stock, until the market digests the news and you can lock into its genuine direction.

## SCENE SIX: THE WHIPSAW CLUB

You're day trading. Strong market, strong stock. You buy at a good entry point. Stock moves up, and then stalls. Rats.

Market goes against you. The stock index futures slip, and the TICK falls off, but the TRIN stays low. Good. You hold your position and start humming "The TRIN always wins."

Suddenly, the futures dive hard. The TICK follows. Oh, no. You're puzzled. Even though indexes and indicators edge down, the TRIN is holding relatively low, under 0.8.

Market makers vanish from the bid. Your stock slides through its immediate support area and through your stop. *Wince.* Support is an "area," isn't it? Lots of books say that. You'll give your stock another 20 cents or so, before you get out.

The 20-cent bid leaves. Just when you're poised to click on your sell order, the stock rallies 25 cents. *Whew.* Close call.

In a nanosecond, the downturn resumes. The TRIN climbs only slightly, while other indicators trickle through support areas. It's a slow decline, like water torture. This is a pullback, right? After all, nothing goes straight up. Retracements happen.

Your stock slides and you see high volume coming into each red candlestick. Enough, already. Bite-the-bullet time. You sell and swallow your point loss. *Double rats.*

Suddenly, you feel vengeful. If this stupid stock is going to fall, you might as well short it. You'll make money on the doggoned thing one way or another. When it rallies (it's easiest to short on a rally where you have the upticks you need to enter the trade via the uptick rule), you short 500 shares and place your stop loss 25 cents above the rebound price. There. Take that, you stupid stock.

The stock hesitates, falls 30 cents, then stalls again. Suddenly the futures bounce, the TICK shoots higher. Your stock hits minor support. The volume spike rockets up. On your Level II screen, a boatload of players appear at the bid. Groan. Please stop. Maybe . . . maybe this is just a rebound in the stock's downtrend. Do you get out now or wait?

The stock steps neatly over your stop point and soars even higher. You grit your teeth and cover your short. Another loss—one going each way. Now you're a card-carrying member of the Whipsaw Club.

Loss avoidance tactic: First, you let the stock slip through your initial stop loss without taking action. If you'd sold then, you would have shrugged off the loss as part of the business, and would have eliminated the need for revenge. "Don't get mad, get even" rarely works in the stock market.

Second, your anger caused you to short the stock just because it was going down. Anger is an emotion we can't afford when trading.

Third, the TRIN truly did tell a story, although prices are the bottom line. I've experienced a few days when the TICK dropped like a sack of moldy potatoes, and the TRIN remained under 0.8 for hours at a time. It's a strange divergence and certainly contradictory. The only way to read such diversion is "confusion." When events like this take place in the market, jump out and stand on the sidelines. We cannot outguess confusion, or a trendless market.

## SCENE SEVEN: GOING BALLISTIC

You know the drill: strong market. You're scanning charts for a day trade on the long side. Suddenly a mutual fund manager on CNBC mentions that *Missile .com* is the new darling of the wireless communications stocks. And, he likes it. He loves their new product, and their CEO is a wonder boy. *Wow. That oughtta' do it.* Wireless stocks scream skyward whenever someone on CNBC sings their name.

You quickly bring up Missile.com's daily chart. *Whoa!* A week ago, it was 11. Today it's 44! It's trading miles over its 20-day MA, and it's way overextended. Still, who can argue with success? A glance at its Level II screen shows hungry piranhas eating through the offer like lightning. It's at $45, $45.50, $45.80, $46, $46.40, $46.70. Awww. Just a half point, or so. That's all you want. That's what Level II is for, right? Ultimate speed. You throw in your offer 5 cents above the current ask, and get hit in a nanosecond: 500 shares at $47. Sold to the highest bidder. You!

Missile.com quivers for a few seconds, then plunges. *No, wait. Hold it!* The time and sales screen turns blood red with downticks. The missile reverts into a fizzle. Your hand freezes on your mouse. *Please stop falling.*

Seconds later it screeches to a halt at 44. You're $1,500 in the hole. How do you climb out of it?

The fund manager on CNBC said Missile's a good stock, didn't he? Well . . . if you buy another 500 shares here, at $44, your net price per share would be $45.50. Better than $47. So you buy 500 at $44 and dig in. Your scalp is now a swing trade.

The next day the market opens down, and the wireless index sings the blues. When Missile hits $41, and holds through lunch, you take it as a sign from above. This is the bottom. Surely it'll breakout from its lunchtime congestion and turn north again. You buy another 500 at $41.

After lunch, though, the candlesticks in the congestion pattern start closing on their lows. Wince. You know what that means. And it does. All fall down. Your stomach churns, your palms sweat. You're in so deep, how do you get out except with a horrendous loss?

You check Missile's daily chart again. You find support around $39. Surely it will bounce off that. By the end of the day, it slips to $39, and hovers there. Okay. Just one more time. Gritting your teeth, you buy an additional 500 shares, maxing out your margin.

During the next few days, the wireless telecom group, already overblown for weeks, gets punctured. You sell other stocks at a loss to avoid a margin call. Missile tanks again, diving through support at $36, and heads for who-knows-where. Wearily, you check the daily chart. The next support is at $28. You can't take it anymore. You sell out at $35. You close your eyes and refuse to look at your account balance.

Loss avoidance tactic: Before we start, if you think this can't happen—it can. This very situation happened once, um, to a friend of mine.

First, it's easy to get caught up in the euphoria of a running stock. When the Level II screen flashes a stream of green, we slip into a hypnotic state. In that trance, we click on the buy button. Next comes the ohnosecond when we realize what we've done. It's always followed by the prayer to the trading god: *Please, please get me out of this trade alive. If you do, I promise I'll be good for the rest of my life.*

If you get sucked into a screaming trade because of a momentary sanity lapse, close it as fast as you can. Fix your mistakes before they turn into big losses. As traders say, "Your first loss is the smallest."

Second, when you see a stock trading way above its 20-day MA on a daily chart, it's overextended. Like a rubber band stretched too far, it's likely to snap back soon. Leave it alone until it pulls back, at least to its 10-day or 20-day MA, which it will inevitably do.

Third, "averaging down" means you nibble on a stock in a downtrend at various points. You hope (not good) that when it rises, your average price will be low enough to save some gains, or at least get out even.

When to average down: If a strong stock in a strong market pulls back to an expected reversal point, then breaks out in a trend continuation, averaging down is acceptable trade management.

**HOT TIP**

If you follow your plan for each trade 90% of the time, and you are stopped out of more than 50% of your trades, re-evaluate your basic trading plan. You may wish to consult a mentor or trusted trading professional for feedback.

When not to average down: When you're trading short term and your stock reverts from strong to weak, don't continue to buy more. Sell your position. If it sinks to a support area, holds, and breaks out on volume with a market reversal trending the same direction, that's when to consider re-entering.

In conclusion, you see that scene one happens regularly as part of this business. Scenes two through seven demonstrate how ignoring a position's initial stop point causes 99% of the agony that follows.

The solution is so simple, and for some reason so hard to follow. As the saying goes, "just do it." Honor your stop-loss points. Each time you make that choice, congratulate yourself. This is a tough business, and success deserves recognition.

# QUIZ
IIIIIIIIIIIIIIIII

## *Questions*

1. What questions will you answer in your Success Journal?
2. You're in a day trade. It's 11:30 A.M., you've made a $2 profit, and your stock is nearing resistance. What should you do?
3. What usually happens to market mood in the afternoon prior to the announcement of an important economic report?
4. True or false? If you are in a trade and the situation gets ugly, simply change the time frame you've designated for the trade, and then lower your stop.
5. A market order placed before the opening bell will get filled at the open at the _____ possible price.
6. Buy the _____, sell the _____.
7. When a stock comes out with a good earnings announcement, how should you treat it?
8. Some traders say, "If it's not a long, it's a short." Is that always true?
9. True or false? If a trade gone sour makes you angry, direct that energy to your next trade.
10. Define an "overextended" stock.
11. What's the least profitable situation in which to average down?

## *Answers*

1. Why did you enter each trade? What can you do to improve your trading performance in the future?
2. Take at least partial profits.
3. The market usually adopts a quiet, lethargic mood.
4. False, false, false
5. highest
6. rumor, news
7. Wait until it trades for two to three days, so you can more accurately predict future price action.
8. No. Trendless stocks in a volatile market make neither successful long nor successful short candidates.
9. False. You're not really angry at the stock. You're angry at yourself. Carried into your trading, anger always results in huge losses. If you feel angry while you're trading, take your positions flat. Then go for a walk, or even take the rest of the day off. You'll feel better and so will your trading account.
10. When a stock trades way above a major moving average. A good example is when a stock shoots several points above its 20-day MA on a daily chart.
11. You're trading short term (swing trades, day trades, and scalps) and your stock reverts from strong to weak.

## CENTER POINT: THE TRUTH ABOUT FEAR

*"Begin difficult things while they are easy, do great things when they are small. The difficult things of the world must once have been easy; the great things must once have been small . . . a thousand-mile journey begins with one step."*

—Lao-Tse

We are all acquainted with fear and the way it makes us feel. Regarded in the proper context, however, it's really a positive emotion. It warns us of impending danger so we can take steps to safety.

Unfortunately, we tend to hold onto fear long after it's outlived its usefulness as a warning device. Then fear twists into all kinds of related detrimental emotions from low self-esteem, to stress, to panic. When fear digs its claws in deep enough, it takes conscious effort to release it. Here are three things that can help.

First, when you feel fear, acknowledge it. Notice how it feels and where it's located in your body. Many of us feel it in our solar plexus. Sit quietly; let yourself feel it in a nonjudgmental way. What thoughts are involved? What message does the fear have for you?

Treat your fear as though it were a small child. If a four-year-old came up to you and cried she was afraid of the bogeyman, what would you do? You'd hug her and ask her to explain her fears. When she finished, you'd assure her that the bogeyman isn't real and soothe her with positive, affirmative thoughts. That's exactly how we should treat that part of ourselves that operates in fear . . . with love and positive emotions. After all, fear is not the truth. Fear is nothing, trying to be something. It has only the power we give to it.

Recall a time in your life when you felt supremely safe, secure, and loved. Draw upon the feeling that memory holds for you. Gently replace your negative feelings with the positive, loving feelings of those memories.

Because love and fear are polar opposites, love drives away fear. Similarly, light is the reality, and darkness is the absence of light. When you let light in, darkness disappears; it is not real.

We recognize fear as the warning tool that it is. We acknowledge it, learn from it, and then let it go. In doing so, we lift ourselves up one more rung on the ladder to happiness and success.

# CHAPTER 13

# Trading Survival Techniques

In this chapter, you'll find a "stew" of trading tips, techniques, and general knowledge I've gained through experience. They're the things I'd tell you if you called me on the phone, and we chatted as friends, and as traders.

## THE "IF, THEN" MENTALITY: HOW IT BOOSTS YOU TO THE RANKS OF PROFESSIONALS

Remember a college math course called Logic? Logic used single sentences that we changed into a mathematical equation to gauge its validity. The first half of the sentence always began with "If"; the second half of the sentence started with "then." Briefly, if both phrases in the sentence were true, the sentence was true. If either phrase was false or uncertain, the entire sentence was false. Naturally, when both phrases were false, the entire sentence was invalid. Logic reveals the truth, and can be a terrific way to evaluate, for example, what a politician says in a speech.

It follows that the further you travel in you trading career, the more you'll recognize correlations between diverse market occurrences. Every time you use those correlations to your advantage, you advance more quickly to the ranks of the victorious.

Therefore, learn to think in terms of "if, then." "If" might translate into a geopolitical event, economic report, or other news event that causes the markets to react. Or, it might state the positions of two indices used as indicators. "Then" represents probable reaction of the market to the "If" premise. Think: action = reaction. Or, "When *this* happens, then *that* usually happens."

Example: Remember that as financial markets open and close around the world, those markets impact each other in a domino effect. If the Asian exchanges sell off at their opens, then that negativity can put negative pressure on European, South American, and U.S. markets for the next trading day.

At various places in this chapter, I'll stress the "if, then" circumstances, so you'll understand why it's important to channel your thoughts along those lines.

## STAY AWARE OF BIG PICTURE DYNAMICS

Even though you may be trading short-term time frames, you'll want to monitor major market trends. It is particularly significant when the market moves into the top of a cycle and reverts to a trendless interval. Cycle tops are always high-risk periods. Remember October 1987 when Black Monday wiped out many accounts within hours? (If you didn't experience it, you've surely heard of it.) Other high-risk periods were October 1997, when the Asian Contagion first infected our market; the disastrous summer and fall of 1998, ignited by a devalued Russian ruble; and the first months of 2000, when our tech markets were overblown and the dot.com bubble burst.

High-risk zones, as illustrated in Figure 13-1, don't have to be accompanied by negative news. Often when the market balances precariously on the top of a cycle, bad news chooses that exact point in time to push the markets over the edge. High-risk zones always produce false buying signals and whipsaw conditions.

Interestingly enough, low-risk periods—when the market is bottoming, or basing—are not low risk on a short-term basis. They emit the same signals and conditions as toppy markets do: false, whippy, and choppy. Why? Because they, too, occur when the market is searching for a new trend.

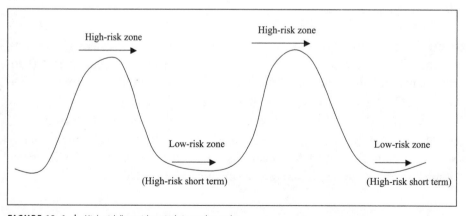

**FIGURE 13-1** | High-risk/low-risk periods in market cycles.

During both periods, you'll hear announcers on financial networks ask their guests, "Is this the top?" "Can the market go higher from here?" Or "Is this the bottom?" "Has enough panic selling occurred that buyers will start nibbling here?"

Savvy investors and traders track market trends because it enables them to position themselves advantageously. At the culmination of a major uptrend, when the market rolls over into a high-risk zone, they build cash reserves and trade in short time frames, only.

When the market bottoms after a downtrend and begins to move sideways in a so-called low-risk area (remember, *it's low-risk long term, not short term*), it's time to cover shorts and again build cash supplies to prepare for selective buying.

See why traders often say, "the trend is your friend"? During a definite uptrend or downtrend, we all agree on which road we're taking. When the camp divides after a protracted move, none of us agree on direction. We end up bumping into each other, and many times, we both get injured.

When the market turns into either one of these cycles, my advice is to observe without playing. A few intraday trades—occasional swing trades of stocks trending on their own, make sense. During these times, many traders switch to their futures accounts and trade the mini stock index futures contracts. More than that is gambling. I've held position trades through reversal patterns early in my trading career. Ouch, did I lose money! I couldn't get on the right side of anything. And I wasn't the only one. Disasters littered trading rooms everywhere.

So, how can you track big-picture dynamics? Check daily and weekly charts of the Dow, NYSE, and NASDAQ 100 or Composite. Draw trendlines, and plot 20-, 50- and 200-day MAs on them. (I like the 30- and 39-week MAs on weekly charts. They correspond to 150- and 200-day MAs on daily charts.)

Ask the usual questions: Are the indices trending or trading horizontally? Where is support and resistance? Are they trading above or below their major moving averages? Which markets are overextended?

You don't buy a stock trading under the 20-day MA, and especially the 50-day MA. Smart traders tread carefully—or not at all—when the broad markets exhibit the same behavior.

If many traders and most investors had followed and interpreted daily or weekly charts of the major indices from January to March of 2000, they would have exited long positions and saved trillions (yes, trillions!) of dollars in profits.

Now you're one of those in the know. You needn't ride out such drastic moves. You know when stocks or indices are overbought, and preparing to rolling over. You have the savvy to protect your principal and your profits.

*If, then:* If the market is in a high-risk or low-risk zone, then trading conditions will be whippy, choppy, and unpredictable. Trade only short-term positions, if at all. Save cash for a stock-shopping spree when the market breaks out of this zone.

## THE ADVANCE-DECLINE LINE AS A SUPERB STORYTELLER

One of the most popular long-term indicators of market breadth—and thus overall market strength—is the NYSE Advance-Decline Line, or A/D line. A breadth indicator uses advancing and declining issues to measure participation in the movement of the market.

When we're in the midst of a strong bull market, a large number of stocks climb upward in orderly patterns. If that market starts to deteriorate, only a small number of stocks make large advances in price. To the uninformed, it appears the bull still feels frisky because those stocks pull the averages up. The appearance is not the reality, though, and the A/D line tells it as it is.

Conversely, as a market bottoms after a downtrend, fewer and fewer stocks decline even though the market indices still slide south.

The A/D line is calculated by subtracting the number of NYSE stocks that declined on the day from the number of issues that advanced. This is added to a cumulative total. Though the actual numbers that designate the line mean little, the pattern it draws tells us a vital story.

If it isn't available on your trading software, you'll find the A/D line published in *Investors Business Daily*, the *Wall Street Journal*, and other financial newspapers. Compare it to the Dow or the S&P 500 Index. Now, look for divergences. Reassuring signs of a strong market combine a rising A/D line with new highs on the preceding indices. But when you see the Dow, for instance, making new highs in an uptrend, and the A/D line is forming a negative divergence by rolling sideways and failing to make new highs, it's time to pull anchor on long-term holds.

*If, then:* If the Dow and the S&P 500 continue to make new highs and the A/D line doesn't, then the market may be headed for a spill.

Go to cash, hop in and out nimbly with intraday trades, and get ready to hold the door open for those who don't have your insight.

*If, then:* If declining issues outnumber advancing issues, then the markets are weak. If advancing issues outnumber declining issues, then the market is strong.

## MEET ANOTHER STORYTELLER: U.S. THIRTY-YEAR TREASURY BONDS

The thirty-year Treasury bond is the benchmark for all bond prices.

Along with the stock index futures, the T-bond futures indicate how the market will open. Since these bonds trade twenty-four hours electronically, the bond futures react to international news, to foreign markets that trade while we sleep, and to U.S. issues active in those markets. Bond futures also watch and react to U.S. economic reports and other important news.

> **HOT TIP**
>
> Treasury debt securities issued by Uncle Sam are classified according to three categories that relate to their maturities: Treasury bills have maturities of one year or less. Treasury notes have maturities of two, three, five, and ten years. Treasury bonds have maturities of ten to thirty years.

Bond prices and bond yields, meaning their interest rates, move in opposite directions. As bond prices rise, their interest rates drop. When low interest rates generated by bonds make them less attractive to investors, those investors look to stocks for more attractive profits. Result? Stock prices rise. Finally, remember that interest rates equal the price of credit, which in turn reflects the growth rate of the economy.

The bond traders watch economic reports with the same intensity of cats staring into gopher holes. Inflation is the bond traders' enemy. It makes sense, because rising prices in goods and services cause the current value of the dollar to shrink in the future.

When good employment numbers or strong economic growth numbers are announced, the bond market turns paranoid. The seemingly positive reports as a sign of rising consumer prices—a negative to bond traders.

Check my Web site, and click on the Econ Calendar view section for the following week's economic reports. As soon as CNBC or another financial network announces those reports, (usually 8:30 A.M. or 10:00 A.M. EST), the bond futures (and mini stock index futures) reveal how Wall Street interprets those numbers.

Say an economic report, such as lower unemployment numbers, infer the economy is strengthening. Translate the report into an if, then equation, such as: If the economy strengthens, then higher interest rates follow, and bond prices fall. How will the market react?

In this case, the stock market may fall because a strong economy can goad the Fed into raising rates to curb inflation. Rising rates mean companies have to pay more to borrow money, which leads to lower earnings. Lower earnings = lower stock prices.

> **HOT TIP**
>
> *Inflation* is the rising cost of goods and services.

Those reasons encourage investors to embark on "a flight to safety." They cash in their stocks and put their money in high-yielding bonds.

Or, say the economy shows signs of mild strengthening, and the general consensus holds that the Fed will not raise interest rates. The stock market rises because stockholders see higher earnings ahead. Again, the T-bond and E-mini S&P futures will tell you immediately which opinion prevails.

If, then scenarios—comparing thirty-year Treasury bond futures to E-mini S&P futures:

➤ If bond yields fall, and the E-mini S&P futures rise, then cyclical stocks—stocks that act best in strong economies (as opposed to stocks with earnings handcuffed to interest rates)—show strength. Cyclical equity groups include paper, aluminum, chemicals, technology, heavy construction, and retailers. Examples are International Paper (IP), Aluminum Company of America (AA), the Dow Chemical Co. (DOW), the Hewlett Packard Co. (HPQ), Caterpillar Inc. (CAT), and J.C. Penney Inc. (JCP).

➤ If bond prices weaken (yields or interest rates rise), then interest-sensitive stocks like banks (Citicorp-C), moneylenders (American Express-AXP), and homebuilders (the Lennar Corp.-LEN) may weaken with them. Higher interest rates mean banks have to pay more to borrow money. Thus, their spread between what they lend, and what they borrow, narrows. In addition, as interest rates rise, people stall on buying new homes.

➤ If bond prices are strong and S&P futures are weak, then cyclicals usually recover strength first.

➤ If bond prices are strong and S&P futures are strong, then look for banks, lenders, and homebuilders to climb.

## HOT TIP

Traders also watch the 10-year Treasury note and the two-year note and compare the yield difference. The yield for the 10-year note should be higher, because investors should be compensated for holding these instruments for a longer maturity. When the yield curve becomes inverted (the two-year yield is higher than the 10-year yield interest rate), it does not necessarily forecast a recession, but historically, this has taken place more times than not.

## OTHER "IF, THEN" SETTINGS

If oil prices rise, then transportation stocks fall, and vice-versa, because higher fuel prices shrink profits.

If signs of inflation climb, then gold and silver stocks rise. Investors buy these instruments to hedge against inflation. Besides individual gold and silver stocks, traders can now buy gold and silver ETFs: iShares Comex Gold Shares (IAU), StreetTracks Gold Shares (GLD), Market Vector Gold Miners (GDX), and the iShares Silver Trust (SLV).

If the U.S. dollar strengthens, then imported goods become more attractive to Americans. Stocks like Nike Inc. (NKE) and the Toyota Motors Corp. (TM) rise. Conversely, American products sold overseas cost more, so stocks like Intel Inc. (INTC) and Johnson & Johnson (JNJ) may suffer.

If the CRB index (Commodity Research Bureau price index of 22 commodities) falls, then inflation is not such a worry. Bond and stock prices rise.

### HOT TIP

Commodities are defined as either raw materials or products nearing the initial construction phase (Think: crude and heating oil, industrial and precious metals, rubber, corn, cattle, hogs, sugar). We say they are "sensitive," because their markets are instantly affected by changes in economic conditions. Rising commodity prices usually indicate impending inflation. If it costs more to buy the commodity to manufacture the products, those prices are eventually passed onto consumers.

## TOO MUCH CHOCOLATE?

The next two overall market indicators represent inverse sentiment. Translated, they suggest that too much of anything, whether good or bad, eventually causes the opposite reaction. Take chocolate, for instance. Chocolate (a good thing), when eaten in huge portions, causes a stomachache (a bad thing).

### Advisors' Sentiment Report

Investor's Intelligence in New Rochelle, NY (*www.investorsintelligence .com*) conducts a weekly poll of investment advisors and publishes the Advisors' Sentiment Report. CNBC routinely announces the report results, and it is closely monitored by the investment community.

The poll tallies how advisors feel about the stock market—bullish, bearish, or neutral. The ratio is calculated by dividing the number of bullish advisors by the number of bullish plus bearish advisors. (Neutral advisors don't count.)

Since it's a contrary indicator, the more bullish the advisors feel, the more bearish the indication. The opposite is also true. For example, if 55–60 percent of the advisors polled are bullish, then that extreme optimism and euphoria usually signals the market is top heavy and ready to fall. If the reading dips to 40 percent, verifying extreme pessimism and bearishness, then the index implies a bullish reversal is in the wind.

### The CBOE (Chicago Board Options Exchange) Total Put–Call Ratio

The CBOE Total Put–Call Ratio tracks both equity and index option put-call ratio. (Puts and calls are options contracts that give participants the right to sell (put) or buy (call) the underlying security at a specified price, during a limited time period.)

You can access the ratios for the Total Put/Call Ratio at *www.cboe.com* (click on "Data," then "CBOE Daily Market Statistics").

Because this is a contrary sentiment indicator, you can interpret it like this: The higher the level of pessimism in the options players, the more optimistic the outlook for the market. The lower the level of pessimism, the more bearish the actual outlook.

Or, the higher the put (Think: selling) trading, the more bullish the indication. The higher the calls (Think: buying) trading, the more bearish the indication. This indicator works best at extremes.

For example, a reading in the CBOE Equity Put–Call Ratio of 0.60 is considered bullish. When the index soars above 1.0, however, that's heading into a very high level of pessimism. Extreme pessimism usually tells us that bulls will soon begin to nibble.

On the flip side, bearish signals flash when the ratio reaches 0.40. When the ratio drifts below that number, market players are too optimistic. Look for an impending market reversal led to the downside by the bears.

## WATCH OUT! IT'S OPTIONS EXPIRATION WEEK

Speaking of options, the contracts expire the third week of each month. During options expiration weeks (especially Wednesday, Thursday, and Friday) market conditions are extremely choppy and volatile, as options traders close out their positions. Quarterly options expiration is named "Quadruple Witching," because four categories of options expire: stock options, stock index options, futures options, and single-stock futures options. Quadruple Witching Fridays cause extreme whipsaw and roller-coaster trading conditions. Please take the day off. I do.

## PROGRAM TRADING: A JOLT OUT OF THE BLUE

If options expiration day feels like a roller-coaster ride, program trading resembles getting shocked by a lightning bolt. When a "sell program," especially, hits the market, the floor gets yanked from underneath most stocks in seconds. Your screen will turn blood red in a nanosecond with downticking stocks.

Program trading takes place when a divergence occurs between two closely related markets, such as the S&P 500 (cash) index and the S&P 500 futures. Arbitrageurs buy one market, short the other, and profit from the difference. This is called index arbitrage.

Another definition of program trading is a computer-aided strategy, usually generated by institutions for profit-taking, or as a hedge against falling stocks.

Either way, it's painful. Sell programs can be mild or wild. Many times stocks plunge straight down—so fast it takes your breath away. One defense tactic against program trading: Keep a ticker of the thirty Dow Industrial components on your screen. If it suddenly turns blood red, a sell program probably went off.

According to the NYSE, program trading accounts for about 45% of the trading volume on that exchange in the course of each trading day.

This is part of trading. If program trading suddenly swoops into the markets, stay calm, and don't lower any of your protective stop orders. Cut your losses and re-evaluate the environment once conditions stabilize.

## LEARN HOW TO CHANGE GEARS

The market never allows you to get comfortable. Just when you think you have it by the tail, everything changes.

World or national events constantly shape and reshape the market environment into new paradigms. Keep an open mind so you can identify the changes. As you identify new patterns and analyze their effects, you can alter your trading techniques to conform and reap gains.

For example, the Asian Contagion drastically altered U.S. stock market behavior. The Contagion started in October 1997, with the fall of Malaysia's market. It spread to Korea and Japan; much later, it contaminated Russia and Brazil. In fact, the Asian Contagion, or "Asian Flu," as it was also called, severely tainted markets on a global basis. Japan's stock market, the Nikkei, along with other Asian markets, assumed the role as the leading daily indicator for the U.S. market's open.

We traders began to watch CNBC much earlier in the morning than we used to. We kept a constant pulse on the Nikkei. Its close—weak or strong—pretty much dictated which way our market would open.

As you can imagine, holding stocks overnight became suicidal. Traders with any sense closed all positions, every night, no exceptions. When the U.S. market closed each evening, we had no clue whether the next morning would bring calm or catastrophe.

We also learned to shun stocks from companies with overseas exposure, particularly those who sold products to countries on the Pacific Rim. Technology companies, drug companies, and many others slid daily. Short sellers raked in profits.

Traders who refused to sell short spent their days hunting for stocks with no ties to Asian countries.

In other words, we had to change gears, and do it quickly, or get left by the side of the road.

Since then, other disasters (unfortunately good news doesn't attract as much volatility) have shaken the U.S. markets. We've experienced September 11th, the subsequent brief selloff, and rally into 2002. We've experienced bear market selloff in the last three quarters of 2002, Hurricane Katrina and a rash of other hurricanes, the rapid rise and fall of the housing markets, and the screaming rise in oil prices and metals and their inflationary effects on the market. Through it all, the traders who survived learned how to stay mentally nimble.

Stop right now and reflect . . . what global events and economic situations are creating an impact in the current financial marketplace? What factors create the present environment?

Lesson: When a major world or national event occurs, think: If this event shapes our market into a different paradigm, then these industries and stocks (list) will benefit. On the other hand, these (list) industries and stocks should be avoided. In addition, I must alter my trading techniques to fit the changing world. Whenever I'm in doubt, I stay out of the market.

## TRADING DAY IN A CAPSULE

What does a typical trading day look like? Although it obviously changes from trader to trader, here's an encapsulated view of my day.

**5:30 A.M.** Rise and shine. While sipping coffee, read *Investor's Business Daily*. Focus on global events and interesting stocks to check out later, along with news on currently held issues. Workout, shower, breakfast. While eating breakfast, scan the *Wall Street Journal*.

**8:00 A.M.** Turn on CNBC. Open trading platform and check mini stock futures, gold, and oil index futures activity. (Traders without futures quotes can see them on CNBC's "bug" in lower right-hand corner of screen.) Are futures trading up or down? How about T-bond futures? (If you don't have those quotes, television announcers talk about them.) Check morning research Web sites I use (*www.briefing.com*) for global market closing levels. Check stock upgrades and downgrades by analysts. Briefly scan daily newsletters that I subscribe to.

**8:30 A.M.** Check account balances for accuracy and cash available to trade. Monitor any economic reports issued. Review target stocks, their setups, and risk-reward analysis.

**9:30 A.M.** Opening bell rings. Monitor mini stock index futures movements, along with NYSE and NASDAQ TICK, TRIN, and other indicators. The only opening-bell trades I make at the open: profit-taking in positions gapping open from night before, or emergency exits.

**9:40 A.M.** May or may not test the waters, depending on market "temperature."

**9:50 A.M.** Observe open positions and possible new trades: How are they handling the 9:45 A.M. reversal period. Are they weak or strong? I find this to be a good weeding technique for discarding weak trades, and possibly adding to strong ones.

**10:10–11:20 A.M.** Trade actively, moderately, or not at all, depending on opportunities and conditions.

**11:20 A.M.** Start peeling off profits on some day trades, depending again on strength of stocks and market conditions. Lunch digests better with a portion of my intraday profits tucked safely under my belt. I especially take profits: (1) if economic reports are due out the following day that will cause this afternoon to slide into sluggishness, and (2) if a stock looks dicey enough to capitulate during the lunchtime moody blues.

**12:15 P.M.–1:30 P.M.** Leave office for lunch.

**1:30 P.M.** Begin scanning daily, then 5-minute charts for strong stocks in an uptrend (downtrend for negative days) that have pulled back a fraction of a point from their session high and are forming lunchtime consolidations. (You know the pattern.) Focus on the best candidates by zeroing in on those with consolidation candlesticks closing on their highs. (Reverse this scene for shorting.)

**1:45 P.M.** Watch for after-lunch volume to surge into breakout candidates. Add to open positions from morning session, if warranted. Trade actively, moderately, or not at all depending on opportunities and market mood and manner. Check open position and swing trades for progress and possible profit-taking.

**3:15 P.M.** Begin cashing in on profits before other traders exit and drive prices down. Consider potential swing trade entries and overnight holds if all systems agree.

**4:00 P.M.** Closing bell rings. Fall out of chair.

**4:30 P.M.** Check trade confirms and reconcile account. Post profits, losses. Enter trades in Success Journal and note lessons learned. Pull up charts and scan for tomorrow's opportunities.

## HOT TIP

Groups that typically perform well in bull market environments: technology, transportation, capital equipment, chemicals, basic materials, consumer cyclicals. At the top of a bull market, energy stocks usually move higher. Groups that normally do well in bear markets (we call them defensive stocks): pharmaceuticals, cosmetics, food, other consumer noncyclicals, utilities; in late bear market, autos, housing, and banks.

## WHERE TO FIND STOCKS TO TRADE

After you've been trading for a while, you'll have built a watch list of favorite, high-quality stocks that you know well, and profit from consistently. Where do you find those stocks?

As mentioned before, in a bull market environment, I suggest you target the leading industry groups—groups that are currently trading in an uptrend, or breaking into one. Then check the component stocks in that group, or related stocks, and scan for high-probability setups.

Again, you'll find a long list of industry groups and a selection of their components on my Web site, on the Sectors & Stocks page.

Other resources:

➤ Newspapers such as *Investor's Business Daily*, the *Wall Street Journal*, and *Barron's*.
➤ There are thousands (!) of Web sites that publish stocks of interest. Please don't enter a position blindly because of a recommendation. Conduct your own analysis.
➤ Hundreds of online subscription services issue daily buy or sell recommendations. Again, always perform your own analysis and make sure the stocks you enter adhere to your personal criteria.
➤ Many online trading chat rooms issue buy or sell recommendations. Some are excellent, with high-quality instructors, who teach as they trade. Others are downright dishonest, leading unsuspecting traders to enter positions that will benefit the chat room leaders. Enter online trading chat rooms with caution.

When developing your list of trading stocks, remember to check average daily volume, (300,000+) for the reasons stated in Chapter 7.

Cross-check selections you make in the *Investor's Business Daily* stock tables. Make sure your selections are active stocks with high (more than 70 is best) composite ratings. Also, stocks listed in these tables with high volume percent changes (200%, or higher) may offer good trading opportunities.

In the first paragraph of this section, you'll see the words *high* and *quality*. Please make sure any stock you trade represents a high-quality company.

Bulletin-board stocks (OTCC) and penny stocks (pink sheets) can result in bad trading bets, especially if there is no market for them. So are relatively unknown stocks you find being hyped in online chat rooms.

Please don't be a scam victim. In every trading situation, think for yourself. If you've done your homework, you don't need someone else making decisions for you. Remember your uppermost goals: Protect your principal, and trade to trade well. When you achieve those goals, your bottom line will expand rapidly.

## HOT TIP

Beware of "Pump and Dump" schemes. Unfortunately, greedy stock promoters, who have managed to dodge the SEC, run a few so-called investor chat rooms. These promoters goad naive traders and investors into buying small-cap and other "growth" stocks. The buyers run up the price of the stock. The promoters sell their previously purchased shares for a profit, then disappear. The stock—which was worthless all along—crashes.

## TRADING FITNESS: YOUR BODY, YOUR MIND

Guess what? Bet you my duck slippers that physically fit traders make more money than couch potatoes. Don't groan, please. Stay with me.

### Your Body

If you weren't aware of it already, the two weeks in Beginner's Boot Camp taught you that trading full-time can stress your body and mind to the max. Besides, sitting in a chair all day is not a healthy way to live.

If you're on an exercise regimen, stick to it, even if you have to get up a little earlier. If you're not—start. Drag yourself outside first thing in the morning and walk fast, ride your bike, run the dog, or swim for a half-hour. Weight-lifting is also fine, but serious cardio exercise works best to clear your head and body of stress.

Exercise helps you think faster and produces wonderful feelings of well-being that combat stress. It will also ward off "traders' spread" from sitting all day. If you can't find the time to exercise before breakfast, try using lunchtime as an exercise break.

### Your Mind

As you already know, trading demands every ounce of concentration you can muster. It also demands courage and self-confidence. When you walk in that trading room each morning, you'd better feel "on top of the world." Not cocky, or self-important, but self-assured and in control.

Have you just broken up with your girlfriend/wife/boyfriend/husband, or had a fight with someone close to you? Is someone in your family critically ill? Are the kids home alone, and you're worried about them?

Did you by any chance party into the wee hours of the morning? Do you have a hangover?

Are you getting the flu? Or, did you lose a bucket load of money trading yesterday, and you're extremely depressed?

Don't trade on the days you feel bad, whatever the reason. *You* will lose money.

## TRADING RULES TO PROSPER BY

All successful traders I know post a list of trading rules near their computer. Please consider doing this, also. Written rules remind you of your goals and boundaries, and have the same effect on the psyche that written stops do: They make those points concrete, nonnegotiable. Think of them as your conscience. Written rules bring us back to "center" when the market hypnotizes us and we think we can fudge.

The following rules are my own. Use them, if you wish, as a base from which your own rules will evolve. Then keep your "Trading Rules to Prosper By" within full view at all times.

### Trading Rules to Prosper By

1. At all times, I protect my principal.
2. I trade to trade well, not to make money.
3. I trade only when top down criteria are optimal.
4. I enter only after conducting my risk-reward analysis.
5. I do not chase stocks. Nor do I "bet the ranch" on a single trade.
6. I enter intraday long positions when the NYSE TICK is above zero, and the TRIN is below 0.9.
7. I write down my protective stop level for every trade. I also enter it with my broker. Manual stops are honored when they are touched.
8. If I have two open trades losing money, I stop trading and reassess what the market is telling me.
9. I never take home a losing intraday trade.
10. When I have a reasonable profit, I take it.

# QUIZ
||||||||||||||||

## Questions

1. True or false? A low-risk zone in a market cycle is the best time to initiate position trades.
2. If the Dow is making higher lows and higher highs, but the A/D line rolls over from an uptrend to a horizontal trend, what might that indicate in the long-term?
3. Bond prices and bond yields move in _____ directions.
4. Interest rates equal _____.
5. If the Fed raises interest rates, why does that indicate stock prices may fall?
6. If bond yields fall, and E-mini S&P futures are strong, what usually happens to bank stocks? Try to answer in an if, then format.
7. What do contrary or inverse sentiment indicators suggest?
8. True or false? During Options' Expiration Weeks, and especially during Quadruple Expiration Weeks, Fridays are good days to go to the beach.
9. Name a good resource in which to locate good trading opportunities.
10. You have the hangover. Your spouse is mad at you. You just got a margin call, and your car payment bounced. To top it off, you feel like you're catching the flu. This is the perfect day to trade hard because hard work is good for the soul. Right?

## Answers

1. False. A so-called low-risk area means the market is in a sideways, basing formation after a prolonged downtrend. The low-risk definition pertains to investors who buy long-term positions with reduced risk of the market going lower. For *traders*, a basing formation is trendless and produces whippy, choppy conditions. Placing long-term position trades *before* the market breaks out to the upside is chancy.
2. If the Dow keeps making new highs, but the A/D line does not, the market may be ready for a major correction in the near future.
3. opposite
4. the price of credit
5. Companies have to pay more to borrow money, which lowers their earnings. Lower earnings = lower stock prices.
6. If bond yields fall and E-mini S&Ps are strong, then bank stocks usually rise.
7. Too much optimism in the market can lead to its downfall. Too much pessimism leads to an eventual reversal to the upside.
8. True. Or go shopping. Or take your spouse/kids/dog on an unexpected outing. Just don't trade.
9. Target component of leading industries in a bull market, and lagging industries in bear markets.
10. Wrong! If you trade today, you'll end up even poorer. Take some aspirin, and some time off to fix things. Tomorrow's a new day.

## CENTER POINT: LIVE CONSCIOUSLY AND SUCCEED!

*"All that we are is the result of what we have thought. The mind is everything. What we think, we become."*

—Buddha

We each have a choice: to live our lives consciously, or unconsciously. When we live consciously, we come from a position of internal power. We enjoy each day and the events it brings with proactive energy.

When we live unconsciously, life happens to us, and we react to it. Instead of learning from our problems, we shove them away. Then we wonder why they keep reappearing in our lives.

The ultimate life process has a role for everything and everyone. One need only look at how perfectly nature orchestrates the forces on this planet to see the truth in this. Each of us has been given a unique talent, and a unique way of expressing it. We are meant to discover our potential, and then achieve it. In doing so, we fulfill our own goals and help those around us.

When we look at life through the lens of our potential, we realize the urgency of purpose. Each day unfolds with new meaning. Instead of rushing through daily events with a just-get-it-done attitude, we view each situation as a learning opportunity. Our decisions come from our core, a nonjudgmental "knowing" that dwells deep inside.

When you choose to wake up and live thoughtfully and consciously, you begin to transform your life. Suddenly, you realize you are far more than you thought you were—more than your background, more than your education, more than your "station in life."

Let's carry out our everyday lives secure in the knowledge that we operate within the context of a greater plan.

Every week, every day, and every hour, we can choose how we will live. When we come from an inner place of peace, power, and consciousness, we bring an entirely new intention to our lives. We rise above personal limitations and realize our lives can be exciting expressions of success.

# CHAPTER 14

# The Future Is Now!

Congratulations! We're galloping into the home stretch.

In this chapter, we'll start with a discussion of a common trading malady, operating in the State of Overwhelm. Next, we'll look at a list of trader-friendly Web sites that will give you educational and research starting points for trading opportunities. We'll also talk briefly about trading chat rooms and subscription services.

Finally, we'll glance into the kaleidoscope of the future. How will the markets and trading change as we race through the initial decades in this brand-new century?

## TRADING FROM THE STATE OF OVERWHELM

Please understand that operating in the State of Overwhelm is a common affliction among novice traders. Most experienced traders venture there periodically, as well. I freely admit to bouts of Overwhelm. After all, the financial markets are so gargantuan, and we have so much information at our fingertips, the scope of it all boggles the mind.

In order to leave the State of Overwhelm and set up shop in the State of Clarity and Calm, please reassure yourself that you cannot possibly know or absorb every nuance of the markets, every day (or ever!).

Wise strategy: Remember, your time and your energy are finite. To make the best use of them, choose to master the trading vehicle(s), time frames, setups, and trade management strategies that best fit your personality and your lifestyle. Specialize in one area, and become good at it.

Think about it. We rarely hear of famous physicians who are general practitioners. We do, however, hear of famous bone specialists, renowned cardiologists, prominent pediatric doctors, and celebrated neurosurgeons. These specialists are wise enough to know that the study of the human body emerges from a universe of nearly immeasurable knowledge.

So, too, is the universe of the financial markets. It's a vast territory of enormous intricacy. In order to succeed, I encourage you to master one corner of it. Perhaps you're attracted to day trading semi-conductors stocks. Or, maybe you'd rather swing trade bank and homebuilder stocks. Or, maybe you'd rather position trade Dow stocks and hedge with the mini-Dow futures, or position trade ETFs, and then hedge with options. You may want to wander into the forex, or currencies markets.

Whatever your decision, I suspect that you, like other professionals who focus on targeted regions of big-territory fields, will succeed faster and with a higher degree of accomplishment than those who scatter themselves across many different areas.

## MICROLIST OF HIGH-CALIBER FINANCIAL WEB SITES

Currently, the wealth of information on the Internet available to investors and traders boggles the mind. Google the words *stocks* or *day trading*, and . . . blam! A zillion Web sites nearly knock you down.

To get you started, the following Web destinations offer a mixture of education and news related to the financial markets. Most you can roam free of charge. Others offer limited free material, along with additional subscription services.

American Stock Exchange: *www.amex.com*
Big Charts: *http://bigcharts.marketwatch.com*
Briefing.com: *www.briefing.com*
DecisionPoint: *www.decisionpoint.com*
Elite Trader: *www.elitetrader.com*
Investopedia: *www.investopedia.com*
*Investor's Business Daily*: *www.investors.com*
MSN Money: *www.moneycentral.msn.com*
NASDAQ: *www.nasdaq.com*
New York Stock Exchange: *www.nyse.com*
Quote.com: *http://new.quote.com*
StockCharts.com: *http://stockcharts.com*
*Stocks & Commodities*: *www.traders.com*
The *Wall Street Journal: www.wsj.com*
TradingMarkets: *www.tradingmarkets.com*
Yahoo! Finance: *http://finance.yahoo.com*

*Exchange Traded Funds Web Sites*
ETF Connect: *www.etfconnect.com* (general)
iShares: *www.ishares.com*
Merrill Lynch HOLDRS: *www.holdrs.com*
PowerShares XTF: *www.powershares.com*
Select Sector SPDRS: *www.spdrindex.com*

Because trading is a solitary occupation, many of us who trade daily from our individual offices enjoy having contact with other traders, using Instant Messaging or a similar form of online connection.

I've found that the best trading groups consist of a network of close trading friends who do not have an interest in my positions, other than to share knowledge and provide a friendly support system.

Still, many novice traders usually gravitate toward online trading chat rooms. Some Web sites offer active threads or chat rooms targeted to specific trading venues. You can hang out, and hopefully, learn something.

Others offer "virtual trading rooms." During market hours, these rooms present intraday stock recommendations and information on a subscription basis.

I have not listed Web site addresses here, as many of them come and go quickly. Your best resource is word-of-mouth from other traders. Trading magazines, such as *Stocks & Commodities, Active Trader, SFO* (Stocks, Futures & Options), and *Futures Magazine* are also good sources for online rooms and sites.

Investigate as many sites as you can before you designate one as your home base. Study their educational materials, if they offer any. Note the tone or thread of the room. Avoid rooms full of self-proclaimed experts. Take members' comments with a grain of salt, until you are sure of their intentions.

As far as trade recommendations go, even if they come from a reliable room, please compare the suggestions to your own criteria before you buy or sell. Think for yourself. Follow your own reasoning. Stay proactive. Don't become reactive.

It's easy to get caught up in a hyped stock, especially if you think everyone's buying it. It's not nearly as much fun to buy a position, and then watch the stock deflate when the hype dissolves into the cyber ether.

If you say, "I totally disagree with this recommendation. This stock is headed south, not north," hold to your position. If the trade does play out in the direction presented, don't regret your own actions. Shrug it off. Then observe the stock to see how it plays out—and whether your assessment was on target. Know that these situations make great learning experiences.

Bear in mind that while you glean knowledge from trading rooms and Web sites, you're doing it with an eye on the future. Though you may enjoy subscribing to a service that gives stock suggestions, or chatting online with other traders, your ultimate goal is to trade from your candidates that fulfill your buying and selling criteria. That's where the most money is made.

## PUMP AND DUMP

As you sample different trading sites, please beware of one unfortunate situation that's cropped up. Although many online trading rooms are run by sincere, honest teachers, a few online chat rooms profit nicely from a deceptive practice called "pump and dump." This is most prevalent with rooms that tout micro-cap, low-volume stocks.

How it works: The guru puts a buy recommendation out on a certain stock; for example, she might say, "Buy Zowie.com immediately! It's going to fly!"

Now, subscribers or members in this online room—maybe hundreds of them— buy Zowie. Result? The demand spikes Zowie's price for seconds to minutes.

If the guru is a "pump and dumper," she quickly sells personal Zowie holdings—bought before she issued the recommendation—into the increased order flow generated by the recommendation. She may have bought the stock a few minutes ago, earlier in the day, or earlier in the week for that matter. Her profit is assured, as room members buy shares and raise the price. Then she takes profits by selling her shares to the people whom she urged to buy.

Now, maybe Zowie.com was poised to fly, and maybe it did. And maybe you made a profit. I truly hope so.

But I've personally seen pump and dumpers make outrageous "it's gonna fly" comments about a stock that's tanking, in a market that's tanking, five minutes before the market close. New traders who didn't know any better jumped in and bought. Whose shares did they buy? They bought the guru's shares. He fled his position fast because the stock was crashing. If these gurus were registered stockbrokers, which they never are, they'd be behind bars.

Lesson: Never buy a stock just because someone tells you to. Always use your own measurements and criteria. And *always* think for yourself.

## SHOULD YOU TAKE A TRADING COURSE?

The more trading explodes as a profession, the more courses and seminars crop up to fill traders' needs.

Early in this book, I stated that knowledge and discipline are the keys to success in this field. When you're sitting in front of your computer screen with your finger on the trigger, about to make a split-second decision that involves thousands of dollars, it doesn't make a darn bit of difference how good-looking you are, what kind of car you drive, or who you know.

All that matters is what you know, and how you apply it.

That's why I recommend you research, and then attend high-quality trading seminars. In other words, you can either go to school, or you can let the market teach you how to trade. From personal experience, the latter is cheaper and more effective.

As you research, you'll encounter two breeds of training. The first is genuine trading seminars and workshops, either online or at a single classroom location. (The classes usually take place over a period of one to five days.)

The second breed *pretends* to be a trading course. In reality, it offers superficial training at best, accompanied by the requirement that you to open an account with their broker. If that's what you want to do, fine. Just be aware of the difference.

Some are pretenders, through and through. If they're not reputable, you'll end up learning a little and losing a lot. They'll get rich off the commissions. And believe me, they do not care if you blow up your account. There's another hopeful right behind you, willing to believe their "you'll get rich by Friday" claims.

How will you know? When you call for information, their reply to your questions will sound something like this: "Nah, you don't have to learn all that charting stuff to make money. Just open an account with us. With our system, we'll show you how to make big bucks—fast. You can start with only $5,000, and by the end of the (week, month) year, you'll probably make $50,000!"

Baloney. *Double baloney.*

It's impossible to trade successfully if you don't know at least basic trading techniques. And, it's even more unlikely that you'll make 1,000% on your money anytime soon. (Experienced professionals are extremely happy when they earn 40% on their account in a year!). Take time to learn traditional methodology and trading tactics, then continue to study while you trade. You'll end up as a prosperous, long-term trader, not a short-term loser.

If you decide to attend a high-quality trading school:

➤ Determine that the instructors are, or have been, expert traders (wannabees don't count).
➤ Make sure the level of training is not too basic, nor too advanced, for your present level of knowledge.
➤ Ask what materials you can study before the class, so you are up-to-speed on the lessons that will be taught.

## IN CONCLUSION

Congratulations! You've journeyed through a long discourse on a heavy subject—trading in the financial markets. Your tenacity shows courage and persistence, two qualities that mold excellent traders. I trust you are on your way to a successful trading career.

In composing this book, I have written each word from my heart. The techniques and strategies in these pages work for me. I hope they will benefit you, help keep you safe, and assist in making your trading experience fulfilling and profitable.

Please remember that prosperous traders are perpetual learners. The Recommended Reading list that follows will guide you to additional books by trading professionals.

May the trading god smile on you, always.

*Toni Turner*

# CENTER POINT: WE ARE ALL CONNECTED

*"We have stopped for a moment to encounter each other, to meet, to love, to share. This is a previous moment, but it is transient. It is a little parenthesis in eternity. If we share with caring, lightheartedness, and love, we will create abundance and joy for each other. And then this moment will have been worthwhile."*

—Deepak Chopra, *The Seven Spiritual Laws of Success*

During interviews, astronauts who've orbited the Earth have commented that viewing our exquisite world from such a glorious vantage point has convinced them that a supreme, cosmic mind is at work.

Scientists tell us our planet formed billions of years ago from stellar debris. Out of that aggregation of cosmic dust, life burst forth and materialized. The sun warmed the Earth, then one-celled plants and animals built the foundation for the chain of development that would unfold through time.

You and I represent an important part of that procession. Our lives form a vital link in a much larger chain that stretches into the future.

When we celebrate our birthdays, we really are celebrating our participation on a planet that, since our last birthday, has orbited the sun one more time. We are part-and-parcel of the Earth's lifetime, just as the cells in our bodies are part of our lifetime.

If we can stretch our minds to observe ourselves and our neighbors as life, itself, in the process of moving toward greater expression and fulfillment, we realize that we are all connected, one to another. Though we have different personal beliefs, skin colors, and cultural boundaries, each of us is born of the intelligence and energy that begets all life. That common thread connects us as brothers and sisters in spirit.

As we go forth in our lives to meet new challenges and opportunities, consider, if you will, that we are each necessary to the progression of life, to the grand scheme of things. Further, that progression connects you and me.

We are separate parts of a perfect whole.

Let's honor one another and strive to make our world harmonious and peaceful. For together, we form links of a magnificent chain that reaches into infinity.

# Recommended Reading List

*Beyond Candlesticks: New Japanese Charting Techniques Revealed* by Steve Nison

*Candlestick and Pivot Point Trading Triggers +CD Rom: Setups for Stocks, Forex, and Futures Markets* by John L. Person

*If It's Raining in Brazil, Buy Starbucks* by Peter Navarro

*High Probability Trading* by Marcel Link

*How I Made $2,000,000 in the Stock Market* by Nicolas Darvas

*Japanese Candlestick Charting Techniques 2nd Ed.* by Steve Nison

*Market Wizards: Interviews with Top Traders* by Jack Schwager

*Mastering the Trade* by John Carter

*Reminiscences of a Stock Operator* by Edwin LeFevre

*Stan Weinstein's Secrets for Profiting in Bull and Bear Markets* by Stan Weinstein

*Technical Analysis from A to Z* by Steven B. Achelis

*The Disciplined Trader* by Mark Douglas

*The New Market Wizards: Conversations with America's Top Traders* by Jack D. Schwager

*Tools and Tactics for the Master Day Trader; Battle-Tested Techniques for Day, Swing and Position Traders* by Oliver Velez and Greg Capra

# Index

## ABOUT THE AUTHOR

Toni Turner is the best-selling author of *A Beginner's Guide to Day Trading Online, A Beginner's Guide to Short Term Trading* and *Short-Term Trading in the New Stock Market.* An investor/trader with sixteen years' experience, she is a popular educator in the financial arena and speaks at trading forums and financial conferences across the United States.

Toni has appeared on NBC, MSNBC, CNN, CNNfn, and CNBC's *Power Lunch.* She has been interviewed on dozens of radio programs and featured in many periodicals including CBSMarketWatch.com, *Fortune* magazine, *Stocks and Commodities, SFO* magazine, *Fidelity Active Trader,* and *Bloomberg Personal Finance.*

Toni is the President of TrendStar Group, Inc. For more information, please go to: *www.ToniTurner.com.*